TALKING ABOUT TORTURE

Talking About Torture

HOW POLITICAL DISCOURSE
SHAPES THE DEBATE

Jared Del Rosso

 COLUMBIA UNIVERSITY PRESS   NEW YORK

COLUMBIA UNIVERSITY PRESS
Publishers Since 1893
New York   Chichester, West Sussex

cup.columbia.edu

Library of Congress Cataloging-in-Publication Data
Del Rosso, Jared.
    Talking about torture : how political discourse shapes the debate / Jared Del Rosso.
        pages cm
    Includes bibliographical references and index.
    ISBN 978-0-231-17092-5 (cloth : alk. paper) — ISBN 978-0-231-53949-4 (e-book)
    1. Torture—Government policy—United States. 2. Extraordinary rendition—Government
policy—United States. 3. War on Terrorism, 2001–2009. 4. Torture—Political aspects. I. Title.

    HV8599.U6D45 2015
    364.6'7—dc23

                                                                    2014044877

Columbia University Press books are printed on permanent and
durable acid-free paper.
This book is printed on paper with recycled content.
Printed in the United States of America

c 10 9 8 7 6 5 4 3 2 1

Cover design: Lisa Hamm
Cover image: AP Photo/Dennis Cook

References to websites (URLs) were accurate at the time of writing.
Neither the author nor Columbia University Press is responsible for URLs
that may have expired or changed since the manuscript was prepared.

CONTENTS

IN THE EARLY YEARS OF the U.S. war in Iraq, the Department of Defense provided no official counts of Iraqi casualties. It would take something else to bring U.S. violence in Iraq back home. On April 28, 2004, a report on detainee abuse, aired by CBS's *Sixty Minutes II*, included digital photographs of U.S. soldiers torturing detainees at Abu Ghraib prison. For many Americans, the photographs taken at Abu Ghraib have come to stand in for the Bush administration's detention and interrogation program more generally. The photographs also provided an opportunity for U.S. culture to reckon with, to co-opt Vice President Dick Cheney's well-worn phrase, the dark side of the U.S. war in Iraq.

The acts of violence photographed at Abu Ghraib are, in many ways, unrepresentative of contemporary U.S. violence. They do not depict the technologies of "shock and awe" that reintroduced the people of Iraq to U.S. force. Nor do they depict the trajectory of U.S. counterterrorism. Missile strikes from unmanned drones and targeted assassinations have come to replace torture. Such forms of violence seem highly controlled and precise. They tend to spark outrage only when there is a breach in that image, as when a video recording of a U.S. Apache helicopter firing on unarmed Iraqis revealed that even technologically sophisticated violence could be committed with ferocity, pursued as an end in itself. The photographs taken at Abu Ghraib prison, however, show violence that appears atavistic. In the photographs, viewers saw older images of cruelty and sadism—the Crucifixion of Jesus or the lynching of African Americans. Others observed "isolated incidents." This book is a study of the political reckoning with Abu Ghraib and of the subsequent debate about U.S. torture. It is, in other words, a study of a form of cruelty that appears, at first glance, anachronistic and outmoded. Yet the political reckoning with torture reveals the contours of contemporary American discourses of violence, the ways that certain expressions of cruelty become palatable to a democracy while others become indigestible.

It is possible that the political reckoning with Abu Ghraib and with torture more generally will stand, for many Americans, as their only sustained encounter with U.S. violence in Afghanistan, Iraq and now Somalia, Yemen, Pakistan, and Syria. As such, the debates considered in this book provide a window, albeit an opaque one, on the meanings of "us" and "them" and the relation that violence forges between.

ACKNOWLEDGMENTS

This book originates in a proposed paper on Abu Ghraib, which I initially abandoned, for Stephen Pfohl's course on visual culture, Images and Power. I benefited from Stephen's generous feedback and guidance, and this book bears the traces of Stephen's mentorship and the intellectual concerns born in his classes. I am also grateful to Sarah Babb and C. Shawn McGuffey for their sustained engagement with this work and, in particular, for teaching me how to practice and write as a qualitative sociologist.

Darius Rejali has, through his scholarship and through bursts of e-mail exchanges, also helped this research along. I owe the conclusion of this book, which seeks to "speak frankly" about torture, to him. My colleagues at the University of Denver have provided advice, feedback, guidance, and support as I developed this work into the form it takes now. I am especially indebted to Paul Colomy, Hava Gordon, Jennifer Reich, and Scott Phillips. My undergraduate advisor, Gila Hayim, introduced me to sociology; her courses on social theory and existential sociology are the foundations on which I built this work. Gordie Fellman's and Bob Irwin's classes on nonviolence cultivated the concerns expressed in this book.

Jennifer Perillo, Stephen Wesley, Michael Haskell, Michele Callaghan, the anonymous reviewers, and Columbia University Press have invested considerable time and energy in seeing this book into publication. Their guidance, advice, and support have been invaluable.

Boston College, the Tufts University Experimental College, and the University of Denver have given me opportunities to teach courses on torture to undergraduates. Through their intellectual curiosity, students in these courses have enriched this research; I have learned much about what is at stake when we talk about torture from their contributions to my classes.

I gratefully acknowledge the support of the Department of Sociology at Boston College, which awarded me a Summer Research Fellowship near the beginning of this project, and Boston College's Graduate School of Arts and Sciences, which awarded me a Dissertation Year Fellowship near its end. I am also grateful to Sarah Hogan, who introduced me to government documents.

I am lucky to have lifelong friends with expertise in other disciplines. Jason Altilio, Steven Altman, Shivang Shah, and Jason Farbman have engaged me on the politics of torture and other serious and not so serious matters.

I am indebted to my family, who have supported and inspired my work and who make up the world beyond my word processor. More than once, Melissa has shared her home with me; spending time with her and her family over holidays and breaks has, I believe, staved off exhaustion. More than once, Jeremy has saved me from technological disaster; his generosity with his time and skills has kept my computers operating against all odds. Andrew's contributions to this work are less concrete but no less certain; his encouragement and occasional provocations have been essential. My parents, Monica and Wayne, taught me to think. Without their support, which has always been unconditional, my work would not have been possible.

Over the past decade, Jennifer Esala has been the first reviewer of my work and my favorite sociologist. Jennifer has walked uncounted miles with me, working out the intricacies of research and the dull ache of the hours in front of a computer. This book is dedicated to her.

*   *   *

Portions of this book have appeared in earlier works, often in different form. Portions of chapters 1, 2, and 3 were previously published as "The Textual Mediation of Denial: Congress, Abu Ghraib, and the Construction of an Isolated Incident," *Social Problems* 58, no. 2 (2011): 165–88 (copyright Society for the Study of Social Problems 2011). Portions of chapters 4 and 5, and the appendix were previously published as "Textuality and the

ON DECEMBER 9, 2014, while this book was in production, the Senate Select Committee on Intelligence released the executive summary of its report on the CIA's detention and interrogation program.[1] The report draws on a review of more than six million pages of CIA documents and took three years to complete and two more for declassification. In it, the committee documents that the CIA employed unauthorized interrogation techniques and used authorized techniques in unauthorized ways and that those techniques did not yield valuable intelligence. The committee also found that the agency consistently misrepresented its use of "enhanced interrogation"; indeed, even the Department of Justice's authorizations of the program were based on a misleading picture of how "enhanced" techniques were used. These general findings had been leaked to the press in the months before the executive summary's release. So the specific details, rather than these general claims, were of particular note. Among them, a few stood out for being especially revealing of the brutality of the CIA's interrogation program.

The report revealed, for instance, what critics of waterboarding long suspected: it was not a careful, restrained technique that CIA interrogators had "enhanced," but, simply put, torture. Waterboarding's supporters claim that it was carefully practiced, with safeguards protecting detainees. As chapter 6 of this book shows, these supporters tell stories that emphasize the brevity of waterboarding's use on two high-value detainees, Abu Zubaydah and Khalid Sheikh Mohammed. Zubaydah underwent, apologists claimed, only thirty seconds of waterboarding before deciding it was prudent to answer his interrogators' questions. Mohammed held out three times as long—a minute and a half. Marc Thiessen, a former Bush administration speechwriter and now an opinion writer for the *Washington Post*, described waterboarding in a 2010 post for the *National Review* as "a few seconds of water being poured over the mouth of terrorists, never entering their stomach or lungs."[2]

The Senate Intelligence Committee's findings discredit these claims. According to the CIA's own documents, Abu Zubaydah, during his first waterboarding session, "coughed, vomited, and had 'involuntary spasms of the torso and extremities'" (*Executive Summary*, 41). A later session left him "completely unresponsive, with bubbles rising through his open, full mouth. . . . [He] remained unresponsive until medical intervention, when he regained consciousness and expelled 'copious amounts of liquid'" (43–44). A medic who observed Khalid Sheikh Mohammed's waterboarding noted that the detainee was "ingesting" and inhaling "a LOT of water" (86). One agency document notes that Mohammed's "abdomen was somewhat distended" after waterboarding and "he expressed water when the abdomen was pressed." The practice, according to the medic, had devolved into "a series of near drownings" (86).

The Intelligence Committee's report also documents that the agency subjected five detainees to "rectal hydration" or "rectal feeding" without medical necessity and threatened others with the practices. Both practices were previously undocumented and, according to Senator Diane Feinstein, the former chair of the Senate Intelligence Committee, never approved by the Department of Justice.[3] The CIA, in its official response to the report, has denied that "rectal hydration" was used for reasons other than "medical necessity":

> The record clearly shows that CIA medical personnel on scene during enhanced technique interrogations carefully monitored detainees' hydration and food intake to ensure [high-value detainees] were physically fit and also to ensure they did not harm themselves. Dehydration was relatively easy to assess and was considered a very serious condition. Medical personnel who administered rectal rehydration did not do so as an interrogation technique or as a means to degrade a detainee but, instead, utilized the well-acknowledged medical technique to address pressing health issues.[4]

While the CIA's response offers no explanation of "rectal feeding," both Michael Hayden, a former director of the CIA, and former vice president

Dick Cheney defended the practice as a medical procedure. In fact, as a medical procedure, "rectal feeding" is badly outmoded. Writing in the *BMJ*, Margaret McCartney claims that the "most recent mention of 'rectal feeding' I can find in the medical literature is from 1913." Broader searches return references to the term more recently, but the majority of writing on the technique appears between 1915 and 1925. The *BMJ* has published just six articles, including McCartney's letter, mentioning the procedure in its 175 years. The *Journal of the American Medical Association* has published seven. The most recent, an editorial published in 1932, notes that the "vogue" of using "nutritional enemas . . . has disappeared almost completely," largely because the human body does not effectively absorb nutrients through the colon. Not surprisingly, doctors who have spoken about "rectal feeding" have rejected Hayden's and Cheney's claims. Vincent Iacopino, a senior medical advisor for Physicians for Human Rights, described the practice as "a form of sexual assault masquerading as a medical treatment."[5]

Though the Senate Intelligence Committee's findings are unambiguous and based on the CIA's own records, it has not ended, at least in the short term, the debate about "enhanced interrogation." Supporters of the CIA's interrogation program, including most Republican members of the Senate Intelligence Committee, have rejected the report as a partisan screed based on inadequate research.[6] They have highlighted the fact that the committee did not speak with CIA interrogators or former directors. And they continue to argue that "enhanced interrogation" yielded critical information that contributed to the prevention of major terrorist attacks.

Given the mixed, often oppositional response to the Senate Intelligence Committee's report, what can we now say about torture in U.S. political culture?

First, the response to the report tells us that political elites who support "enhanced interrogation" remain unwilling to make a case for torture. They also remain unable to admit, let alone defend, facts that suggest that "enhanced interrogation" is torture. This is so despite the fact that recent public opinion polls show that a slight majority of Americans approve of the use of torture.[7] Evidence for this can be found in what the primary supporters of "enhanced interrogation" said in response to the report. Cheney, in an interview with Chuck Todd of *Meet the Press* soon after the report's release, claimed, "We were very careful to stop short of torture." Later in the interview, he claimed that waterboarding—"the way we did it"—is not

torture. In an editorial for the *Wall Street Journal*, three former CIA directors and four former deputy directors rejected the report's finding that the
agency used unauthorized techniques, citing the Department of Justice's
investigation of the program, which did not pursue charges in connection
with the interrogation program, as evidence that "no prosecutable offenses
were committed." Marc Thiessen, in an op-ed written for the *Washington Post* after the report's release, noted that "the CIA contends that the
techniques did not constitute torture" even as he celebrated the fact that a
recent public opinion poll found that a majority of Americans support torture.[8] None acknowledges the specific details of waterboarding's use that
appear in the committee's report.

Even more telling is how the CIA and Intelligence Committee republicans responded to the report. Committee republicans, in their three
"minority views" reports, never address the specific claims about waterboarding or rectal hydration and feeding, even to refute them.[9] The CIA,
in its official response, addressed claims about waterboarding's use and
include some of the quotes from the Intelligence Committee's reports that
I reproduced above. They do not, however, specifically refute or affirm
those claims. Instead, the agency's response notes that waterboarding was
last used in 2003, was only used on three detainees, and the Office of Legal
Counsel reaffirmed the legality of the practice after a CIA request for
review. The CIA's response also disowns the most egregious aspects of the
program by referring to them as errors that occurred in the program's "early
days" and fell below the standards "later established at detention sites."[10]

None of this is especially surprising. If one wishes to contend that a
practice is legal and even moral, one is likely to downplay, if not outright
ignore, the most disturbing details of its use. But critics of torture can and
should take some comfort in the fact that the highest-profile supporters of
"enhanced interrogation" continue to deny that "enhanced" practices constitute torture and refuse to affirm or defend the most brutal aspects of the
program, despite public support for torture. By their denials, supporters of
"enhanced interrogation" recognize—implicitly at least—the legitimacy of
the legal prohibition of torture and the moral force of human rights norms.
Until Cheney, Thiessen, Hayden, and other political elites begin offering
full-throated defenses of torture, rather than "enhanced interrogation," or
defend waterboarding as a practice that leaves detainees unconscious and

bubbling at their mouths, the "torture debate," which Thiessen declared won by his side, favors critics.

Second, the response to the Senate Intelligence Committee's report suggests that it has shifted the empirical ground of the debate about torture—even though supporters of "enhanced interrogation" have attempted to invalidate the report's findings as flawed, biased, and partisan. Since the report's release, stories and claims that emphasize waterboarding's precision and restraint have been conspicuously absent from the debate. Thiessen, perhaps the most consistent teller of these stories, made no mention of them in his first two op-eds written after the report's release. The CIA, though downplaying errors associated with the program, did feel compelled to admit some excesses. It seems, though it may be too early to tell, that the report's contribution to the documentary record of U.S. torture has diminished the credibility of these claims.

Finally, the response to the report suggests that the CIA's decision to destroy videotapes of its use of waterboarding remains a definitive "contribution" to the documentary record of U.S. torture. Supporters of "enhanced interrogation" have called the report flawed because the Intelligence Committee relied, exclusively, on an analysis of documents to support its findings. There is an irony in this. Hayden had told the committee, according to Feinstein, that the destruction of the tapes

> was not destruction of evidence, as detailed records of the interrogations existed on paper in the form of CIA operational cables describing the detention conditions and the day-to-day CIA interrogations. The CIA director stated that these cables were "a more than adequate representation" of what would have been on the destroyed tapes.[11]

The videotapes of CIA interrogations would not have ended debate about the program. They would not have told us much, for instance, about the effectiveness of "enhanced" techniques. But if they still existed, the debate about this report would be profoundly different. There would be an intense, coordinated effort to declassify the tapes, and the release of the tapes, if it occurred, would be a major media event. The footage might have become especially provocative B-roll, running behind and cutting against the grain of interviews with supporters of "enhanced interrogation." And we would be able to triangulate claims about CIA interrogation, checking commentators' arguments against both the Intelligence Committee's report and the agency's own videos.

All this is speculative. What the rest of this book shows, though, is that the documents produced by the Americans who engaged in or directly observed torture influenced the debate about the practice in ways that executive and congressional investigations did not. The former seem unvarnished; we do not hear the Abu Ghraib photographs, the FBI's e-mails about Guantánamo, or the military's interrogation log of Mohammed al-Qahtani described as partisan. The Senate Intelligence Committee's report has now introduced portions of the documentary record produced by CIA agents into the public domain. Though the CIA's videotapes have been destroyed, a rich, important, and still-classified record remains: photographs of the military's torture of detainees in its custody, videos of force-feedings at Guantánamo, the CIA's internal reviews, and those six million pages of documents that the Senate Intelligence Committee analyzed. It is possible, though unlikely, that President Obama, who came to office expressing an interest in looking away from American torture (by "looking forward as opposed to looking backwards"), will declassify some of these documents over the final years of his second term. It is obvious that Congress will resist such efforts. In fact, the Senate Select Committee on Intelligence, now under Republican leadership, is trying to reverse its own work by recalling copies of its full report, which has not yet been publicly released, from the executive branch.[12]

Nothing that these documents contain is likely to be definitive or undeniable. If they are released, public opinion may remain hardened in favor of torture, and Thiessen, Cheney, Hayden, and others will continue to rationalize "enhanced interrogation." The scandal of American torture may remain frozen, as Mark Danner described it in 2008.[13] But with each leak of a firsthand account of U.S. torture, apologists for "enhanced interrogation" have rhetorically retreated, ceding portions of their discursive territory to critics. This book maps that terrain and the shifting borders of American torture talk.

NOTES

1. Senate Select Committee on Intelligence, *Committee's Study of the Central Intelligence Agency's Detention and Interrogation Program: Executive Summary*, United States Senate, 113th Cong., accessed January 22, 2015, http://

www.intelligence.senate.gov/study2014/executive-summary.pdf; further references to this source will be made directly in the text.

2. Marc Thiessen, "Yglesias Admits His Ignorance," *National Review*, February 9, 2010, http://www.nationalreview.com/corner/194573/yglesias-admits-his -ignorance/marc-thiessen.

3. Senate Select Committee on Intelligence, *Committee's Study of the Central Intelligence Agency's Detention and Interrogation Program: Findings and Conclusions*, United States Senate, 113th Cong., accessed January 22, 2015, http://www .intelligence.senate.gov/study2014/findings-and-conclusions.pdf, 4; Dianne Feinstein, "Fact Check: CIA's Use of Rectal Hydration, Feeding Not Medical Procedures," accessed January 22, 2015, http://www.feinstein.senate.gov/public /index.cfm/press-releases?ID=e8f730c3-43c8-4931-94f6-c478f25d8bbb.

4. Central Intelligence Agency, *Comments on the Senate Select Committee on Intelligence's Study of the Central Intelligence Agency's Former Detention and Interrogation Program*, accessed January 22, 2015, https://www.cia.gov /library/reports/CIAs_June2013_Response_to_the_SSCI_Study_on_the _Former_Detention_and_Interrogation_Program.pdf, 55.

5. Margaret McCartney, "Rectal Feeding Is Torture Masquerading as Medicine," *The BMJ* 349 (2014): g7859, accessed January 22, 2015, http://www.bmj.com /content/349/bmj.g7859, doi: http://dx.doi.org/10.1136/bmj.g7859; "The Rectal Administration of Sugar," *The Journal of the American Medical Association* 98, no. 20 (1932): 1747, accessed January 22, 2015, http://jama.jamanetwork.com /article.aspx?articleid=280015; Physicians for Human Rights, "Medical Professionals Denounce 'Rectal Feeding' as 'Sexual Assault Masquerading as Medical Treatment,'" December 2014, accessed January 22, 2015, https://s3.amazonaws .com/PHR_other/fact-sheet-rectal-hydration-and-rectal-feeding.pdf.

6. See, for instance: Senate Select Committee on Intelligence, *Committee Study of the Central Intelligence Agency's Detention and Interrogation Program: Minority Views of Vice Chairman Chambliss Joined by Senators Burr, Risch, Coats, Rubio, and Coburn*, United States Senate, 113th Cong., accessed January 22, 2015, http://www.intelligence.senate.gov/study2014/minority-views.pdf; George J. Tenet, Porter J. Goss, Michael V. Hayden, John E. McLaughlin, Albert M. Calland, "Ex-CIA Directors: Interrogations Saved Lives," *Wall Street Journal*, December 10, 2014, accessed January 22, 2015, http://www.wsj.com /articles/cia-interrogations-saved-lives-1418142644.

7. Adam Goldman and Peyton Craighill, "New Poll Finds Majority of Americans Think Torture Was Justified After 9/11 Attacks," *Washington Post*,

December 16, 2014, http://www.washingtonpost.com/world/national-security /new-poll-finds-majority-of-americans-believe-torture-justified-after-911 -attacks/2014/12/16/f6ee1208-847c-11e4-9534-f79a23c40e6c_story.html.

8. NBC News, 2014, "Meet the Press Transcript—December 14, 2015," *Meet the Press*, accessed January 25, 2015, http://www.nbcnews.com/meet-the-press /meet-press-transcript-december-14-2014-n268181; Tenet, Goss, Hayden, et al., "Ex-CIA Directors: Interrogations Saved Lives"; Marc Thiessen, "Democrats Lose the 'Torture' Debate," *Washington Post*, January 5, 2015, accessed January 25, 2015, http://www.washingtonpost.com/opinions/marc-thiessen -democrats-lose-the-torture-debate/2015/01/05/5e5347ca-94da-11e4-927a -4fa2638cd1b0_story.html.

9. Senate Select Committee on Intelligence, *Committee Study of the Central Intelligence Agency's Detention and Interrogation Program: Minority Views*; Senate Select Committee on Intelligence, *Committee Study of the Central Intelligence Agency's Detention and Interrogation Program: Additional Minority Views of Senator Coburn, Vice Chairman Chambliss, Senators Burr, Risch, Coats, and Rubio*, United States Senate, 113th Cong., accessed January 25, 2015, http://www.intelligence.senate.gov/study2014/additional-minority.pdf; Senate Select Committee on Intelligence, *Committee Study of the Central Intelligence Agency's Detention and Interrogation Program: Senators Risch, Coats, and Rubio Additional Views*, United States Senate, 113th Cong., accessed January 25, 2015, http://www.intelligence.senate.gov/study2014 /additional-minority-views.pdf.

10. Central Intelligence Agency, *Comments*, 54.

11. Dianne Feinstein, 2014, "Statement on Intel Committee's CIA Detention, Interrogation Report," accessed January 25, 2015, http://www.feinstein .senate.gov/public/index.cfm/2014/3/feinstein-statement-on-intelligence -committee-s-cia-detention-interrogation-report.

12. David Johnston and Charlie Savage, "Obama Reluctant to Look into Bush Programs," *New York Times*, January 11, 2009, accessed January 25, 2015, http://www.nytimes.com/2009/01/12/us/politics/12inquire.html; Mark Mazzetti, "C.I.A. Report Found Value of Brutal Interrogation Was Inflated," *New York Times,* January 20, 2015, accessed January 25, 2015, http://www .nytimes.com/2015/01/21/world/cia-report-found-value-of-brutal-interroga tion-was-inflated.html.

13. Mark Danner, 2008, "Frozen Scandal," December 4, 2008, accessed January 25, 2015, http://www.markdanner.com/articles/frozen-scandal.

TALKING ABOUT TORTURE

Introduction

IN THE FINAL QUESTION OF the first presidential debate of 2008, Jim Lehrer asked the two major party candidates—Senators John McCain and Barack Obama—to evaluate the likelihood of "another 9/11-type attack on the continental United States."[1] In place of prognoses, both candidates offered optimism tinged with insecurity: the nation had become "safer" since September 11, 2001, but "we are far from safe" (Senator McCain) and "we still have a long way to go" (Senator Obama). Why the ambivalence? In their responses, the candidates cited torture:

McCAIN: We've got to ... make sure that we have people who are trained interrogators so that we don't ever torture a prisoner ever again.

OBAMA: I give Senator McCain great credit on the torture issue, for having identified that as something that undermines our long-term security.

In an otherwise divisive campaign, the convergence of the two candidates' positions on the "torture issue" represented a political breakthrough. The 2004 presidential debates occurred in the aftermath of the release of photographs showing U.S. soldiers torturing detainees at Abu Ghraib prison in Iraq. In fact, the Senate Armed Services Committee held their final hearing on Abu Ghraib only three weeks—to the day—before the first 2004 presidential debate. Even so, during the 2004 debates, the word "torture" was used only once, by President Bush, and only in reference to Saddam Hussein's human rights crimes.[2] Between the two presidential elections, the recognition that the United States had tortured detainees in its custody moved from the periphery to the center of U.S. politics as Democrats and Republicans alike acknowledged its use. The torture issue had become a political fact.

It is tempting to view this development as simply one whose time had come. After all, the 2008 election was contested as a referendum on the Bush administration.[3] In the months preceding the election, most national polls showed that less than 30 percent of the public approved of Bush's performance as president.[4] With public support for the president so low, McCain and Obama both had much to gain by distinguishing their policies from those of the sitting administration. The candidates also had well-known personal stakes. McCain is a survivor of torture, and Obama is a former professor of constitutional law. Taken together, these political and personal motives offer a seemingly robust explanation of the candidates' rejections of torture.

As commonsensical as this explanation is, it is insufficient to account for the rise and persistence of the "torture issue" in U.S. politics. Simply put, this explanation leaves out far too much. It leaves out, for instance, the political debate over the trickle of revelations about the treatment of detainees in U.S. custody, including the failed efforts of the Bush administration and its supporters in Congress to make torture a political non-issue. It also erases the expenditure of governmental resources, in the form of official investigations and congressional committee hearings, spent on studying and drawing public attention to the treatment of detainees in U.S. custody. Political issues have histories, even if they may be deployed strategically in political competitions.

It is also not clear that the political acknowledgment and disavowal of torture was an idea whose time had truly come. McCain proved himself an outlier among the Republican candidates for president by unequivocally rejecting waterboarding and other "enhanced interrogation" techniques as torture,[5] a position that other leading candidates, including Mitt Romney and Rudy Giuliani, did not take.[6] After the debates, after Obama's November election victory, and even after Obama signed an executive order revoking the CIA's ability to use painful interrogation techniques, the "torture issue" remained unresolved. The convergence of Republican and Democratic positions, so poignant in 2008, gave way to bitter partisanship. On May 21, 2009, President Obama and former vice president Cheney gave dueling national security speeches. Obama, in his, rearticulated his antitorture position. Cheney, in turn, made a case for the necessity of "enhanced interrogation." The killing of Osama bin Laden in May 2011 and, subsequently, the dramatization of that event in the film *Zero Dark Thirty* further renewed the debate about torture. Romney, the Republican's nominee for president in 2012, again expressed his support for "enhanced interrogation."[7] Deep into Obama's second term, Americans continue to debate whether the detention and interrogation practices authorized by the Bush administration were legal, humane, and effective.

THE SOCIAL CONSTRUCTION OF TORTURE

The terms of the U.S. debate about interrogation have shifted over time. Indeed, the very meaning of allegations of U.S. torture—at Abu Ghraib, Guantánamo, and CIA secret prisons or "black sites"—have changed, in fits and starts, over the past decade and a half. Taking these observations as its point of departure, this book retrieves, documents, and analyzes the evolution of the "torture issue" in the United States. To do so, I examine the ways that relatively small but influential groups of political elites—members of Congress and, particularly, members of the House and Senate Judiciary and the House and Senate Armed Services Committees—debated torture. To study the evolution of torture as a political problem, I take a constructionist approach to the practice. This means that I study torture not, primarily, as the application of pain on a detained person but as the subject of "torture talk."[8] This is a study of the language that U.S. politicians use to talk about torture—the meanings, historical associations, and images that officials attach to the practice and the arguments that they make about it.

A constructionist approach to torture allows us to understand how it is that torture becomes a matter of public concern in the first place. It is well documented that political problems must be defined and publicized; people must draw attention to evidence about their presence and harms.[9] Moreover, public and political responses to evidence of problems are rarely proportional to changes in those indicators.[10] Those that evidence suggests have significant social harms can be effectively ignored for extended periods of time; this is a core observation of Stanley Cohen's work on denial.[11] Torture was more intensely debated in the months before and after the 2008 election than those preceding and following the 2004 election. This occurred even though the most controversial instances of torture occurred in 2002 and 2003 and became public knowledge in 2004 and 2005. Political attention to detention, interrogation, and torture did not change incrementally in proportion to changes in information regarding the treatment of detainees in U.S. custody. Congress largely overlooked problems— including reports of detainee abuse at the Metropolitan Detention Center in New York in late 2001 as well as March 2004 reports of detainee abuse at Abu Ghraib prison—until photographs taken at Abu Ghraib became public in April 2004. To understand why this is so, this book considers the interaction between political attention to torture and the available evidence of torture's use, rather than assuming that the former straightforwardly follows the latter.

Typically, research focuses on the direct study of torture, examining its historical use and prevalence. Such studies use accounts of torture— survivors' testimony, official investigations, human rights reports, and investigative reporting—as data that provide more or less transparent windows onto the underlying reality of the practice. Such studies—many of which I cite in this book—have laudable aims. By studying the historical and geographic distribution of torture, these studies have uncovered the social, cultural, political, and institutional conditions out of which torture emerges. By interviewing and examining victims of torture, such studies also expose the social, psychic, and physical damage that torture causes, as well as the efficacy of the medical and psychological treatment of victims.[12] And, by interviewing and examining perpetrators, such works also show that the practice has harmful consequences for torturers.[13]

Given the lengths that governments go to practice torture covertly, it remains necessary for scholars, human rights investigators, and the press to continue compiling evidence of the use and harms of torture. This is particularly true at a moment when what really happened to detainees in U.S. custody remains contested. Why, then, study *talk* of torture, rather than take up the important work of documenting its use, the causes of its use, and its consequences? Would it not be more appropriate to study this problem directly, to learn more about U.S. detention and interrogation operations, and to contribute to our understanding of how to control or prevent the abuse and torture of detainees? I am sympathetic to these questions, particularly since I, too, am interested in what really happened in U.S. detention facilities and the consequences of those occurrences. Likewise, I accept the control and prevention of torture to be a political good.

This book is meant to supplement—and surely not to take the place of—the litany of studies published over the past decade that have analyzed the legal reasoning and policy decisions of the Bush administration that contributed, directly or indirectly, to U.S. interrogators torturing detainees in their custody. Such studies do important work. Not only do they document how the administration put policies permissive of torture in place, they also reveal the historical continuities between U.S. torture and other instances of torture, such as British use of it against the IRA and French use of it in Algiers. Nor is this book meant to establish for the reader what, precisely, occurred in U.S. detention facilities, either military or CIA. This book does not establish, for instance, how, exactly, the CIA used waterboarding and whether that use led to effective information.

Rather, in studying torture talk, I explore the rhetorical techniques that both sides of the debate use to strengthen their arguments and weaken those of their opponents'. I consider how evidence of torture, when leaked in the press or compiled in the form of an official investigation, affects the debate, making some arguments less credible and others more so. I also show how broad shifts in the political context—particularly as it pertains to the war on terror—affected how U.S. politicians understood allegations of torture. Finally, I consider how U.S. politicians understand the administration's interrogation policies in relation to historical precedents and national values

There is practical value to studying debate about torture. Political discourse is entangled in the very socio-political conditions—which Ronald D. Crelinsten refers to as a "torture-sustaining reality"—out of which torture emerges.[14] On the one hand, discourse may—by dehumanizing enemies, rationalizing violence, downplaying the suffering of victims, and isolating incidents—neutralize laws and social norms against torture. In so doing, political discourse may, intentionally or not, sustain the cultural, institutional, and social psychological environments in which torture thrives. On the other hand, political discourse may promote norms against torture by challenging rationalizations and acknowledging harms. Discourse is one—not the only, but *one*—of the factors that enables or prevents torture's use. As we will see, the emergence of a discourse that acknowledged "enhanced interrogation" as torture cleared the way for Barack Obama's order, as president, that banned the CIA from using such practices.

Contemporary torture, which leaves few lasting, physical marks, is notoriously difficult for observers to document.[15] This, the political scientist

Darius Rejali argues, entangles political communities in doubt. Survivors struggle to articulate their experiences to others. Those receiving allegations of torture struggle to confirm those allegations. Recognizing this, this book considers the effect of various types of evidence, such as official reports, statistics, photographs, and interrogation logs, on the U.S. debate about torture. My hope is to contribute to the development of a public "literacy," as Rejali refers to it, of torture by identifying the qualities of evidence that facilitate political recognition of the practice.[16] Throughout the book, I reflect on the role of evidence in the transition in U.S. politics from denial to acknowledgment. I also consider, in the conclusion of the book, the limitations of the particular forms of evidence that U.S. politicians prefer when debating torture.

Finally, by studying discourse of torture, this book explores the contemporary meaning of the practice in the United States. This is a cultural project that allows us to see how U.S. self-identity, national values, and violence align. As chapter 1 documents, torture, as a cultural object, has a long and consequential history. The vocabularies surrounding the practice have changed in the centuries since the practice went from being an official part of the penal system to being considered beyond the pale of an enlightened nation. So, too, have the laws. Today, the word "torture" carries significant, symbolic power, so much so that those governments accused of torture deny it vehemently. What, then, happened when torture arrived on the U.S. political scene? How were painful interrogation practices woven into the cultural and moral fabric of the country? How were they unraveled? Who are we Americans who advocate violence against those in our custody? Who are we Americans who resist these practices? This book provides partial answers to these questions, addressing them by considering what the country's elected officials made of torture.

Congressional Hearings as a Stage for Political Discourse

To address these issues, I conducted a discourse analysis of the published transcripts of forty-two congressional hearings held between 2003 and 2008 on detention and interrogation policy, as well as detainee abuse and torture, in the context of the U.S. "war on terror." Readers will find, however, that I draw from other government and media texts. Political discourse is thoroughly intertextual. Public officials frequently support their arguments by reference to evidence and arguments that appear in other documents. I strive to identify such sources and reflect on the ways that those sources' portrayals of detainee abuse and torture influence political debate. Still, the overarching structure of this study and the majority of examples that I use to illustrate my claims come from my analysis of congressional hearings.

Congressional hearings take several forms. In the House, they cluster into legislative, oversight, and investigative types.[17] In the Senate, committees call these three types of hearings and also call confirmation hearings to question presidential nominations for executive and judicial positions.[18] Data in this study come from all four types of hearings; however, the bulk of it comes from investigative and oversight hearings. Investigative hearings are especially relevant to my study. In such hearings, Congress may receive information about allegations of wrongdoing, either by public officials or private citizens whose behavior is sufficiently consequential as to demand legislative action (as when Congress received testimony from the CEOs of Ford, Chrysler, and General Motors in 2008). Specific legislative proposals are not the primary aim of investigative hearings; they may be more symbolic in nature, aiming to influence public understandings and discourse surrounding problems, controversies, and scandals.

A chair, who is typically the committee member of the majority party with the most seniority, wields considerable power to influence the agenda of his or her committee. Chairs select the issues on which committees will focus. They also are largely responsible for the witness lists of hearings. Chairs may use hearings to "provide the opportunity for representation of different interests, although chairs have been known to 'pack' the hearings with spokesmen."[19] Members of committees recognize this. In a study of nonlegislative hearings, Jeffrey C. Talbert, Bryan D. Jones, and Frank R. Baumgartner interviewed a staff member for a Republican member of the House Energy and Commerce Committee. At the time of the study, Democrats controlled the House. During the interview, the staff member admitted, "Hearings are not much use to us because the chairman is from the other party, and the hearings are usually stacked against us."[20] House and Senate procedures allow for the minority party to call "witnesses of their choice on at least one day of a hearing, when the chairman receives a written request from a majority of minority party members."[21] But, as the staff member told Talbert, Jones, and Baumgartner, the minority party's influence on the agenda and witness list of hearings is minimal and came at an expense: "It was possible, but it would expend considerable resources."[22]

Even so, hearings do provide an opportunity for members of both parties to contribute their preferred framing of problems and controversies to the public record. Representatives of both major parties—typically, the majority party's committee chair and the ranking member of the minority party—offer lengthy statements that seek to clarify or criticize the agenda of the committee's hearings. These statements assign meaning to the topics covered in the hearing, articulate the stakes of the topics before the committee, and, because they are largely scripted, provide insight into the overarching frames in which political elites situate the facts of political problems. Witnesses, too, offer scripted statements that may amplify the claims of one or both political parties or offer unique vantages on political problems. Opening statements, then, tend to signal the discursive "borders" of the broader political concern about issues.[23] Typically, statements are followed by lengthy question-and-answer periods, in which each representative in attendance is allotted time to question witnesses. Through these exchanges, hearing participants negotiate the meaning of political problems and current events. At times, these negotiations result in the repetition of well-worn claims and beliefs. At other times, they may test incompatible claims about an issue. In these negotiations, the very meaning of political problems and current events is at stake.

Congressional hearings also illuminate the processes by which information, allegations, and evidence about issues are transformed into taken-for-granted facts about the practice. They also result in the production of a public record to which future congressional investigations orient.[24] The Senate Armed Services Committee, for instance, produced an investigation of American detention and interrogation practices, the *Inquiry Into the Treatment of Detainees in U.S. Custody*. To produce this report, the committee built on its public hearings and churned up layers of records that documented the previously classified or undocumented behavior of U.S. officials in the spread of torture. More frequently, though, congressional committees operate as clearinghouses of information. On the stages provided by committee hearings, government and nongovernment experts testify about social problems and public issues, offering statistics and analyses of those problems. Committee members amplify or refute that information and, in some cases, incorporate it into their understandings of public problems.[25] The information presented at hearings is not always valid or accurate.[26] Still, by publicizing information, congressional committees participate in the construction of social problems and public issues. We find, in Congress's hearings on issues of detention and interrogation, a public arena for the synthesis of expert knowledge, a space in which torture becomes a meaningful social object.

There are, however, limitations to the study of political discourse through congressional hearings. Political claims are processed, and thus altered, through the media and actively interpreted by audiences.[27] While hearing transcripts are well suited to the research questions that I have posed, they do not provide information on the media's or the public's reception and subsequent framing of congressional discourse. I address this limitation by providing some contextualizing details about media and public understandings of torture; I also address media coverage of torture at greater length when discussing the effect of leaked and declassified documents on congressional responses to torture. It is also important to note that the transcripts of hearings only partially preserve the background work by which congressional committees arranged hearings. Elements of the organization of hearings can be detected in their timing, titles, and witness lists. I am attuned to what these signal about how committees stage torture as a political issue. These hearings, however, do not allow me to draw conclusions about the "motivating cause" of political behavior, "such as the shifting preferences of the ruling class."[28] This is not simply a limitation of the data. Sociological theorists of elites, such as C. Wright Mills and G. William Domhoff, are skeptical of the role of the U.S. Congress in effecting foreign policy.[29] For those interested in the trajectory of U.S. foreign policies of detention and interrogation, this limitation may be lethal as the discursive action, as it pertains to torture, would be found in the executive.

There are, however, good reasons to investigate discourse beyond the executive. For one, the contours of executive discourse are well documented. In legal memoranda and public statements, Bush administration officials and lawyers constructed the "war on terror" as an unprecedented struggle against a shadowy, barbaric enemy who refused to conform to the laws of war, resisted traditional interrogation techniques, fabricated stories of abuse and torture, and posed an imminent and existential threat to democratic civilization.[30] With this construction of the enemy as its discursive grounds, the administration argued that international laws of war did not apply to the U.S. war on terror and that U.S. interrogators could lawfully use pain-inducing interrogation techniques, which did not meet the administration's interpretation of the legal definition of torture, to acquire the intelligence necessary to prevent imminent terrorist attacks. We know, however, far less about congressional discourse, the extent to which it replicated or challenged the administration's discourse, and *how* it accomplished its replication or resistance.

There is, moreover, conflicting evidence about the role of ruling elites in authorizing and implementing torture. In his study of torture in democracies, Darius Rejali considers the possibility that "democratic states are ruled by an elite who, for whatever reason, want to hide their exploitative state in the guise of a genuinely democratic government" and so authorize interrogators to use torture practices that are difficult to document.[31] Rejali finds, however, that—while "both political elites and lower-level police and military have, at different times, initiated stealth torture"—more commonly "torture began with the lower-downs, and was simply ignored by the higher ups."[32] While the recent experience of the United States appears to be a notable exception to this—after all, the administration authorized CIA and Guantánamo interrogators to use painful interrogation practices—one must still ask why those who authorized torture denied that the practices they permitted constituted torture and repeated that the United States "does not torture."[33] These denials suggest, at a minimum, that the administration believed they "were being watched and judged by others in how well they respect human rights and they believe at least a thin veneer of legitimacy is necessary."[34] Those who watch the executive may not shape "events from invulnerable positions behind the scenes," but the fact of their watching and their insistence, particularly discursively, that the United States conform to human rights norms mediates elite behavior.[35]

Congress is one of the institutions that monitors the executive's behavior. Compared with the work of human rights monitors, however, congressional response to torture is uneven. Congress may refuse to monitor the executive for a variety of reasons. Congressional leaders may agree with the executive's policies on interrogation. They may wish to protect the policy makers who authorized torture. Other topics, too, may require more urgent consideration.

But, as this book makes, clear, Congress did respond to allegations of U.S. torture. The nature of that response, though, is complex; the simple fact that Congress is talking about allegations of torture should not be mistaken for an authentic attempt to prevent torture or hold policy makers accountable for its use. At times, Congress collaborated with the executive to maintain a facade of legitimacy by performing "oversight" of torture without implicating those who authorized the practices. This, I think, fairly describes what the Republican-run Congress did in 2004 and 2005 when it debated detainee abuse at Abu Ghraib and Guantánamo. Congress may, however, participate in the production of antitorture discourse, shifting the cultural and political grounds on which the executive considers detention and interrogation policy. We witnessed just such a shift in discourse starting in late 2005, continuing into 2006, and crystalizing over the final two years of the Bush administration. This book focuses on this shift, accounting for it by highlighting the changes in public knowledge of torture and the political context that drove it.

Analyzing Congressional Discourse: A Note on Methodology and Methods

This book is based on a discourse analysis of congressional talk about detention, interrogation, detainee abuse, and torture. Discourse analysis involves the "structured and systematic study of texts" to discern how those texts "contribute to the constitution of social reality by *making* meaning."[36] The discourse analyst explores "how socially produced ideas and objects that populate the world were created in the first place and how they are maintained and held in place over time."[37] Attuned to both the meaning and content of texts and their social production, discourse analysis permits me to document the shifting contours of political definitions of detainee abuse and torture, as well as the social processes that produced those definitions and the political and cultural contexts that nourished them.[38]

For this analysis, I did not randomly sample data but examined the particular texts that would best allow me to address my research topic and questions.[39] Specifically, I have analyzed congressional committee hearings called to review allegations of detainee abuse or executive branch policies of detention and interrogation. I have not, in other words, examined a random sample of all congressional references to torture, detainee abuse, or interrogation. There are, however, sound reasons for focusing on congressional hearings. The hearings that I examined are saturated by torture talk. Unlike statements that appear in the congressional record, they are systematically and socially arranged around relevant topics. By focusing on congressional hearings, I provide both an in-depth analysis of political discourse of torture and a commentary on how hearings, as an expression of political power and social activity, influence that discourse.

Discourse analysis is also particularly well suited to the idiosyncrasies of congressional hearings. The transcripts of congressional hearings are, in important ways, records of social activity. The activity of meaning making is represented in the exchanges between witnesses and committee members. Discourse and qualitative textual analysis allows for analysis of text "much like an ethnographer's technique for analyzing his or her field notes."[40] This approach enables a rich study of torture talk. It permits me to document the content of congressional discourse—the forms of denial and specific claims employed at given moments. It also allows me to analyze the interpretive processes, such as the interactions among hearing participants, that sustain particular accounts and claims within political discourse. By allowing the analyst to take an ethnographic stance toward texts, discourse analysis further permits the researcher to uncover how texts relate to context, a topic that I discuss at length in chapter 1. Congressional discourse, particularly on the stage of committee hearings, occurs within an organizational, political, and cultural context. Hearings are arranged affairs, and how hearings are arranged affects what is said during them. By studying, to the extent that I can, congressional discourse within its institutional and political context, this study shows how three contextual factors affected the debate about torture: (1) the documentary record related to U.S. interrogation policy and practices; (2) political power, as expressed in the control of congressional committees; and (3) the interpretive frames that gave allegations of torture their meaning. I also argue that U.S. discourse of torture is oriented to a broader cultural context in which torture—and even the word "torture"—is toxic and the democratic state's use of violence appears legitimate only so long as it can be credibly said to have been deployed in a restrained, goal-oriented manner. Today, we tend to associate torture with Nazis, communists, the imperial Japanese, and even the interrogators of the Spanish Inquisition. If the seven-letter word "torture" attaches itself to a practice like waterboarding, those sorts of associations come rushing in. Both sides of the debate about interrogation understand this. Those who support a practice like waterboarding take pains to distinguish the practice from the *real* torture practiced by despots. Those on the other side of the debate mention waterboarding in the same breath as these historical precedents, exploiting the political and cultural baggage that these precedents carry.

OVERVIEW OF BOOK

Chapter 1, "The Torture Word," positions the U.S. debate about torture in its cultural and social context, reviewing the set of illiberal associations that the word "torture" now carries. These associations date to the eighteenth century, when broad legal and social changes led to the legal abolition of torture and its moralization. Given the contemporary meaning of torture, states now tend to use the practice in secret and then deny having done so. Focusing on denial, I present a typology of it grounded in literature on the subject. I then discuss the role of evidence, political power, and interpretive frames in state denial of torture.

Chapters 2 through 6 present my analysis of congressional discourse of torture. The chapters are, roughly speaking, organized chronologically. This allows me to trace the shifting contours of political discourse. It also permits me to account for these shifts by drawing attention to the dynamic contextual factors that influenced the debate.

Chapter 2, "The Heartbreak of Acknowledgment: From Metropolitan Detention Center to Abu Ghraib," compares Congress's response to the abuse of the "September 11 detainees" at the Metropolitan Detention Facility (MDC) in Brooklyn, N.Y., with its response to the release of photographs taken at Abu Ghraib prison in Iraq. While Abu Ghraib provoked a significant political crisis, Congress did not respond to the earlier allegations at MDC with the same urgency and intensity. I consider how evidence and the political context shaped these different responses. The abuse at MDC was, when Congress first considered it, verbally alleged by victims and verbally denied by the accused perpetrators. The violence at Abu Ghraib, in contrast, was represented in digital photographs that secured the reality of the violence and foreclosed its outright denial. Congress also understood the abuse at MDC as occurring in the chaotic wake of the September 11, 2001, terrorist attacks, when aggressive actions were necessary to prevent follow-up attacks. This framing provided Congress with powerful rationalizations, grounded in a "national security" frame, for the mistreatment of the "September 11 detainees." Congress framed the abuses at Abu Ghraib within the context of the Iraq War, the improvement of human rights in Iraq, and the precarious political relationships required to win the war. Within this framework, U.S. abuse of detainees at Abu Ghraib appeared to be a disruptive force, a threat to the war's legitimacy and to the bonds that tethered U.S. public support and Iraqi "hearts and minds" to the war.

Chapters 3 and 4 build on chapter 2 by detailing how Congress, the military, and official investigators accounted for Abu Ghraib. Chapter 3, "Isolating Incidents," examines claims about the geographic extent of abuse. This chapter shows how the gradual buildup of evidence forced Congress and the military to recognize that abuse had been pervasive in Iraq. At the same time, it shows how this widespread abuse was disaggregated into politically tolerable forms—inadvertent occurrences during the arrest of detainees—and intolerable forms—the intentional and especially pathological violence photographed at Abu Ghraib. By doing this, military officials, investigators, and Senate Republicans isolated Abu Ghraib and downplayed the allegations of mistreatment that occurred beyond the facility. Chapter 4, "Sadism on the Night Shift: Accounting for Abu Ghraib," examines the causal isolation of Abu Ghraib. It details the arguments that absolved high-ranking ranking military and executive branch officials, as well as the policies that they authorized, of blame for the abuse of detainees at the facility. Taken together, these two chapters explore the rhetorical strategies and types of evidence that permitted the Bush administration, high-ranking military officials, and Senate Republicans to contain the Abu Ghraib scandal.

While Congress debated Abu Ghraib, concern for Guantánamo was minimal as only a few, minor instances of abuse were acknowledged at the latter facility. Chapter 5, " 'Honor Bound': The Political Legacy of Guantánamo," shows how this view of Guantánamo transformed, morphing the facility into the domestic and global problem it now is. To account for this, I isolate two key changes in the documentary record of Guantánamo: the release, in December 2004, of FBI e-mails describing detention and interrogation practices at the facility and the leak, in June 2005, of the military's interrogation log of Mohammed al-Qahtani to *Time* magazine. These documents suggested that significant instances of abuse, comparable to those at Abu Ghraib, had occurred at Guantánamo. Along with these additions to the documentary record, I also show how two developments in the political environment further contributed to the stigma surrounding Guantánamo. First, the Supreme Court ruled against the administration in the landmark case of *Hamdan v. Rumsfeld*. This decision forced Congress to reckon with military and international standards of justice and elevated the rule of law in Congress's discourse surrounding Guantánamo. Subsequently, the 2006 midterm election reconfigured political power, permitting congressional Democrats to employ committee agendas to broaden the discursive scope of their investigations of torture. By incorporating legal scholars, human rights workers, and former members of the executive critical of the Bush administration's policies, the Democratic committees further elevated human rights and the rule of law as interpretive frames in political debate about torture. Within this context, a discourse that acknowledged and criticized U.S. torture finally solidified.

Chapter 6, "The Toxicity of Torture: Waterboarding and the Debate About 'Enhanced Interrogation,'" examines political discourse surrounding waterboarding in 2007 and 2008. Because the CIA destroyed—and admitted destroying—videotapes of its interrogations, U.S. politicians competed to define the practice. Proponents of waterboarding attempted to portray it as effectively, appropriately, and precisely used. Doing so, they attempted to neutralize comparisons between waterboarding and torture, voiding the illiberal associations that the latter form of violence carries. Opponents, however, mobilized these associations, describing waterboarding as a dangerous, difficult to regulate practice that had been historically used by notorious nondemocratic regimes to produce compliant detainees who would say anything to stop the pain. These incompatible images of waterboarding reside precariously next to each other. This, I argue, has to do with the lack of a definitive, firsthand, official or quasi-official account of the practice. Lacking such a definitive description of waterboarding, neither side possesses the resources necessary to settle the debate.

In chapter 7, "From 'Enhanced Interrogation' to Drones: U.S. Counterterrorism and the Legacy of Torture," I reflect on the contested legacy of U.S. torture. I highlight the lack of consensus about the legality and effectiveness of "enhanced interrogation," explaining the partisanship surrounding these techniques as, in part, the product of gaps in the documentary record of U.S. torture. I also discuss the transition in U.S. counterterrorism policy from "enhanced interrogation" to drones. I argue that this transition bears several traces of the debate about torture. Drones, I argue, are an especially attractive technology, because they dodge the problem of where to hold and what rights to give detained terrorists; these are issues that remain hotly contested in U.S. politics. Drones are also attractive because they are easier to fit to our understanding about how U.S. violence should be deployed. Both President Bush and President Obama used a rhetoric of restraint, lawfulness, necessity, and instrumental rationality when legitimating "enhanced interrogation" and drones, respectively. But, as this book makes clear, the reality of torture troubles advocates' claims about painful interrogation practices. Drones, in contrast, are easier to discursively fit to democratic principles because of their technological sophistication and apparent precision. I also consider how the U.S. debate about torture facilitated the transition to drones by avoiding a confrontation with the human costs of the country's interrogation program. This dodged confrontation might have provided an opportunity for the country to meaningfully reckon with the implications of its violence, as well as the political relationships and ethical obligations forged by that violence. Having avoided this reckoning, members of Congress who repudiated torture rejected only that single form of violence, not global violence more generally, and left the foundation set for the Obama administration's transition to drones. I conclude by highlighting the work of Physicians for Human Rights, showing how their report *Broken Laws, Broken Lives: Medical Evidence of Torture by U.S. Personnel and Its Impact* permits readers to encounter and reckon with the lives and losses of survivors of U.S. torture.

CHAPTER | **1**

The Torture Word

ON MAY 4, 2004, Secretary of Defense Donald Rumsfeld held a press briefing on the abuse of detainees at Abu Ghraib prison in Iraq. During the briefing, Rumsfeld was asked about U.S. use of torture: "Mr. Secretary, a number of times from the podium you've said U.S. troops do not torture individuals . . . does this report undercut your notion that the U.S. doesn't torture?" Rumsfeld responded:

> My impression is that what has been charged thus far is abuse, which I believe technically is different from torture . . . I don't know if . . . it is correct to say what you just said, that torture has taken place, or that there's been a conviction for torture. And therefore I'm not going to address the torture word.[1]

Rumsfeld's nimble response is a form of denial that the sociologist Stanley Cohen refers to as "interpretive."[2] By casting instances of violence as "abuse" rather than "torture," Rumsfeld tried to neutralize the cultural associations and legal implications that the latter form of violence carries. This chapter describes those associations and their origin. I then review the forms of denial that governments typically use to neutralize allegations of torture. I conclude by situating official denial within a broader social and political framework.

TORTURE AS A CULTURAL OBJECT

The word "torture" may refer to a practice—the infliction of severe pain by public officials against a detained person for the collection of information, the production of confessions, or social control and dominance. Torture, however, is also a cultural object, one that has a lengthy and important history in Western imaginations. "Torture" refers not only to particular practices but also to a knot of associations and images that give the practice its contemporary meaning. Darius Rejali describes these associations as a "modern memory" of torture.[3] They are, however, not so modern. As Rejali puts it, the modern memory of torture is "a blissful nineteenth-century memory residing untouched by the horrors of the twentieth century."[4]

This "blissful" nineteenth-century memory and the historical changes that produced it are vital to understanding contemporary responses to torture, including in the United States. Between the mid-eighteenth and early nineteenth centuries, most nations of Europe abolished judicial torture, "the use of physical coercion by officers of the state in order to gather evidence for judicial proceedings."[5] Orbiting the development was a second one: torture moved from a "specifically legal vocabulary . . . into a general vocabulary of moral invective."[6] The moral vocabulary of torture lacked the legal vocabulary's specificity and neutrality. In it, torture opposed human progress and dignity; it became a practice whose persistence in the contemporary world signaled the legacy of irrational, uncivilized, and outmoded forms of dominance.

This view is detectable in Enlightenment critiques of the practice. Cesare Beccaria, in his 1764 treatise *On Crimes and Punishments*, listed torture as one of the legal practices that emanated "out of the most barbarous ages" and described its persistence in Europe through the eighteenth century as "an enduring monument to the ancient and savage legislation of an age when ordeals by fires and boiling water and the uncertain outcome of armed combat were called 'judgments of gods.' "[7] Voltaire offered a comparable condemnation, juxtaposing the seeming cultural and social sophistication of France with its continued reliance on torture:

> Foreign nations judge France by its plays, novels and pretty poetry; by its opera girls, who are very gentle of manner; by its opera dancers, who are

graceful . . . They do not know that there is no nation more fundamentally cruel than the French. The Russians were considered barbarians in 1700, and it is now only 1769; an Empress has just given to that vast state laws. . . . The most remarkable is universal tolerance; the next is the abolition of torture. . . . Woe unto the nation which, though long civilized is still led by ancient atrocious customs![8]

The association of torture with "the most barbarous ages" and "ancient atrocious customs" affected modern understandings of torture. In the nineteenth century, studies of the practice often described its legal prohibition in the moral vocabulary's terms. The nineteenth-century historian Henry C. Lea, for instance, referred to the practice as a "relic of medieval barbarism."[9] A contemporary, W. E. H. Lecky, used similar language to describe torture's abolition:

> Torture was abolished because in the progress of civilization the sympathies of men became more expansive, their perceptions of the sufferings of others more acute, their judgments more indulgent, their actions more gentle. To subject even a guilty man to the horrors of the rack seemed atrocious and barbarous, and therefore the rack was destroyed.[10]

This understanding of torture persisted into the twentieth century. The historian Edward Peters documents its particularly acute resonance with international actors after World War II, whom he describes as endeavoring to achieve "a new Enlightenment, one with universal civil and political (as well as social and economic) consequences for all people."[11] The humanitarian principles associated with the moral vocabulary—such as the inherent dignity and inalienable rights of all humans—have been inscribed into international instruments that prohibit torture, such as the United Nations' *Universal Declaration of Human Rights* and its *Convention Against Torture and Other Cruel, Inhuman, or Degrading Treatment or Punishment*. The *Universal Declaration*, adopted three years after the end of World War II, noted that "disregard and contempt for human rights have resulted in barbarous acts."[12] This is a noncontroversial description of the violence of the first four decades of the twentieth century, but to describe violations of human rights as barbarous is to employ a word heavy with social otherness and echoes Beccaria's, Lea's, and Lecky's language.[13]

Other, more specific statements on the nature of torture circulated in the background from which international instruments prohibiting torture emerged. F. S. Cocks, a contributor to a draft of *The European Convention of Human Rights*, proposed language for the *Convention* similar to Lea's:

> All forms of torture, whether inflicted by the policy, military authorities, members of private organizations or any other persons are inconsistent with civilized society, are offences against heaven and humanity and must be prohibited.... [The Consultative Assembly] believe that it would be better even for Society to perish than for it to permit this *relic of barbarism* to remain.[14]

The atrocities of the Second World War solidified, rather than eroded, the cultural meaning of torture as antithetical to modernity. Rejali documents the emergence of the "modern memory" of torture following the war. This "memory" involved collective amnesia surrounding democratic histories of torture and a collective remembrance of, if not an outright preoccupation with, Nazi and Soviet practices. One Allied poster, reprinted on the cover of Rejali's book, communicates this message with uncommon clarity. "Torture," the poster reads. "This is the method of the enemy" and then, "WE FIGHT FOR A FREE WORLD." As this book shows, the modern memory of torture is, in contemporary U.S. political discourse, broader than how Rejali originally described it. Remembered with Nazi and Soviet atrocities are those of imperial Japan, China, the Khmer Rouge, Iran and Iraq. The U.S. memory of torture is also deep; it recalls, still, the water tortures of the Spanish Inquisition. Still, a generalizable point of Rejali's holds: The modern memory of torture disavows the practice's historical use by democracies.

CONTEMPORARY TORTURE AND THE AMBIGUOUS LEGACY OF THE MORAL VOCABULARY

Torture, the method of the enemy. Four centuries of meaning are well represented in those few words. This cultural configuration—which associates torture with barbarism, repression, and notorious illiberal regimes and aligns the practice against democracy—has had a profound, albeit ambiguous, influence on the contemporary use of torture and the rhetoric surrounding it.

The abolition of judicial torture and the emergence of a moral vocabulary of torture did not vanquish the practice. Instead, torture went elsewhere, from formally recognized judicial proceedings to "the hidden interrogation rooms of police stations, in the personal interaction between guard and prisoner."[15] Lea, in fact, observed this, documenting a case in Switzerland "in which, a man suspected of theft was put on bread and water from Oct. 26th to Nov. 10th, 1869, to extort confession, and when this failed he was subjected to thumb-screws and beaten with rods." Still, Lea remained optimistic that modern sensibilities would immunize society to torture: "It is to be hoped that the scandal caused by the development of this barbarism may render its repetition impossible."[16]

The twentieth century, of course, would not oblige. Writing in 1959, Jean-Paul Sartre listed the countries—Hungary, Poland, the Soviet Union—that had employed torture since the Second World War. Cutting himself off, Sartre concluded with resignation: "I could go on: today it is Cyprus and it is Algeria; all in all, Hitler was just a forerunner."[17] Less than two decades later, Amnesty International published its first international study of torture and found that the practice had "developed a life of its own and become a social cancer"; torture was "a practice encouraged by some governments and tolerated by others in an increasingly large number of countries."[18] Amnesty's subsequent studies have consistently documented the use of torture in more than one hundred nations.[19] The use of torture by the United States represents only the most recent example of a Western democracy relying on the practice. In this, the United States follows Israel's use of torture against Palestinians, England's practices in its colonies and against members of the IRA, and France's use of it in Algeria.[20] U.S. interrogators at the turn of the twentieth century in the Philippines and later in Vietnam also employed torture.

Despite the historical record, it is indisputable that the eighteenth and nineteenth centuries instigated long-lasting changes in the laws governing, uses of, and rhetoric surrounding torture. The practice is now, after all, prohibited by international and, in most countries, domestic laws. Public monitors of state behavior mobilize around such laws, attempting to influence state behavior by documenting incidents of torture, participating in domestic and foreign "moral consciousness-raising," and exerting institutional and grassroots pressure.[21] Such efforts may involve the mobilization of the illiberal associations of torture to "shame" an offending state into conforming to international human right norms.[22] In response, many nations that torture and most democracies that torture now attempt to do so secretly and with techniques that leave few, lasting physical marks.[23] The use of nonmarking or "clean" torture techniques makes it difficult for observers to document the practice and also helps governments that torture to maintain international legitimacy by *appearing* to conform to human rights norms.[24]

The Rhetoric of Denial

The institutionalization of the moral vocabulary has had a second effect. When allegations of torture become public, governments usually use what Stanley Cohen calls a "rhetoric of denial" to minimize the effect of allegations.[25] The rhetorical techniques of denial cluster into three types: literal, interpretive, and implicatory.[26] Cohen's research also shows that governments often find it difficult to sustain denial. Despite this, full acknowledgment of human rights violations is rare; when pressed beyond the rhetoric of denial, officials will engage in qualified or "partial acknowledgement."

LITERAL DENIAL

"Literal denial" is the "laconic disavowal that 'nothing happened.'"[27] This form of denial often involves discrediting the "reliability, objectivity and credibility of the observer."[28] Literal denial may also involve "magic denial," the argument that "the violation is prohibited by the government, so it could not have occurred."[29] Literal denial is also inscribed into acts of state violence. Disappearances and clean torture produce little evidence that violence occurred, are more difficult for observers to document, and are easier for governments to outright deny.[30]

INTERPRETIVE DENIAL

Given international monitoring of torture, literal denial is difficult for most states to maintain. "Interpretive denial" is the rhetorical strategy by which officials "admit the raw facts . . . but deny the interpretive framework placed on these events."[31] What a critic calls torture an official may describe as a legitimate state practice, such as "an alternative set of procedures."[32] Interpretive denial also involves disputes over the legal category that an alleged incident of violence satisfies: "abuse," "ill treatment," or "torture."[33]

It can involve efforts to reframe accountability for torture; the claim that the violence at Abu Ghraib reflected the actions of a "few bad apples" is a well-known instance of this variant of interpretive denial. As with literal denial, the flexibility needed for interpretive denial is inscribed into torture practices. An "alibi"—that the alleged incident was not torture but a legitimate investigation—is built into torture by the torturer's use of ordinary investigative tools, such as flashlights, or practices, such as strip searches or force-feeding, to inflict pain on victims.[34] What Eric Bonds refers to as "surrogacy"—one state's reliance on another's use of violence, as in the case of extraordinary rendition—also facilitates interpretive denial, particularly denial of responsibility.[35]

IMPLICATORY DENIAL

"Implicatory denial" refers to the rhetorical strategies that officials use to justify alleged incidents of torture. Officials may challenge the legitimacy of human rights norms, argue that violence is necessary for defense of the state, blame victims, or contrast the violations of their own state with violations of enemy states.[36] Officials may also justify torture by citing instances when it proved effective.[37] As a variant of the claim of necessity, the hypothetical "ticking-bomb" scenario, in which an interrogator confronts an enemy known to have knowledge of an impending attack, has become one of the leading images used to justify torture.[38]

PARTIAL ACKNOWLEDGMENT

In the face of domestic or international pressure or because of the emergence of persuasive evidence that torture has occurred, denial sometimes gives way to acknowledgment. Yet full acknowledgment is rare, as states tend to qualify wrongdoing with "three devices": "spatial isolation," "temporal containment," and "self-correction."[39] "Spatial isolation" refers to the claim that an alleged incident is an "isolated incident" unrepresentative of state practices.[40] "Temporal containment" locates the alleged incident in a past that is no longer politically relevant. Finally, "self-correction" involves the argument that the criticized state is effectively addressing its violations.

Contemporary human rights work often involves efforts to shame nations accused of human rights violations.[41] These efforts mobilize the association of torture with illiberal cruelty to disrupt claims that states respect modern human rights norms. By denying or only partially acknowledging allegations of detainee abuse and torture, public officials engage in repair work that, like the "official discourse" employed in response to other forms of misconduct, aims at "verbally bridging the gap between action and expectation."[42] The rhetoric of denial, in other words, aims to bridge the gap between prevailing ideas about the illegality and immorality of torture and its actual use.[43] If successful, denial may maintain or restore the credibility of the offending government by downplaying or rationalizing the harms of torture, euphemizing alleged instances so that they are not perceived as torture in the first place, or representing the alleged incident as unsanctioned by state officials. Repair work may also involve rhetorical efforts to associate some political actors, such as low-ranking officials or soldiers, with torture, while cordoning off others from its toxic, symbolic effects.

THE SOCIAL CONTEXT OF OFFICIAL DENIAL

As this book makes clear, Cohen's typology of denial and partial acknowledgment provides a useful guide to the U.S. political discourse of torture. To address the question that this study poses—how did U.S. discourse transition from denial to acknowledgment—we must consider the social and political factors that influenced how American politicians responded to allegations of detainee abuse and torture. Congressional discourse of torture occurs within a dynamic political and social environment. This environment provides the resources—evidence of torture's use, access to political power, and interpretive frames for understanding that evidence— that political actors employ when debating the practice.

Evidence as a Resource for Debating Torture

Political discourse is not, in a traditional sense, evidence based. Political actors may support their claims with unprovable evidence, as when politicians support their arguments with allusions to classified or privileged knowledge. They may also support their claims with dubious data.[44] Even so, politicians, when debating issues, present some claims as facts and, frequently, will use some sort of supporting evidence—even if of dubious accuracy—to support their arguments.

In this book, I document and reflect on the types of evidence political actors use to support their claims about U.S. detainee abuse and torture, regardless of whether that evidence is especially compelling. This focus allows me to document how an act—torture—practiced in settings with virtually no public oversight becomes a matter of public concern. It also allows me to document the types of evidence that matters to political actors and how those types affect their arguments about detainee abuse and torture.

Most participants in congressional hearings on detainee abuse and torture did not and certainly could not view detention and interrogation practices as they occurred. Instead, documents, such as photographs and investigations, enabled them to do so indirectly. The inscription of an event into textual or visual form makes that event durable and mobile.[45] By durable, I mean that an account of an event that is written up, photographed, or otherwise documented may be preserved even after the event has ended. Without taking some sort of documentary form, the event of torture would disappear into its own enactment, lost to the historical record. By mobile, I mean that documents have the capacity, by their materiality or digitality, to be passed on and shared between people. Inscribing accounts or representations of events into written and visual documents gives those events a "real and immediate *virtual* presence" at sites of political discourse.[46] This allows political actors to scrutinize or "read through" those documents to establish "what actually happened," in this case in U.S. detention centers and interrogation rooms.[47]

All documents, however, are not created equal. Some are bureaucratic, replacing the lived experience of those who practiced or suffered torture with a stiff and, typically, euphemistic official vocabulary. Some take the form of photographs, which carry substantial, evidentiary weight in contemporary societies. Because viewers must visually decode photographs before linguistically describing them, photographs may also evade the euphemistic powers of official discourse. Other documents are somewhere in the middle—produced by a bureaucrat but providing a rich, detailed, and vivid account of detainee abuse and torture nonetheless.

The debate about torture occurred within a dynamic textual environment made up of an ever-changing documentary record. This documentary record makes up the "reality" of U.S. torture; it provides the basic facts of the matter. Officials may selectively draw on the realities inscribed in these documents to ground their own or weaken competitors' claims about torture. This book tracks these changes in the documentary record, focusing on the different forms that evidence of detainee abuse and torture took and the impact of those different forms on the congressional debate.

Power and Knowledge in the Debate About Torture

The production of evidence of torture—particularly of instances that occurred in a prison far from the political center—requires access to facilities, classified documents, organizational actors, and perpetrators and victims that most political actors do not possess. Those with access, however, are capable of influencing the form and content of the documentary record. In this book, I situate political discourse within the "shifting positions of political parties in Congress," as well as within the shifting organizational dynamics between Congress, executive agencies, the media, and human rights organizations.[48] In so doing, this book reveals how power, as expressed in the control over the documentary record, shaped public debate about torture.

Of particular importance is how actors wield their control over the documentary record to expose or obscure the physical and mental anguish experienced by detainees in U.S. custody. Evidence is neither neutral nor complete; it provides a vantage on particular representations of reality and not others. To access the "event" or "experience" of torture—the physical contact between torturers, their weapons, and victims and the contortion of bodies in pain—we must pass, first, through a selective witnessing of those experiences. Perpetrators, bystanders, and victims cannot attend to the "whole act itself" but to particular aspects of the experience. Elements of the scene of torture fall away as victims give testimony to International Committee of the Red Cross inspectors, human rights monitors, lawyers, official investigators, journalists, and their own communities. Those who receive testimony themselves transform it. Summarizing or transcribing testimony, they erase certain communicative aspects; body language, pauses, and intonation may be lost in the production of written accounts of torture. And so it goes . . . Personal testimonies may be aggregated to produce composite accounts of the standard treatment of detainees in a facility. These, in turn, may be transformed into elementary facts: whether a particular form of torture occurred in a particular place and time.[49]

Because our access to the reality of torture is always mediated by these sorts of partial accounts, our knowledge of it is always selective and incomplete.[50] These remarks are not meant to belittle the work of those who document torture, nor are they meant to suggest that all accounts of torture will or even *ought to* be recognized as valid. Representational practices, even if they cannot fully represent reality, are what allow us to engage in the crucial work of transforming the practice of torture into relatively permanent and stable traces. These very transformations are a precondition of the collective acknowledgment—and, yes, denial, too—of human cruelty and suffering.[51] Recognizing this, we may study how actors document the experience of violence, eking toward an understanding of how communities come to recognize or deny the suffering of others. If we take it as a good that torture be acknowledged and addressed, as I do, then such studies might help us clarify the conditions, as well as the forms that evidence can take, that promote the acknowledgment of suffering.

The American executive branch, because it controls and has access to the sites where interrogation and torture occurs, is uniquely situated to control official representations of interrogation. Official denial of torture is sustained by the executive's production of evidence that silences the "distinctive local historical character" of torture—the ebb and flow of torturers' violence, the excesses of torture's implementation, and the embodied experience of the sufferer's pain.[52] These features of torture tend to be, with high fidelity, represented in survivors' narratives, human rights accounts, and photographs; they trouble dominant justifications of the practice because they activate the illiberal associations that torture carries.

The debate over "enhanced interrogation" is a case in point. Advocates attempt to maintain the legitimacy of "enhanced interrogation" by portraying the practice in instrumentally rational terms. As chapter 6 documents, supporters of the CIA's controversial interrogation program tell stories about its use that highlight the program's restraint, effectiveness, and precision. In doing so, they craft accounts of the practice that neutralize the ferocious qualities of interpersonal violence, the very qualities that recall the illiberality of torture and give the practice its toxicity.

This image of the agency's program, though, is challenged by evidence of torture that retrieves the distinctive local character of U.S. detention and interrogation. The challenge comes from the ways that interrogators tend to inflict pain and the ways that human bodies suffer. Because interrogators lack a science of pain, the implementation of "enhanced interrogation" rarely, if ever, conforms to the interpretive contours of prevailing images of its use. Interrogators cannot increase or adjust pain inclemently and predictably; instead, they creatively deploy, combine, and improvise torture techniques in the hope of approaching a victim's pain threshold.[53]

Torture, moreover, is a culturally mediated activity.[54] Torturers may describe their techniques as derived from a feared, historical inflictor of pain—particularly, the Nazis—to increase their notoriety.[55] Torturers also learn from the cultural traumas enacted on members of their own societies and, in the U.S. case, fictional presentations of the practice, such as those offered by the television show *24*. Because torture is a practice that attacks, in addition to bodies, the social worlds of victims, ethnocentric, sexist, and racist beliefs frequently shape the practice of torture.[56] Gender, sexuality, religion, and the family all may be mobilized to attack the victims.[57] Contemporary torture, even though it is typically presented as callous, clinical, and restrained, often is, in fact, ferocious and ritualized.[58] It may appear, as Don DeLillo describes it, "a drama . . . old as human memory . . . actors naked, chained, blindfolded, other actors with props of intimidation . . . nameless and masked, dressed in black" and so fail to negate the associations of torture with illiberal cruelty.[59] And, while interrogators may use "clean" torture practices that do not produce bodies that carry lasting marks of torture, the suffering body rarely suffers cleanly; more frequently, it appears mangled, contorted, vulnerable, and leaky. Victims of clean torture—including "enhanced interrogation" techniques—bleed, blister, choke and gag, vomit, and lose control over their bodily functions. When rendered visible, through photographs and videos, or legible, through written accounts, these outward signs of an assault on a person's bodily integrity tend to shock the conscience. They remind us of torture's illiberal history and its aim "to strip away from its victims all the qualities of human dignity that liberalism values."[60]

The executive branch has an interest in filtering out these features of torture. Evidence that retrieves the disorders of interrogation, the propensity of interrogators to creatively practice their "art," and the leakiness of suffering human bodies are difficult to accommodate into justifications of painful interrogation practices. Occasionally, documents emerge—photographs, e-mails, interrogation logs—that preserve aspects of these disorders and excesses. Such documents tend to shock the conscience; they are difficult to square with claims that painful interrogation practices are used with restraint and precision. Critics of torture understand this, dwelling on such documents and drawing attention to the ways that the U.S use of the practice fails to conform to standards of professionalism, restraint, and precision.

Notably, these arguments apply to collective responses to other forms of state violence, such as war and capital punishment, particularly in democracies. The democratic practice of violence should appear instrumental, rational, and proportional to the threat it addresses.[61] It must also appear— or be made to appear—to be regulated by rule and law.[62] And, even as violence targets human bodies, it must avoid unnecessarily or excessively violating the dignity of those bodies.[63] Violence that appears to violate the dignity of victims is likely to appear to modern observers as barbaric, repressive, if not sadistic and may also elicit unfavorable comparisons to historical instances of disowned forms of violence, such as lynching.[64] For instance, the "ideal" American execution preserves the appearance that the dignity of the condemned is protected by producing no visible signs of suffering. "Botched" executions, in contrast, produce just such signs. Electric chairs, on the one hand, might burn the flesh of the condemned and cause execution rooms to fill with smoke; lethal injections, on the other hand, might cause bodies to writhe, sometimes for extended periods of time, as in the recent case of Clayton Lockett. Unsurprisingly, botched executions are symbolically potent events and death penalty abolitionists frequently mobilize around them.[65]

Those who approve of "enhanced interrogation" tend to view it as an uncomfortable, perhaps painful, but certainly not brutal practice. The suffering body is effaced through techniques of denial. Apologists describe severe practices—waterboarding, for instance—as briefly used and causing no lasting harm. They compare other practices, such as stress positions and sleep deprivation, to everyday discomforts, such as standing at work or the college student's all-nighter respectively.[66] As the subsequent chapters make clear, the documentary record frequently betrays these portrayals. The release of documents that capture the excesses and disorders of U.S. torture—first, the Abu Ghraib photographs then FBI e-mails about Guantánamo, and, finally, the Guantánamo interrogation log of Mohammed al-Qahtani—profoundly altered how Congress discussed detainee abuse and torture. These documents portrayed terrified, exposed, and vulnerable detainees. They are, for this reason, difficult—though as this book demonstrates, not impossible— to accommodate within modern sensibilities of violence.

These documents have a second important quality. They are official or quasi-official accounts, produced by agents of the state working within military, law enforcement, and intelligence agencies but not always sanctioned by the institutions in which those agents worked (as in the case of the Abu Ghraib photographs). Given their sources, these documents were especially difficult to deny. The tactics of literal denial, in which the source is discredited, cannot easily be applied to American soldiers and FBI agents, who are viewed, in Congress, as credible witnesses to torture with no stake, as human rights organizations or detainees are often said to have, in portraying the country in a poor light.[67] These documents also resist efforts to reinterpret what they document from serious instances of abuse and torture to lesser forms of misconduct. When an FBI agent describes, in an e-mail, the military's use of "torture techniques," one is brought up short.[68] Surely, FBI interrogators know torture when they see it. This is not to say that such allegations cannot be reinterpreted. From Congress's perspective, it is simply harder to do so, as chapter 5 shows, when the allegation comes from a hardened interrogator rather than a journalist or human rights organization.

Political Context, Interpretive Frames, and the Meaning of Evidence

To be recognized as legitimate, violence practiced by liberal democracies should appear rational, restrained, and, even, humane. Because of this, proponents of state violence have difficulty accommodating two qualities of torture into their arguments: those who use painful interrogation techniques are rarely able to control their violence and those who suffer violence rarely suffer it cleanly. Facts, though, have "no absolute size"; they lack, in other words, an objective social meaning.[69] Instead, "every fact belongs to a series and has relative importance only within its series."[70] As I argued earlier, the importance of evidence of abuse and torture derives, in part, from the long-standing, illiberal associations that torture carries. The resonance of evidence of torture also derives from the interpretive frames available for understanding that evidence. An interpretive frame is a "central organizing principle that holds together and gives coherence and meaning to a diverse array of symbols."[71] Frames allow people to "make sense of the raw data" of experience and make "events meaningful."[72]

In the U.S. debate about torture, the balance between national security and the rule of law as political values and interpretive frames is particularly important. In the months and even years following the September 11,

2001, terrorist attacks, U.S. politicians generally referenced allegations of detainee abuse and torture in the context of terrorism and the executive branch's effort to prevent follow-up attacks. This context depressed political concern for those allegations as the abuse of foreigners, some of whom were said to have ties to terrorism, seemed to pale in comparison with the alternative: the return of terror to U.S. cities. Gradually, a rule-of-law frame became available for speaking about detainee abuse and torture. In fact, some U.S. politicians actually fused national security to the rule of law, arguing that the country would only be secure if it pursued counterterrorism policies that emphasized civil liberties and human rights. Within this frame, torture appeared a significant political problem that had actually weakened the country by betraying core national values and fraying the international alliances that the country had built on the presumption that its behavior was restrained by law. Over the course of this book, I track the changes is the political context that enabled U.S. politicians to employ this frame in the debate about torture.

The meaning of torture derived not only from politicians' framing of it but also from how politicians performed its meaning.[73] By the timing of hearings, the titles of hearings, and by inviting particular actors and not others to appear on the stage of a committee hearing, representatives—and particularly committee chairs—exercise the power to "display for others the meaning of their social situation."[74] This is another way that access to political power, in the form of control over congressional committees and expressed in symbolic and performative work of agenda setting, influenced the debate about torture. Between 2003 and 2008, changes in the political context set the conditions in Congress for a discourse that acknowledged torture to emerge. Over the course of this book, I highlight three changes that contributed to this.

The first was the Iraq War. As it became clear, in late 2003 and into 2004, that significant stockpiles of weapons of mass destruction would not be found in the country, the Bush administration turned to human rights and the rule of law as legitimating claims for the war. When the Abu Ghraib photographs became public in April 2004, they profoundly disrupted the narratives that the administration and its supporters in Congress used to justify the war. In part, the acute resonance of the photographs can be explained by this and, in Congress, a protracted reckoning with the violence at the facility followed the photographs' release.

The second and third key changes in the political context came in 2006. In June 2006, the Supreme Court issued a ruling in *Hamdan v. Rumsfeld* against the Bush administration's military commissions at Guantánamo. The decision shifted, albeit in small ways, the balance of power between Congress and the executive on issues pertaining to detainee rights. The ruling required Congress to authorize the commissions. The ruling also required that the commissions be designed to be consistent with the U.S. Code of Military Justice and Geneva Conventions. The decision, then, required Congress to take a more active role on detainee rights than it had previously and forced Congress to involve spokespeople for military and international law in the debate.

The final change that this book highlights is the 2006 midterm election, which swung control over both Houses of Congress from the Republicans to Democrats. The difference in the frequency, tenor, and agenda of congressional hearings on detainee abuse and torture before and after the election is notable. Before the election, the Republican-controlled committees largely limited their witness lists to representatives of the executive; legal experts, human rights organizations, and detainees' lawyers, among others, were, with a few exceptions, excluded from the debate. This narrowed Congress's discourse, which was characterized by denial of torture and the exoneration of administration policies. Following the election, the Democrats opened committee hearings to a diverse group of political actors. Suddenly, human rights claims and antitorture positions were consistently heard during congressional hearings.

CONCLUSION

"Denial," the sociologist Stanley Cohen writes, "is the normal state of affairs."[75] Recognizing this, Cohen articulates a research agenda for the study of political and cultural responses to atrocity:

> Instead of agonizing about why denial occurs, we should take this state for granted. The theoretical problem is not, "why do we shut out?" but "why do we ever not shut out?" The empirical problem is not to uncover yet more evidence of denial, but to discover the conditions under which information is acknowledged and acted upon.[76]

This book accounts for the shift in elite political discourse from denial to acknowledgment of U.S. torture. Congress's discourse of acknowledgment applied the "torture word" to U.S. interrogation practices and construed the use of those practices as a significant political problem. Given the dominance of denial, there are few studies of acknowledgment. Those studies that do focus on acknowledgment—such as Leigh Payne's excellent book *Unsettling Accounts: Neither Truth nor Reconciliation in Confessions of State Violence*—include analyses of cases quite unlike this study's.[77] Payne examines the struggle over state violence that follows nondemocratic states' transitions to democracy. We have in the case of the United States an instance in which acknowledgment occurred within a democracy and during the administration that authorized torture. The case of this study also differs from those Payne studied—Argentina, Chile, Brazil, and South Africa—in that the United States primarily tortured foreign prisoners and did so within the context of international conflicts, rather than domestic ones.

While these distinctions may limit the generalizability of the U.S. case, we have, in this case, an instance in which acknowledgment emerged even as the military conflicts in which torture was practiced persisted. This book, then, sheds light on the social conditions, political processes, and forms of knowledge that permit a government to work itself, at least partially, out of the discourses that sustain torture. As the rest of this book documents, the emergence of a discourse critical of torture is related to changes in several key factors. Members of Congress encountered an evolving documentary record that retrieved the disorders and excesses of detention and interrogation. These representations of detention and interrogation served as resources to establish the illiberal reality of U.S. torture. Members of Congress also encountered—and under Democratic leadership after the 2006 midterm elections helped produce—a change in political culture that fused the pursuit of national security to the protection of human rights and the rule of law. In this frame, torture appeared a betrayal of core U.S. values and a threat to U.S. interests. The emergence of the discourse of acknowledgment is, then, a story of changes in political knowledge, understandings, and power.

CHAPTER | 2

The Heartbreak of Acknowledgment

FROM METROPOLITAN DETENTION CENTER TO ABU GHRAIB

ON APRIL 28, 2004, CBS broadcast photographs showing U.S. soldiers abusing detainees held at Abu Ghraib prison in Iraq.[1] Taken, predominantly, by Americans working the night shift of Tier 1A, a cellblock reserved for high-value detainees, the photographs showed soldiers posing with naked detainees and, most famously, a hooded detainee standing on a box, arms by his side and electrical wires running from his body to the wall.

Eight days after the release of the first photographs, President George W. Bush offered an apology to the king of Jordan and publicly recounted, "I told him I was sorry for the humiliation suffered by the Iraqi prisoners and the humiliation suffered by their families."[2] That same day, the president offered another apology in an interview with Egypt's Al-Ahram International.[3] Despite the apologies, the damage to the president was apparent. The first poll conducted by ABC News/*Washington Post* after the release of the photographs found public approval of Bush's performance as president to be below 50 percent for the first time.[4] John Kerry's presidential campaign and several major news publications called for Secretary of Defense Donald Rumsfeld's resignation.[5]

After April 28, 2004, U.S. politicians confronted what the sociologist Jeffrey Alexander refers to as a "fundamental social crisis."[6] While the majority of political debate involves the "relatively mundane level of goals, power and interest" that do not conflict with "more general values and norms," a crisis occurs when there exists broad consensus that an event has threatened core social institutions, norms, and values.[7] A decade later, the publication of the Abu Ghraib photographs continues to reverberate

within U.S. political culture as a "lasting point of demarcation" within narratives of U.S. detention and interrogation policies.[8] This point is well illus-
trated by general and then-commander of U.S. Central Command David
Petraeus, who described Abu Ghraib as "nonbiodegradable."[9]

The release of the Abu Ghraib photographs was a revelation. Yet it did
not provide the American public and government its first opportunity to
confront, post-9/11, the abuse of detainees in U.S. custody. In June 2003,
the Department of Justice's Office of the Inspector General released an
investigation into the abuse of detainees held by the FBI in connection
with the bureau's investigation of the September 11, 2001, terrorist attacks.
The allegations of abuse, which occurred at Metropolitan Detention Center (MDC) in Brooklyn, New York, did not provoke nearly as intense a
political response as the allegations of abuse at Abu Ghraib did. In Alexander's terms, the allegations of abuse remained on the level of "mundane
politics"; there existed no consensus that these allegations threatened core
U.S. institutions or values.

This chapter addresses a series of questions about the political response
to detainee abuse at MDC and Abu Ghraib. How did U.S. politicians'
downplay the abuse at MDC? Conversely, how did their response to Abu
Ghraib contribute to it becoming a political crisis? And why did these two
events provoke such dramatically different responses?

The juxtaposition of congressional responses to MDC and Abu Ghraib
is instructive for two reasons. First, unlike the photographed abuse at Abu
Ghraib, U.S. politicians initially encountered the mistreatment of prisoners
at MDC as merely verbal allegations. The comparison allows us to detect
how differing forms of evidence influenced political responses to these two
cases. Second, the juxtaposition provides the opportunity to clarify the
limits of the influence of the Abu Ghraib photographs. Like the violence
at Abu Ghraib, the abuse at MDC was, in fact, visually documented. In
December 2003, the inspector general released a supplemental report to
its investigation that included stills from video recordings from MDC.
That this development inspired no significant political response suggests
the need to turn our attention from the forms of evidence that abuse takes
to the context in which politicians respond to that evidence. By presenting
an analysis of proximate cases—the Senate Judiciary Committee reviewed
the abuse at MDC in June 2003, the Senate Armed Services Committee began its review of Abu Ghraib in May 2004—this chapter does this,

documenting changes in the political context over this time and showing how these changes provided interpretive frames that rendered MDC mundane and Abu Ghraib a crisis.

BEFORE ABU GHRAIB: THE ABUSE OF
THE "SEPTEMBER 11 DETAINEES"

After the September 11, 2001, terrorist attacks, the FBI opened a broad, nationwide investigation. Code-named PENTTBOM ("Pentagon, Twin Tower Bombing"), the investigation was the largest in the bureau's history and involved more than half of all FBI employees.[10] Its purpose was to identify those involved with the September 11, 2001, terrorist attacks and to prevent future such events.[11] According to the inspector general, over the first two months of the investigation, the FBI and other law enforcement agencies detained more than 1,200 U.S. citizens and foreigners.[12] While many of those detained were subsequently released without charge, by August 2002 at least 762 foreigners were held by the Immigration and Naturalization Services.[13]

The detentions quickly raised concerns. Media reports and human rights investigations suggested that detainees may have been racially profiled, typically lacked information relevant to the FBI's investigation, were subjected to unfocused interrogations, if they were subjected to interrogations at all, and were denied counsel. Reports also suggested that detainees were held in inhumane conditions and were verbally and physically abused by corrections officers and cellmates.[14]

The Department of Justice's Office of the Inspector General opened an investigation into these allegations in March 2002.[15] The report focused on two detention facilities—Passaic County Jail in Paterson, New Jersey, and MDC—which "held the majority of September 11 detainees and were the focus of many complaints about detainee mistreatment."[16] The inspector general's office released its report on June 2, 2003.[17] It documented that eighty-four "September 11 detainees" held at MDC in Brooklyn were kept in " 'lock down' for at least 23 hours per day," were held in cells that were lit for twenty-four hours a day, were maintained in a "a '4-man hold' with handcuffs, leg irons, and heavy chains any time [they] were moved outside their cells," and were limited to a single legal and a single social call per month.[18] At MDC, prison employees "frustrated efforts by detainees' attorneys, families, and even law enforcement officials, to determine where the detainees were being held" and, in some cases, provided incorrect information to people inquiring about the detainees.[19] The IG's report affirmed allegations that officers at MDC had forcefully pulled detainees out of the vehicles that transported them to the prisons, slammed detainees against walls upon their arrival, dragged them by their arms, and "twisted their arms, hands, wrists, and fingers."[20] The report also documented that corrections officers at MDC taunted and threatened detainees, referring to them as "Bin Laden Junior" and telling them that "you're going to die here," "you're never going to get out of here," "you will be here for 20–25 years like the Cuban people," "you will feel pain," and "someone thinks you have something to do with the World Trade Center so don't expect to be treated well."[21]

Staging MDC as Mundane Politics

On June 25, 2003, three weeks after the publication of the inspector general's report, the Senate Judiciary Committee convened a hearing to receive testimony about the IG's findings. This chronology is itself significant. Reports of the abuse at MDC emerged within weeks of the September 11 terrorist attacks; however, the Office of the Inspector General began conducting research for its report about a half-year later and published its report in June 2003, nearly twenty-one months after the September 11 attacks. The Senate Judiciary Committee, too, responded slowly, allowing nearly a month to pass before reviewing the IG's findings. The relative lethargy of political responses to the abuse of the "September 11 detainees" both suggests and displays its political insignificance. In the eyes of the committee—or, at least, its Republican Chair, Orrin Hatch—the abuse of the "September 11 detainees" was not a matter that required an urgent response.

The makeup of the hearing had a similar effect. Of the committee's nineteen members, only seven—Hatch, ranking Democrat Patrick Leahy, Republicans Saxby Chambliss and Arlen Specter and Democrats Russ Feingold, Diane Feinstein, and Charles Schumer—attended the hearing. (Feinstein, though, offered no statement and did not question witnesses.) Only Hatch and Feingold were in attendance to question both of the committee's two panels of witnesses. Absent were several high-profile committee members, including Republicans Jeff Sessions, Lindsey Graham, and

John Cornyn, all of whom also served at the time on the Senate Armed Services Committee, and Democrats Ted Kennedy, Joe Biden, and John Edwards. As Hatch explained, the Senate's attention was split that day, as there were several votes on amendments to legislation reforming Medicare that committee members attended. The absence of thirteen members should not be interpreted as a reflection of the committee's utter disregard for the treatment of the "September 11 detainees." Still, the members' poor attendance at the hearing reflects where the treatment of the "September 11 detainees" stood among the committee members' many priorities.

The witnesses called to account for the treatment of the "September 11 detainees" reflected something similar. The first panel featured Glenn A. Fine, the inspector general of the Department of Justice. Fine's appearance before the committee is typical of congressional hearings that focus on an investigation produced within the executive branch; ordinarily, the head investigator or investigators testify about their findings. The second panel of witnesses, however, included no high-ranking official within the Department of Justice or the FBI. Director Harley G. Lappin represented the Federal Bureau of Prisons; David Nahmias, counsel to the assistant attorney general of the Criminal Division of the Department of Justice, represented the Department of Justice; and Michael E. Rolince, the acting assistant director in charge of the Washington field office, represented the FBI.[22]

Early in the hearing, Leahy and Feingold drew attention to the absence of Attorney General John Ashcroft, Deputy Attorney General Larry Thompson, and Director of the FBI Robert Mueller. Leahy did so in his opening statement. After thanking Fine and his office for their report, Leahy lamented that "we do not have the Attorney General or other senior witnesses from Main Justice and the FBI, or even outside experts who could shed light on the Department's performance at this hearing. Their absence calls into question the hearing's value."[23] During the subsequent question-and-answer portion of the hearing, Feingold returned to the issue, questioning the legitimacy of the hearing given the attorney general's absence:

> I find it very troubling that neither the Attorney General nor the Deputy Attorney General are here to testify today. . . . The absence of a high-level official from Main Justice frustrates legitimate and meaningful oversight of the Department. This is unfortunate. Imagine, the Attorney General or the Deputy Attorney General are not here to respond to an Inspector General's report about serious abuses within the Justice Department.[24]

The sociologist Nancy Naples, in a study of welfare reform, writes that policy makers

> are situated in a position of power to control whose voices will be represented in the legislative hearings. The organization of congressional hearings establishes spaces for certain actors to perform on the discursive stage, inhibits others from participating, and renders silent the voices of those whose perspectives do not fit.[25]

Naples's claims require some adjustment to account for the effect of Ashcroft's absence from the Senate Judiciary Committee's hearing. In 2003, as the Republican chairman of the Senate Judiciary Committee, Senator Orrin Hatch was "in a position of power to control whose voices will be represented" at the committee's hearing. It would be peculiar, though, to argue that Hatch excluded and so silenced Attorney General John Ashcroft, who is both a member of Hatch's political party and himself a former chairman of the Senate Judiciary Committee, because Ashcroft's perspective did not fit that of the hearing. Instead, Hatch's exclusion of Ashcroft mattered in a different way: it dramatized the perceived political insignificance of the issues before the committee. The attorney general is the highest-profile official from which the Senate Judiciary Committee will generally receive testimony. His involvement would have signaled that the abuse of detainees at MDC demanded an urgent and full political accounting. Ashcroft's absence, however, signaled the opposite; the treatment of the "September 11 detainees" was insufficiently important to compel the attorney general to testify.

After Feingold finished questioning the inspector general, Hatch responded to Feingold's criticisms by noting that the attorney general would appear before the committee at an upcoming oversight hearing. Hatch also claimed that the attorney general's presence was not necessary to effectively oversee the Department of Justice and stated that "time spent complaining about who the witnesses are today is wasted time."[26] This elicited a contentious exchange between Feingold and Hatch in which the two Senators competed to define the symbolic significance of the issues before the committee:

FEINGOLD: The symbolic importance of an Inspector General's report about abuses within the Justice Department I think requires the top person to be here—
HATCH: Well, he will be here.

FEINGOLD: —to respond. But in a context—

HATCH: So will the FBI Director.

FEINGOLD: Mr. Chairman, if I may finish, in a context where that is the focus of the entire hearing, not one of these around-the-world hearings where we all bring up 8,000 different issues, as we must, in a general oversight hearing.[27] This is unique, this is important, and this should be the exclusive focus of a hearing where the Attorney General should respond.[28]

In the exchange, Feingold makes his view of the stakes of the hearing explicit by claiming that the "symbolic importance" of the inspector general's report demands the presence of the attorney general. Feingold's criticism, like those of Leahy earlier in the hearing, attempts to build up the abuse of the "September 11 detainees" into a significant and pressing political problem. Senator Hatch's response—as well as his early decision not to invite any of the witnesses listed by Senator Leahy to the hearing—suggests a different construction of the issue, one that plays down its importance by portraying it as insufficiently consequential to compel the presence of the attorney general. The very fact of the competition signals the lack of political consensus about the symbolic importance of the allegations.

The Senate Judiciary Committee's response to the release of the inspector general's report on the "September 11 detainees" was lethargic and low key. The committee called no high-ranking official in the executive to account for the abuse of detainees at Metropolitan Detention Center in New York. In fact, a majority of the committee's members were absent from the hearing. It is important to note that this disinterested response to the inspector general's report was not the committee's alone. Media coverage of the hearing was scant. The *New York Times* devoted just over 800 words on page 18 of its June 26 edition to the hearing.[29] The *Washington Post* published an even briefer, 468-word article on page 3 of its edition the day after the committee's hearing.[30] Neither article provided much original reporting, straightforwardly juxtaposing the inspector general's findings with the Department of Justice's response.

Staging Abu Ghraib as Crisis

Compared with the Senate Judiciary Committee's response to the release of the IG's report on the "September 11 detainees," the political response to the public release of the Abu Ghraib photographs was rapid and intense. Within a week and a half, both the president and the secretary of defense had apologized. One congressional committee, the Senate Armed Services Committee, opened a series of seven public hearings on detention and interrogation on May 7, 2004, nine days after CBS's report. Twenty-three of the committee's twenty-five members attended this hearing. Only Republicans John Ensign and James Inhofe were absent. The committee was joined by Senator Bill Frist, a Republican and then Senate majority leader.

The witnesses included the secretary of defense, Donald Rumsfeld, and the chairman of the Joint Chiefs of Staff, Richard Myers. The inclusion of these two men contrasts, dramatically, with the absence of Ashcroft, Thompson, and Mueller from the Senate Judiciary Committee's hearing on MDC. Rumsfeld's and Myers's presence before the Senate Armed Services Committee, not ten days after CBS's broadcast and before the release of any official investigation, signaled the seriousness of the event, as well as the immediate need for a political accounting of it. This was apparent in the buildup to the hearing. The C-SPAN video archive of the hearing opens by following Secretary Rumsfeld, surrounded by security, military officials, and others, as he makes his way to the committee room. As Rumsfeld enters the room, he is swarmed by members of the media, who stand to capture photographs, video, and audio of the secretary. The sporadic flash of camera bulbs is apparent as Rumsfeld makes his way to the witness desk (see figure 2.1). The sounds of photography—the snap of shutters opening and closing— crescendos when the secretary and the other witnesses are sworn in.

The very staging of the Armed Services Committee's first hearing on Abu Ghraib expresses the urgency and importance with which it treated the allegations of abuse at the facility. Hearing participants also built up the Abu Ghraib scandal through their use of rhetoric. During the Senate Armed Services' May 7 hearing, there was broad and bipartisan consensus that the publication of the Abu Ghraib photographs was a significant political event. In their opening statements, the committee's chair, Republican John Warner, the committee's ranking Democrat, Carl Levin, and Secretary of Defense Donald Rumsfeld all elevated their rhetoric, referencing the U.S. Armed Forces and the Nation itself while describing the dire consequences of the release of the Abu Ghraib photographs. Warner opened the hearing by describing the allegations of abuse at Abu Ghraib as "as serious as an issue of military misconduct as I ever have observed."[31] He then noted that

FIGURE 2.1. Secretary of Defense Donald Rumsfeld (*seated at center*) prepares to testify to the Senate Armed Services Committee on May 7, 2004.

Source: Getty Images. Photograph by Scott J. Ferrell.

the reports of abuse could "seriously affect this country's relationships with other nations, the conduct of the war against terrorism, and place in jeopardy the men and women of the Armed Forces wherever they are serving in the world."[32] The ranking Democrat in the committee, Carl Levin, followed Warner by observing, at the very top of his opening statement, that

> the abuses that were committed against prisoners in U.S. custody at the Abu Ghraib prison in Iraq dishonored our military and our Nation, and they made the prospects for success in Iraq even more difficult than they already are. Our troops are less secure and our Nation is less secure because these depraved and despicable actions will fuel the hatred and fury of those who oppose us.[33]

Rumsfeld, for his part, used his opening statement to take responsibility for the events at Abu Ghraib and to apologize to the "Iraqis who were mistreated by members of the U.S. Armed Forces. It was inconsistent with the values of our Nation. It was inconsistent with the teachings of the military to the men and women of the Armed Forces. It was certainly fundamentally un-American."[34]

In addition to describing the abuse at Abu Ghraib as a threat to core national values and institutions, these statements also suggest relative consensus among the involved actors—the Republican chair, the ranking Democrat, and the Republican secretary of defense—about the meaning of Abu Ghraib. In fact, over the course of the hearings, Republican and Democrat claims converged, at least when addressing the implications of the abuse of the detainees. Nine of the hearings' twenty-nine participants—including Democrats Levin, Jack Reed, and Ben Nelson, Republicans Warner, Jeff Sessions, John McCain, and Frist, Secretary of Defense Rumsfeld, and Joint Chiefs of Staff Myers—lamented that the photographs had dishonored the U.S. military. Five—Democrats Levin and Mark Pryor and Republicans Warner, Susan Collins, and Elizabeth Dole—observed that U.S. soldiers would face increased dangers abroad because of the release of the photographs. Six—Levin, Warner, McCain, Dole, Myers, and General Lance Smith, deputy commander of U.S. Central Command—expressed worry that the photographs would undermine the U.S. war in Iraq. Eight—Democrats Levin, Kennedy, Pryor, and Reed; Republicans Collins and Dole; Secretary Rumsfeld; and Smith—noted that that the release of the photographs undermined the reputation of the United States.

DENIAL AND THE POWER OF VISUAL EVIDENCE

Why, though, did the committees respond in the ways that they did to these events? There is an obvious difference in the ways that MDC and Abu Ghraib arrived on the political scene. Abu Ghraib arrived, famously, as photographs. MDC arrived, initially, through the verbal allegations of those who suffered abuse and, then, through the inspector general's report. In this section, I consider the influence of these different forms of evidence on political discourse.

MDC and the Contested Reality of Abuse

Senator Hatch's decision not to involve the attorney general and other high-ranking officials depressed the symbolic importance of the hearing.

It also set the stage for the performance of the abuse of the "September 11 detainees" as an inconsequential political issue. This performance began with the condemnations of the physical abuse that the IG reported. Hatch offered a representative condemnation in his opening statement:

> But without a doubt, the most disturbing aspect of the IG report relates to the allegations of abuse and mistreatment of several detainees who were housed in the MDC. Let me state this unequivocally: abuse of inmates, no matter what the actual or potential charges, is wrong. It cannot be tolerated. And should any of the allegations in the IG's report be sufficiently corroborated, the responsible parties should be prosecuted to the fullest extent under the law.[35]

There are two things of note in this condemnation. First, and unlike the condemnations of Abu Ghraib that I discussed above, it did not describe the allegations of abuse as consequential; that is, Hatch did not describe the allegations of abuse as interfering with any national projects or interests. Nor did Hatch describe the allegations of abuse as inconsistent with specific institutional or national values. Although Hatch described the allegations as disturbing, wrong, and intolerable, he was not moved to elevate his rhetoric, mobilize taken-for-granted beliefs of American civil society, and interpret the allegations in relation to them.[36] Put simply, Hatch's condemnation suggested that nothing—neither the country's interests nor the reputations of its institutions—had been threatened by the reports of abuse.

Second, Senator Hatch described the abuse of the detainees at MDC as allegations awaiting sufficient corroboration, rather than substantiated incidents of abuse. This description contrasts with the inspector general's opening statement to the Senate Judiciary Committee, as well as the text of the IG's report. In his opening statement, Inspector General Fine definitively acknowledged that abuse had occurred at MDC: "With regard to allegations of abuse, we concluded that the evidence indicates a pattern of physical and verbal abuse by some correctional officers at the MDC against some September 11 detainees."[37]

The construction of facts is, in part, a rhetorical process by which people gradually disconnect statements from their initial speakers.[38] To usher "allegations" of abuse to a "pattern" of abuse is to disconnect "abuse" from the specific individuals who first alleged it; it is to turn a subjective claim into an intersubjective reality. This is what the inspector general attempted in his statement to the Senate Judiciary Committee. To draw attention to the fact that abuse is "alleged," as Hatch did, is to portray the allegations as bound to the subjective positions of those who made the allegation; it is also to implicitly call into question whether those alleged instances of violence actually occurred.

Over the course of the Senate Judiciary's hearing, several other participants challenged the very reality of abuse at MDC. During the question-and-answer portion of the hearing, Chambliss asked Fine where he got his information from. This elicited an exchange that highlighted the contested nature of the allegations of abuse:

FINE: We got it from a number of sources, some of them from the detainees themselves; some of them from the attorneys; some of them from the Bureau of Prisons, who had received complaints; some of them from public documents.

CHAMBLISS: How about from the prisons guards and the prison personnel? Did any of the information come from them?

FINE: The initial allegations did not, but we have spoken to the prison guards and the prison personnel.

CHAMBLISS: Do they agree that that took place?

FINE: The officers who were the subjects of the inquiry denied it, as we point out in the report. There are at least some that have confirmed it, but the subjects have denied it.[39]

Chambliss did not draw any conclusions from the fact that, as the inspector general testified, "The officers who were the subjects of the inquiry denied it." Nor did he explicitly state that an observer of the hearing should be skeptical that abuse, in fact, occurred. Yet he also did not explicitly state that an observer of the hearing should accept the IG's findings of a "pattern of physical and verbal abuse" on the grounds that the IG's office collected information from diverse sources, including some prison personnel who confirmed the allegations. The transformation of the allegations of abuse to fact idles in the exchange, caught up in the denials of those accused of abuse and the confirmations of other corrections officers.

In the second part of the committee's hearing, Harley Lappin, director of the Federal Bureau of Prisons, directly contested that abuse occurred at

MDC. In his opening statement, Lappin testified that, "To our knowledge, all allegations by the post-September 11 detainees housed at Brooklyn have either been investigated and found to be without substantiation or are currently being investigated."[40]

Officials frequently deny human rights violations by engaging in "literal denial," the outright rejection that alleged incidents occurred.[41] Chambliss' exchange with Fine approaches literal denial; while Chambliss makes no outright denial of abuse, the back-and-forth between the senator and the IG disrupts the transformation of alleged incidents of abuse into substantiated abuse. Lappin's statement goes further, construing allegations to either be "without substantiation" or still of uncertain validity ("currently being investigated").

Participants in the Senate Judiciary Committee's hearing on MDC treated the abuse there as alleged, rather than established. The claims of detainees, corrections officers who witnessed the abuse, and the inspector general were insufficient to establish the reality of the violence at the prison. When encountering Abu Ghraib, however, U.S. politicians confronted violence inscribed in digital photographs. This had a profound influence on political discourse.

"Things That Did, in Fact, Happen": Abu Ghraib and the Objectivity of Photographs

The Abu Ghraib photographs disturbed American politics. They were, first and foremost, empirically undeniable. Here, an oft-cited passage from Roland Barthes is instructive. In his study of photography, Barthes asserted, "in Photography I can never deny *that the thing has been there.*"[42] In a response to a question, posed by Chairman Warner, about the impact of the release of the photographs, Secretary of Defense Donald Rumsfeld implicitly acknowledged this quality of photographs when he stated:

> We have been enormously disadvantaged by false allegations and lies for the better part of a year . . . by terrorists and terrorist organizations alleging things that weren't true. So we have taken a beating in the world for things we were not doing that were alleged to be done. Now we're taking a beating, understandably, for things that did, in fact, happen.[43]

The release of the Abu Ghraib photographs made it impossible to engage in literal denial. To refer to the abuse at Abu Ghraib prison was to refer to visual documents of it. With the authenticity of the photographs established and, given prevailing attitudes toward the evidentiary value of photography, the abuse at Abu Ghraib prison could be *seen*, witnessed.[44] In this way, the photographs foreclosed much of the debate that surrounded MDC—whether, in fact, the alleged instances of abuse corresponded to actual instances.

The Abu Ghraib photographs, moreover, show blood, nudity and sexual violence, and military dogs attacking unarmed, naked detainees. For some viewers, the photographs conjured dark associations. Like photographs of lynching, the violence depicted in the Abu Ghraib photographs appears staged for an immediate audience that includes celebratory perpetrators and bystanders. Also like lynching photographs, the images from Abu Ghraib also appear to have circulated among audiences—other soldiers at the facility—who would sympathize with, if not take pleasure from, viewing the actions of the photographed perpetrators.[45] Viewers of the photographs also noted similarities between the photographs and Christian iconography, especially the Crucifixion.[46] This is particularly true of the now iconic photograph of a hooded detainee on a box attached to wires—a technique, in fact, known to English soldiers during World War I as the crucifixion.[47] Other images of detainees in stress positions also resemble the Crucifixion, a fact not lost on Specialist Sabrina Harman, one of the military police officers who took and posed in photographs at Abu Ghraib. Harman, in an October 20, 2003, letter, described how a handcuffed detainee "looked like Jesus Christ."[48]

Although we do not always know what politicians saw when they looked at the Abu Ghraib photographs, they often described themselves or were described by spokespeople as having been reduced to nonverbal communication, if not outright silence, by the photographs. In his opening statement, Rumsfeld told the committee and its audience:

The photographic depictions of the U.S. military personnel that the public has seen have offended and outraged everyone in the DOD. If you could have seen the anguished expressions on the faces of those in our Department upon seeing those photos, you would know how we feel today.[49]

Others in the hearing made comparable statements. McCain worried that Americans would have the same impulse that he had when viewing the photographs, "and that's to turn away from them."[50] Pryor observed that he "had trouble explaining the photographs and what's going on inside that prison, with my 10-year-old son. They're very hard to explain."[51] Not even the president was immune to the silencing power of the Abu Ghraib images. An aide to President Bush described that the president simply "shook his head in disgust" upon viewing the photographs.[52]

Evidence, Knowing, and Political Crisis

At the Senate Judiciary Committee's hearing on the "September 11 detainees," the very reality of "detainee abuse" was questioned. Hearing participants spoke of "allegations" of abuse or outright denied that any substantiated incidents of abuse had been documented. This occurred despite the inspector general's relative confidence—expressed in his testimony and in his office's report—that evidence, collected from both detainees and some corrections officers at MDC, supported the claim that abuse had occurred in the facility. The fate of Abu Ghraib was different. While there were questions about the extent of detainee abuse across Iraq (see chapter 3) and the causes of that abuse (see chapter 4), no participant in the Senate Armed Services' hearing doubted that "things had, in fact, happened" at Abu Ghraib.

Research suggests that that the objectivity or reality of an event is insufficient to account for collective responses to it—whether it will, in other words, lead to a crisis or scandal.[53] Instead, collective, intersubjective understandings of events, rather than events themselves, are said to account for the onset, nature, and fate of a crisis. Congress's different responses to detainee abuse at MDC and Abu Ghraib suggest the need to qualify this understanding of collective responses to events. The representational form that events take—rather than "events themselves"—may influence collective responses to them. In 2004, the "detainee abuse" problem at Abu Ghraib may have met a similar political fate as did the earlier allegations of abuse at MDC were it not for the existence and publication of the Abu Ghraib photographs. Or, at least, the political consensus that the abuse of detainees at Abu Ghraib occurred may have been far more difficult to establish, as in the case of MDC, without the photographs. This point is consistent with broader studies of representations of violence, as well as the documentary strategies of medical professionals and human rights workers, who have developed diverse representational strategies, including photographic ones, to make torture visible to political communities.[54]

"Events," moreover, are never interpretively available in their entirety; they must be processed and transformed into written, visual, or auditory representations to be interpretively accessible.[55] Such transformations may involve the production of a textual or visual reality and, as I show in the next chapter, those textual or visual realities may vary based on the "extent" of reality they represent and the proximity of that reality to lived experience. It is important, though, to recognize the diversity of forms that accounts of reality can take. In the cases of MDC and Abu Ghraib, the forms that allegations of abuse took clearly influenced the consensus, or lack thereof, about whether abuse occurred. With the release of the photographs from Abu Ghraib, U.S. politicians were compelled to admit that something—whether they called it abuse, mistreatment, or torture—had occurred there. In contrast, participants in the Senate Judiciary Committee enjoyed considerable leeway to cast doubt on the mistreatment of the "September 11 detainees," which was textually, but not visually, documented at the time of their hearing.

Representational forms are diverse and, in that diversity, they present actors with different opportunities and challenges for interpretive work. Interpretive work, however, still occurs within a particular social and historical context that enables and constrains discursive possibilities. In fact, about six months after the Senate Judiciary Committee held its hearing on the inspector general's report on MDC, the inspector general's office released a supplement to it that made reference to and included visual records of the abuse at MDC.[56] The supplement updated the initial investigation as a result of the IG's office's acquisition of 308 videotapes of officer-detainee interactions that confirmed many and "did not refute any of the detainees' allegations."[57] Included in the supplemental report are several stills taken from these videotapes that show corrections office pushing detainees faces against concrete walls, twisting detainees' arms and wrists, and forcing them to stand in front of a t-shirt with an American flag and the slogan "These Colors Don't Run." The inspector general also reported that the videotapes revealed that detainees had been laughed at when they underwent strip searches, many of which the report found were unnecessary. Still, the abuse at MDC barely registered. Media coverage of the release of the supplemental report and the video stills was limited. Only the *Washington Post* and the *New York Daily News* provided original coverage of the report.[58] The Senate Judiciary Committee did not revisit the IG's report.

The Abu Ghraib photographs affected many of their viewers in profound ways and the political controversy following their release was magnitudes greater than to earlier official announcements and media reports concerning detainee abuse in Iraq and at Abu Ghraib. On March 20, 2004, the Coalition Provisional Authority in Iraq announced criminal charges against six military personal for "conspiracy, dereliction of duty, cruelty and maltreatment, assault, and indecent acts with another."[59] Between then and the first release of images from Abu Ghraib on April 28, thirteen articles mentioning Abu Ghraib prison and detainee abuse or mistreatment appeared in U.S. and international newspapers. This total was eclipsed in the forty-eight hours following the release of the images and, in the first week of May, these publications ran approximately 729 articles mentioning the abuse.[60]

This, coupled with the public statements of outrage of political elites, signals the photographs effect and affect. Yet the photographs' capacity to disturb is not the whole story of the social and political response to them. Studies of photography consistently observe that photographs alone are insufficient to move public opinion; instead, what Susan Sontag refers to as a "context of feeling and attitude" must be present for a photograph to register at all.[61] The fact that some of the photographs openly circulated at Abu Ghraib prison and were used within the prison to humiliate detainees is evidence of the unevenness of responses to them.[62] To develop a more robust understanding of government responses to both MDC and Abu Ghraib, it is necessary to avert our attention from the evidence of abuse at both prisons and direct it to the political contexts in which officials responded to that evidence.

THE CONTEXT OF MUNDANE AND CRISIS POLITICS

The different political responses to MDC and Abu Ghraib were not simply matters of fact. Members of Congress encountered MDC and Abu Ghraib within different political contexts; these contexts shaped how participants in the Senate Judiciary and Armed Services committees spoke about these two events. Specifically, the Senate Judiciary Committee understood the abuse at MDC as occurring within a political context defined by the pursuit of national security after September 11, 2001. In this context, the abuse at MDC appeared a regrettable, but tolerable mistake. U.S. politicians, in contrast, understood Abu Ghraib within a context defined by the pursuit of U.S. and Iraqi support for the war on Iraq. In this context, the abuse at Abu Ghraib threatened to weaken the political relationships necessary for the U.S.'s political and military projects in Iraq.

September 11 and the Competing Values of National Security and Civil Liberties

For members of the Senate Judiciary Committee, the mistreatment of the "September 11 detainees" occurred in the long shadow of the September 11, 2001, terrorist attacks. The attacks are stamped into the label that the detainees were and remain known by, even though few of them were found to have ties to terrorist organizations or activities, let alone the September 11 attacks. Every participant in the hearing referenced the September 11 attacks. Even those who made statements most critical of the Department of Justice and the FBI, such as Leahy and Feingold, spoke of the uncertainty that the attacks unleashed and the efficiency of those who investigated it. This bipartisan acknowledgment of the terrorist attacks indicates that "September 11" had, in 2003, a relatively uncontested meaning for members of the committee. The events of September 11 were unavoidable; they were the primary facts against which all other ones about law enforcement's behavior would be interpreted. A statement by Hatch, at the start of the question-and-answer period of the second panel, illustrates this well:

> As we consider these criticisms with 20/20 hindsight nearly 2 years after the 9/11 attacks, it is important to recognize the monumental challenges our country, the Government, and in particular the Justice Department faced in the immediate aftermath of the September 11 attacks.[63]

The September 11 attacks provided powerful interpretive frames for understanding the behavior of law enforcement officials. In the aftermath of the attacks, law enforcement agencies—Hatch, Chambliss, Schumer, and all four witnesses acknowledged—acted and were correct to act as if more attacks might be impending, a fact highlighted in *New York Times* coverage of the hearing.[64] In his opening statement, Rolince, the FBI's representative at the hearing, described at length the challenges the agency faced after the September 11 terrorist attacks. His description touched on the well-known—the threat of follow-up terrorist activity, the anthrax attacks, and the kidnapping of Daniel Pearl. Rolince, however, went further, emphasizing that, pre-9/11, the FBI lacked the institutional resources to adequately investigate terrorism. Post-9/11, the agency, particularly in New York City, faced institutional chaos due to the attacks even as the agency's investigation "became the largest and most complex investigation in the history of the FBI. In spite of operating under severe handicaps, the New York office—relocated to a garage on 26th Street, and lacking a proficient infrastructure—began a 24/7 operation utilizing 300 investigators from 37 agencies."[65]

Under these circumstances, a particular political good became valued over all others: national security. Statements about law enforcement's behavior in light of the perceived threat of terrorism implied a consequentialist calculus that pitted the abuses that the IG documented against the devastation and political fallout of a hypothetical terrorist attack. In an exchange with the Fine, Chambliss implicitly referenced this calculus:

CHAMBLISS: Did you take into consideration the fact that there is a great likelihood that because of the actions of the FBI both here with respect to these detainees and also with other work that they were doing, the FBI has been pretty successful in having no further attacks take place within the United States?
FINE: Yes, we have taken note of that. Everyone, I think, has taken note of that. That is certainly a fact.[66]

Later in the hearing, Schumer made a pointed statement to this effect:

I am sure if you did nothing and then, God forbid, one of these people committed a terrorist act, all the articles would be the other way: What the heck? Why didn't you do it? You didn't move quickly enough. These are very easy things to guess in hindsight, and I think the Justice Department didn't do a great job, but under the circumstances, as long as they move to correct it in the future, the changes, you know, doesn't deserve the kind of opprobrium that I have heard from some quarters about this.[67]

Hatch followed Schumer's statement by offering, "that is my view as well."[68] At the close of the hearing, Hatch referred back to Schumer's statement to minimize the prolonged detention of the "September 11 detainees":

> I can just hear the screaming and wailing and shouting if we had had another terrorist attack because you let some of these people go prematurely. I think Senator Schumer is absolutely right when he indicated that you would never live it down. And even at that, we know that there are known terrorist organizations and terrorists in this country that we are monitoring that we are pretty sure may try to do something like this in the future.[69]

This framing of the treatment of the detainees at MDC, however, carried a symbolic risk. Even as national security emerged as the primary frame for the debate, it was spoken of in relation to a second national value, roughly sketched as "cherished freedoms" or "cherished liberties." The "civil liberties/national security" dichotomy is one that is well-recognized historically and continues today in the United States.[70] Several participants in the Judiciary Committee's hearing explicitly referred to the need to balance security and liberty. In his opening statement, Hatch acknowledged the committee's obligation to "ensure that these agencies are able to investigate, detect and prevent terrorist attacks on our country without threatening or undermining our country's cherished freedoms."[71] Later in the hearing, Schumer described the dichotomy as "the age-old problem of how to balance security and liberty."[72] Rolince, in his opening statement, reflected on the dichotomy's relevance to the FBI:

> The FBI acknowledges that our success is measured not only by how effectively we disrupt acts of terrorism, but also by how well we protect the constitutional rights and cherished liberties of American citizens in the process. We will continue to work to find new ways to meet both of these crucial missions.[73]

The claim of civil liberties might have enabled a countertelling of the legal mistreatment and physical abuse of the "September 11 detainees" as events that threaten the core American value of liberty. Such a framing, in other words, might have amplified the symbolic significance of the violence against MDC detainees. Several participants in the hearing, however, rhetorically neutralized such a framing by placing the victims of abuse at MDC outside the boundaries of the rights and liberties frame. They did so in several ways.

First, and as Senators Hatch, Schumer, and Specter, as well as the inspector general and Nahmias and Rolince observed, nearly all the detainees at MDC were in violation of U.S. immigration laws and not one was a U.S. citizen. (In their reporting on the hearing, the *Washington Post* similarly highlighted the legal status of the detainees, describing the detainees as "762 foreign nationals—all but one of whom had violated immigration laws.")[74] This meant, to participants in the hearing, that holding the "September 11 detainees" was legal. It also meant that the "cherished liberties" that the country must "balance" with national security were, for the most part, not applicable to those detained at MDC. Thus, the symbolic import of Rolince's statement that the FBI is judged by how well they protected the "cherished liberties of *American citizens*" (emphasis mine) as well as of Senator Schumer's similar, but far more explicit, statement:

> There are some who believe anyone should have all the panoply of the Constitution, whether they are a citizen or not. I do not agree with that. That has never been the philosophy of this country, and there should be some rights and there should be rules. But it does not mean that you get the same rights as being an American citizen.[75]

By mobilizing the detainees' status as "illegal" immigrants, hearing participants neutralized claims of liberty and rights, rendering them irrelevant to the particularities of the case at hand. As "illegal aliens," the "September 11 detainees" were also criminals. Their "criminality" was inscribed into their status as "illegal" aliens, yet the meaning of their criminality exceeded these violations. Senator Hatch and Nahmias both cited an earlier inspector general investigation that found that 87 percent of "illegal" immigrants who had been ordered to be deported, in Hatch's words, "fail to honor deportation orders and slip back into our society."[76] Nahmias built on this fact, tethering it to a national security frame by noting that the high risk of having "illegal" immigrants avoid deportation was, "after our experiences on September 11, 2001, . . . too great."[77] Hatch and Nahmias heightened the criminal threat posed by "illegal" aliens by alluding to historical instances in which "illegal" immigrants who had been previously detained and released committed significant crimes against U.S. citizens. Nahmias, in fact, noted that the inspector general had admonished the Department of Justice for failing to prevent these crimes.

The inspector general testified that for the "vast majority" of MDC and Passaic detainees, he was unsure that there was an "indication" that the detainees were associated with the September 11 terrorist attacks or, more generally, terrorism.[78] This observation, however, was not sufficient to disqualify participants from justifying the detention of the detainees on grounds that they posed a threat to national security. Rolince, Nahmias, and Lappin argued and Senators Hatch and Schumer accepted that a reasonable link between the detainees and terrorism existed. Nahmias and Lappin made this argument by describing this link for particular detainees who might, implicitly at least, stand in for all the detainees. For instance, Rolince noted, in his opening statement, that

> one immigration detainee who pled guilty to conspiracy to commit identification fraud and aiding and abetting the unlawful production of identification documents traveled overnight with two of the hijackers. The name and address of another immigration detainee, who pled guilty to identification fraud, was used by Al-Qaeda cell members in Hamburg, Germany, to attempt to obtain U.S. visas.[79]

As "illegal immigrants" or "illegal aliens," the "September 11 detainees" were portrayed as criminals who also posed a risk of terrorism. As a legal, political, and cultural construct, the illegal immigrant, illegal alien, or, simply, the alien is a typified person whose label produces a symbolic border between those who belong to the nation and, thus, receive the full protection of law and those who do not.[80] In the aftermath of the September 11 terrorist attacks, this construct intersected with ethnicity: Arab citizens and immigrants became targets of formal and informal racial profiling.[81] During the Senate Judiciary Committee's hearing, Senator Feingold raised this issue with Rolince, who denied that the high prevalence of, in Feingold's words, those who "share the same religion or ethnicity of the September 11th hijackers" among the "September 11 detainees" was evidence of racial profiling.[82] The issues of race and ethnicity were otherwise absent from the committee's hearing. Indeed, the illegality and the criminality—statuses that were, in fact, conflated—of the "aliens" detained at MDC, coupled with their putative link to terrorism, was sufficient to render them non-citizens and, thus, outside the symbolic boundaries of the political debate about rights and security.[83]

The abuses at MDC were publicly narrated in reference to the September 11, 2001, terrorist attacks and the uncertainty about follow-up or second wave attacks. Such a telling involved the construction of political interests and actors in a way that resulted in the minimization of the abuse at MDC. By narrating the abuse at MDC in relation to the September 11 terrorist attacks, participants in the Senate Judiciary hearing elevated national security to the pinnacle of political goods. What mattered in this framing was national security; in it, the behavior of U.S. law enforcement officers and, more broadly, the executive branch would be weighed against a bleak alternative: the return of terrorism to U.S. cities. In this narrative, the U.S. citizenry figured as passive political actors, if actors at all. They were dependent on law enforcement officers to preserve national security; they were, as described by several hearing participants, *grateful* to law enforcement agencies for preventing terrorist attacks after September 11. Dependent and grateful, the American people were treated as firmly bound to the post-9/11 projects of law enforcement.

With political consensus that the September 11 terrorist attacks put the nation's and its populace's safety at risk, national security, as one tie that binds the citizenry to its government, is a chain. Members of the Senate Judiciary Committee largely assumed public support of PENTTBOM and the quest to prevent terrorism. Finally, the dual identities of the victims as "September 11 detainees" and illegal aliens placed them outside the symbolic boundaries of the rule of law; the victims were noncitizens, criminals with alleged ties to terror. Members of the Senate Judiciary Committee did not perceive the detainees as belonging to an identifiable political group whose cooperation with U.S. political projects mattered and who could, in the name of the "September 11 detainees," press moral or political claims against the country.

Hearts and Minds: Abu Ghraib, Operation Iraqi Freedom, and the Promise of Human Rights

Participants in the Senate Judiciary Committee framed the abuse of the "September 11 detainees" within a context that depressed the symbolic significance of the events at MDC. Conversely, participants in the Senate Armed Services Committee hearings on Abu Ghraib encountered the photographs and the violence that they depicted within the precarious political context of "Operation Iraqi Freedom." Although the Bush administration initially framed the war as one pursued for the sake of national security, it was never described as solely about this. The administration's arguments for the war frequently cited Saddam Hussein's human rights violations, strengthening its claim that Hussein was an irrational political actor who could not be trusted with weapons of mass destruction.[84] After no major stockpiles of these weapons were found in Iraq, the protection of human rights and the establishment of the rule of law became important legitimating claims for the war.

The risks of this transition were readily apparent. On July 29, 2003, Deputy Secretary of Defense Paul Wolfowitz appeared before the Senate Foreign Relations Committee. After Wolfowitz gave an opening statement that emphasized the brutality of Saddam Hussein's reign, Democrats and Republicans alike sharply criticized the deputy secretary for, in the words of Republican Lincoln Chafee, "shifting justifications," avoiding discussion of weapons of mass destruction, and focusing, primarily, on "what a despicable tyrant Saddam Hussein is."[85]

As the point of reference for debating Abu Ghraib, the U.S. invasion of Iraq raised another problem. In political perceptions of the invasion, U.S. and Iraqi citizens figured as crucial political actors, whose support, if not cooperation, was necessary for the success of the mission. Indeed, domestically and internationally, the U.S.'s invasion of Iraq provoked questions about the political legitimacy of the executive branch's actions that were not as salient in debates about the executive's response to the September 11 terrorist attacks.[86] Given a steady drop, beginning in late 2003, in public support for the war and given the political recognition that the success of the invasion demanded winning over Iraqi "hearts and minds" and maintaining U.S. popular support, the problem of legitimacy became increasingly pressing.[87] The claim of human rights was a rhetorical effort to sustain the legitimacy of the war in the face of these difficulties. Human rights, in other words, became one way of attempting to bind U.S. and Iraqi hearts and minds to the invasion.

The human rights crimes in Iraq and, later, the release of the Abu Ghraib photographs weakened the credibility of this framing. In media reporting before the release of the photographs, Iraqis who had been detained by U.S. soldiers compared their treatment to conditions under Hussein; such comparisons eroded the dichotomy between Hussein and the United States that the administration mobilized in their justifications for war.[88] During the Senate Armed Services Committee May 7 hearing on Abu Ghraib, participants expressed concern for the consequences of these developments on these significant political relationships. McCain did so by mobilizing the legacy of Vietnam.[89] Specifically, McCain observed that "we risk losing public support for this conflict. As Americans turned away from the Vietnam War, they may turn away from this one unless this issue is resolved, with full disclosure, immediately."[90]

Others, including Warner, Dole, and Levin, expressed concern that the abuse of detainees at Abu Ghraib would reverse the successes of the war. Dole made a particularly acute comment to this effect: "Trust among the Iraqi people had slowly been established, bonds have been made, and, sadly for now, many of those bonds have been broken."[91] Warner similarly worried about the condition of U.S. international relations after the release of the photographs. Having lamented in his opening statement that the photographs could "seriously affect" the U.S. relationships abroad, Warner later observed that "it's obvious to all of us that the impact of the facts of this case as they are unfolding is affecting our relationship with other nations, our foreign policy."[92]

Kennedy and Reed took a different approach, describing particular photographs as symbols that would come to represent the United States to global communities, particularly those in the Middle East. Kennedy's statement is illustrative. "To the people in the Middle East . . . the symbol of America is not the Statue of Liberty, it's the prisoner standing on a box wearing a dark cape and a dark hood on his head with wires attached to his body, afraid that he's going to be electrocuted."[93] Collins similarly worried that global viewers' would mistake "the real America," which "to a degree unprecedented in human history, has sacrificed its blood and treasure to secure liberty and human rights around the world," with what the photographs showed.[94]

These types of statements recognized a global array of political actors—"people in the Middle East," for instance—as central to U.S. political interests. This fact is further observed in the administration's multiple apologies for the abuse. In his opening statement to the Senate Armed Services Committee, Secretary Rumsfeld offered a lengthy apology that recognized the victims of U.S. violence as both "human beings" and citizens ("Iraqis") with basic, human rights. Rumsfeld also apologized to members of the Armed Forces, the president, Congress, and the American people, implicitly recognizing the moral and political tug of each:

> I feel terrible about what happened to these Iraqi detainees. They're human beings, and they were in U.S. custody. Our country 'had an obligation to treat them right. We did not, and that was wrong. So to those Iraqis who were mistreated by members of the U.S. Armed Forces, I offer my deepest apology. . . . Further, I deeply regret the damage that has been done. First, to the reputation of the honorable men and women of the Armed Forces, who are courageously, responsibly, and professionally defending our freedoms across the globe. . . . Second, to the President, Congress, and the American people; I wish I had been able to convey to them the gravity of this before we saw it in the media.[95]

Rumsfeld's willingness to apologize to a range of actors sharply contrasts with the Department of Justice's refusal to apologize for "finding every legal way possible to protect the American public from further terrorist attacks" after the inspector general released his report on the abuse of the "September 11 detainees."[96]

The stakes of the hearing were also apparent outside Congress. Protestors interrupted Rumsfeld's opening statement to the committee, shouting, "What about other abuses in Iraq?" and "Fire Rumsfeld!"[97] Coverage of the hearing, too, was intensive. On the day of the hearing, *USA Today* devoted a cover article to the Abu Ghraib scandal, noting that Rumsfeld was to face "blunt questioning" when he confronted Congress later in the day.[98] The day after the hearing, the *New York Times* ran a page one article on the hearing and, published excerpts from the transcript. The *Times* also ran an editorial criticizing Rumsfeld for "dodging responsibility." Citing McCain's statement, the editorial concluded that, "as Americans turned away from the Vietnam War, they may turn away from this one unless this issue is quickly resolved with full disclosure immediately. We strongly agree."[99] Coverage in the *Washington Post* was similar, with an editorial sharply criticizing Rumsfeld for not accepting the "fundamental nature of the problem."[100] The *Post* also covered Rumsfeld's testimony on its front page and included excerpts of the hearing transcript.

The concerns expressed in the Senate Armed Services Committee's hearing—about U.S. public support of the Iraq war, Iraqi support of the U.S. mission, and international relations—suggest that U.S. politicians confronted a dramatically different political environment when debating Abu Ghraib from the one that they did when examining the MDC abuses. This environment, in turn, provided interpretive frames in which officials situated the allegations of abuse. The "power" of the Abu Ghraib photographs—their capacity to disturb or outrage viewers—mattered because those viewers, in turn, mattered to prevailing understandings of salient political projects. Members of the Senate Armed Services Committee, as well as its high-profile witnesses on May 7, viewed the war in Iraq as a project that depended on a web of political relationships that the photographs had weakened.

CONCLUSION

An individual may view a photograph of an atrocity and become outraged or disturbed. The photograph might wound that viewer, activating an emotion that typically lies dormant. Then again, the feeling may pass. Many feelings, in fact, do. Outrage—the disturbance of a photograph—may remain a private, temporary feeling. A photograph may make no mark.

The video stills from MDC are forgotten—or, more accurately, never encountered—relics from the aftermath of the September 11, 2001, terrorist attacks. Media coverage of their release was scant and, after the release of the stills, the Senate Judiciary Committee returned to the abuse of the "September 11 detainees" in passing and never on its own terms.[101] The allegations of abuse at MDC emerged within a political environment largely impervious to their influence. Members of the Senate Judiciary Committee accepted that the executive branch's investigation and prevention of terrorism involved highly paternalistic and nationalistic political relations. The support and cooperation of the U.S. citizenry was taken for granted; American citizens appeared, within the rhetoric of committee members, as grateful and passive actors. If segments of the U.S. public were outraged by the abuse at MDC, that outrage remained invisible to participants in the Judiciary's hearing. The "September 11 detainees," for their part, appeared before the Senate Judiciary Committee as criminal foreigners—illegal aliens—whose treatment was irrelevant to ongoing debates about civil liberties.

The Abu Ghraib photographs, however, left a mark on the American body politic. They did so because they were empirically undeniable, contradicted the prevailing framework that the Bush administration had constructed for the Iraq War, and resonated with domestic and international viewers. That resonance mattered because U.S. politicians understood viewers of those images—particularly, U.S. citizens and Iraqi citizens—as political actors whose support of and cooperation with the country's occupation of Iraq was highly consequential.

The committee's work, however, did not end with their worry over the global impact of the photographs' release. The purpose of the committee's hearings was to repair the "bonds," as Dole put it, that the photographs had broken. Secretary of Defense Rumsfeld was not alone on May 7 in articulating his hope that the committee's hearings and the Department of Defense's investigations would resolve the crisis that the images provoked; Senators Levin, Byrd, Wayne Allard, Frist, Dole, and Collins all spoke of a similar hope. Rumsfeld offered, though, the most elaborate statement to this effect:

> Mr. Chairman, I know you join me today in saying to the world, "Judge us by our actions. Watch how Americans, watch how a democracy, deals with wrongdoing and with scandal and the pain of acknowledging and correcting our own mistakes and our own weaknesses." After they have seen America in action, then ask those who teach resentment and hatred of America if our behavior doesn't give the lie to the falsehood and the slander they speak about our people and about our way of life. Ask them if the resolve of Americans in crisis and difficulty and, yes, in the heartbreak of acknowledging the evil in our midst, doesn't have meaning far beyond their hatred.[102]

In the next two chapters, I document the task that Rumsfeld described—the work of the committee, and particularly its Republican members and witnesses from the executive branch—to contain, if not resolve, the Abu Ghraib scandal.

CHAPTER | 3

Isolating Incidents

IN MAY 2004, THE BUSH administration confronted a political crisis provoked by revelations of detainee abuse at Abu Ghraib prison. In the months
leading up to the November presidential election, the crisis threatened the
tenure of Bush's Secretary of Defense, and John Kerry appeared primed to
make Abu Ghraib a campaign issue.[1] By October, however, the Abu Ghraib
scandal had lost much of its political resonance. During the three presidential debates, torture was mentioned only once—by President Bush and in
reference to the human rights violations of Saddam Hussein.[2] Abu Ghraib
and the broader issues of detainee abuse and U.S. detention and interrogation policies were similarly overlooked.

The containment of Abu Ghraib involved the successful portrayal of
the violence at the prison as an isolated incident, unrepresentative of U.S
detention and interrogation practices under the Bush administration.[3] This
portrayal of the violence, in combination with the "few bad apples" account
of it, downplayed the responsibility of high-ranking military and civilian
officials for the abuse and minimized the political harm suffered by the
Bush administration. The geographic isolation of Abu Ghraib prevented
the photographs taken there from coming to represent the U.S. conflicts in
Iraq and Afghanistan, as well as the U.S. detention facility in Guantánamo.
The causal isolation of Abu Ghraib prevented blame for the violence from
climbing up the military and civilian chains of command. Ultimately, the
administration and its supporters in Congress interpretively sealed off Abu
Ghraib, preventing the violence there, at least temporarily, from polluting
the broader political projects of the Bush administration.

This chapter and the next show how Abu Ghraib became an isolated incident. Here, I focus on the geographic dimension of political accounts. During the debate about Abu Ghraib, U.S. politicians and military officials acknowledged that detainee abuse was widespread in Iraq and Afghanistan. How, then, did Abu Ghraib become an isolated incident? The answer, this chapter shows, has to do with developments in the documentary record of detainee abuse. Specifically, accounts of "what really happened" at U.S. detention operations emerged in the spring and autumn of 2004, filling in the gaps in knowledge that politicians faced when discussing detainee abuse in Iraq, Afghanistan, and Guantánamo. During the Senate Armed Services Committee's hearings, U.S. officials processed these developments in the documentary record and competed to define the geographic extent of detainee abuse. I present this process in three parts that loosely correspond to the chronology of the hearings. I begin by describing the lack of consensus, at the start of the committee's hearings on May 7, about the geographic extent of abuse. I then document the emergence of the claim that abuse had occurred throughout Iraq. This claim, which a few hearing participants suggested on May 7, was undisputed by May 19. Finally, I show how, on May 19, July 22, and September 9, hearing participants rationalized "widespread abuse," gave it quantitative form, and isolated the abuse at Abu Ghraib from mistreatment of prisoners that occurred elsewhere.

THE QUESTION OF A "BROADER PROBLEM":
THE LIMITS OF THE ABU GHRAIB PHOTOGRAPHS

As I showed in the previous chapter, the photographs from Abu Ghraib foreclosed literal denial, the claim that nothing had happened at the prison. Participants in the committee's hearings took for granted, as Secretary of Defense Donald Rumsfeld put it on May 7, that "things, in fact, happened" at Abu Ghraib. The photographs permitted a global community of viewers to peer into the prison at Abu Ghraib, observing U.S. violence that might have, had the photographs not been taken, largely gone unwitnessed outside the facility.

Despite their evidentiary value, the photographs suffered from a limitation: the events that they depicted were confined to those that occurred at Abu Ghraib prison and, in truth, only sections of the facility. The photographs, in other words, are relatively "large-scale" depictions of U.S. detention operations; they represent a fairly small portion of reality.[4]

The photographs did not provide, then, the evidence needed to answer a question that Senator Robert Byrd posed to Secretary Rumsfeld on May 7: "How do we know that there isn't a broader problem here?"[5]

To respond to this question, participants in the hearing referred to documents—leaked or officially released reports—that covered a more geographically extensive terrain than did the Abu Ghraib photographs. Citing these documents, hearing participants took up a vantage point from which they could speak about "things that did, in fact, happen" throughout Iraq and Afghanistan. Attempts on May 7 to establish the geographic extent of detainee abuse illustrate this. Two witnesses, General Richard Myers, chairman of the Joint Chiefs of Staff, and General Lance Smith, deputy commander of the United States Central Command, introduced a finding from the Taguba report as evidence that detainee abuse was not widespread. Myers', for instance, noted: "The *Taguba Report*, if you recall, looked at four installations where the 800th MP Brigade had operations. They found abuse in only one, and that's Abu Ghraib."[6]

As evidence to establish the geographic extent of detainee abuse, the Taguba report is an upgrade from the photographs from Abu Ghraib; the report provides an account of the treatment of detainees in four, rather than a single, U.S. detention facility. Smith's and Myers's references to the report were, however, insufficient to foreclose counterclaims on May 7, and the generals' statements sit precariously next to claims that abuse occurred more widely. Citing different sources, Byrd and Ted Kennedy argued that abuse occurred in locations beyond Abu Ghraib prison. Byrd noted that "reports," including those of the International Committee of the Red Cross (ICRC), suggested that detainee abuse had occurred in "more than just the Abu Ghraib prison."[7] Kennedy offered a more specific statement, citing the military's criminal investigations to support his claim that abuse had occurred in Afghanistan and Iraq: "35 criminal investigations into alleged mistreatment of detainees in Iraq and Afghanistan, 25 of these investigations involving deaths. . . . In particular, in December 2002, military doctors at the Bagram Air Base in Afghanistan ruled that two Afghan men in U.S. custody died from blunt-force injuries."[8]

To support their arguments, Kennedy, Byrd, Myer, and Smith drew on reports that provided divergent accounts of the extent of abuse. None of the hearing participants was able to end debate on the topic by referencing the conclusions of a single document; none, in other words, was able to establish, for others at the hearing, whether detainee abuse was widespread in Iraq and Afghanistan. At this point in the committee's review of detainee abuse, this divergence at the level of fact did not trigger a sustained attempt to pin down the reality of detainee abuse across Iraq and Afghanistan.[9] Hearing participants likely understood that major investigations into detainee abuse were ongoing, the documentary record of detainee abuse was still developing, and the simultaneous presence and absence of abuse across the fronts of the war on terror would be parsed later.

BEYOND "ONE SET OF INCIDENTS PHOTOGRAPHED AT ONE PRISON": THE REALITY OF WIDESPREAD ABUSE

On May 7, hearing participants drew on different documents to produce contradictory claims about the geographic extent of detainee abuse. As the hearings advanced, the committee and its witnesses confronted an evolving documentary record. Several major investigations and reports, which provided scaled-down representations of detention operations in Iraq and, eventually, Afghanistan, became available. This development in the documentary record made it increasingly difficult for hearing participants to argue that detainee abuse was limited to Abu Ghraib prison.

This first consequential development in the documentary record came, in fact, on May 7, when the *Wall Street Journal* published a front-page story that included selections from a leaked February 2004 report of the ICRC; the full report was posted on the *Journal's* website on May 10.[10] The ICRC's investigation spanned the first nine months of the U.S. war in Iraq and included evidence gathered from twenty-nine visits to fourteen U.S. prisons in the country The report documented that "ill-treatment during capture was frequent" and that

> persons deprived of their liberty under supervision of the Military Intelligence were at high risk of being subjected to a variety of harsh treatments ranging from insults, threats and humiliations to both physical and psychological coercion, which in some cases was tantamount to torture, in order to force cooperation with their interrogators.[11]

The release of this text profoundly affected the public debate about Abu Ghraib. The *Wall Street Journal's* initial article on the report, aptly titled

"Red Cross Found Widespread Abuse of Iraqi Prisoners," opened by noting that the ICRC's report "concluded that abuse of prisoners in Iraq by U.S. military intelligence personnel was widespread"; it closed by describing the ICRC's allegations of abuse at a military intelligence section of Camp Cropper in Iraq. The allegations included

> soldiers "taking aim at individuals with rifles, striking them with rifle butts, slaps and punches and prolonged exposure to the sun." One prisoner claimed he was "urinated on, kicked in the head, lower back and groin, force-fed a baseball, which was tied into the mouth using a scarf and deprived of sleep for four consecutive days."[12]

The ICRC report also resonated in Congress. During the committee's first of two hearings on May 11 (hereafter, referred to as May 11 a.m.), Kennedy and fellow-Democrat Mark Dayton cited the report to support their claim that detainee abuse was widespread in Iraq. Kennedy's statement is illustrative: "The ICRC collected allegations of ill treatment following the capture that took place in Baghdad, Basra, Ramadi, and Tikrit . . . It isn't only focused on this one prison camp, but lists the others, as well. I think we have to be aware of that."[13]

Paralleling this development was a second one. From May 11 on, hearing participants who spoke of detainee abuse as *limited* to Abu Ghraib consistently qualified their claims. Unlike Myers and Smith, who earlier suggested outright that abuse had only occurred at Abu Ghraib, hearing participants began differentiating between abuse at Abu Ghraib and abuse that occurred elsewhere. For instance, at the May 11 a.m. hearing, General Antonio Taguba twice made claims of this sort. Taguba testified to Senators Hillary Rodham Clinton and Ben Nelson that his investigation had not found evidence of abuse in other facilities in Iraq that was similar to the abuse that occurred at Abu Ghraib. Those abuses, Taguba told Nelson, were "in terms of slapping a prisoner" and were "not to the gravity that was exposed" at Abu Ghraib.[14]

At the committee's second hearing on May 11 (hereafter, designated as May 11 p.m.), Republican Senator James Inhofe questioned two military witnesses—General Keith Alexander, the Army's deputy chief of staff for intelligence,[15] and General Ronald Burgess, the director of intelligence for the Joint Chiefs of Staff—about Taguba's findings that serious instances of abuse were limited to Abu Ghraib. During the exchange, Alexander and Burgess affirmed Taguba's claim that significant instances of abuse were limited to Abu Ghraib. Inhofe, in turn, used the occasion to criticize *Washington Post* reporting on the ICRC's investigation that indicated otherwise:[16]

INHOFE: Okay. Now, you were here, I think, when General Taguba was testifying this morning, and I asked him a series of questions, in terms of did he really feel that the offenses, that the reprehensible acts, were confined to cell block 1A and 1B of one prison, and then, in addition to that, that we don't have any evidence that this is going on at any of the other 25 prisons. He agreed to that. Do the three of you agree with that?

ALEXANDER: Yes, sir.

INHOFE: As far as you know.

ALEXANDER: Of this sort.

BURGESS: As far as I know.

INHOFE: I think that's very important, because there's an article this morning in the *Washington Post* that alleged abuses like those in the prison are widespread, and not isolated, and I just think it's a bad message to send out since the message is wrong, and I wanted to hear all of you express yourselves.[17]

The influence of the ICRC report on political discourse may be observed in the emergence of the claim that abuse occurred throughout Iraq and in the qualifications built into the argument that serious abuse, of the kind photographed at Abu Ghraib, was unique to the facility. Not all participants in the hearings, however, presented the ICRC report as providing indisputable proof of widespread abuse in Iraq. At the committee's afternoon hearing on May 11, Alexander attempted to alter the prevailing meaning of the report by arguing that the serious abuses documented in the ICRC report were those photographed at Abu Ghraib prison.

Alexander first made this argument when asked by McCain about contradictory accounts of abuse. McCain cited the fact that Taguba had testified "that these abuses were somewhat confined to a relatively small area."[18] After Alexander agreed that Taguba's report found that "abuses of this nature" were not widespread, McCain continued by pointing out that the committee was aware that "the ICRC issued a long series—a number of reports concerning prisoner abuses."[19] McCain concluded "something doesn't connect there."[20] Alexander responded by arguing that the events documented by the ICRC were identical to those documented in the photographs: "when . . . you look at the allegations, and you look at the pictures, you immediately make the connection that what the ICRC had and what the pictures said are the event."[21]

Later in the hearing, Dayton returned to the issue, questioning Alexander about the report:

DAYTON: General Alexander . . . are you asserting that the *Taguba Report*, the ICRC Report, and the pictures of the prisoner abuses that we saw last week all refer to the same limited number of events that were carried out by a few MPs, with a couple of unidentified low-level MI officials perhaps interacting with them to lead them to those actions?

ALEXANDER: Sir, I'd note that in the ICRC Report it says that one of the detainees had women's underwear on their head. I, you, the American public saw that photo on TV. That led me to make that statement that those same things that they noted in their report we see in a photograph.[22]

In this testimony, Alexander argued that ICRC report and the photographs largely depicted the same events, minimizing the problem of abuse by confining it to Abu Ghraib prison. By suggesting that the ICRC report and the photographs documented a single incident—"the event" at Abu Ghraib prison—Alexander attempted to alter the meaning of the ICRC report, eroding its evidentiary value for those claiming that serious incidents of abuse were widespread. But congressional hearings are interactive affairs and, in their exchanges, Alexander, McCain, and Dayton debated what, precisely, the ICRC report documented. For their parts, McCain and Dayton both met Alexander's statements with considerable resistance. McCain responded by arguing that "the ICRC alleged, as I understand it, that these situations were widespread, and not confined to just one small area."[23] Later in the hearing, Dayton rejected Alexander's interpretation of the ICRC report and, in fact, succeeded in walking Alexander back from the core of his claim.

DAYTON: The report, as I read it, refers to other abuses that occurred in that prison to other prisoners that didn't fit the descriptions in those pictures. But I guess I just wanted to clarify . . . what you're implying here, because, as I read the ICRC Report, it refers to . . . a total of 14 detention centers or prisons, and I don't know how to quantify the extent of the violations that they are alleging, but it certainly appears to be far broader and more systemic than one set of incidents photographed at one prison. Would you concur with that sir, or do you—

ALEXANDER: Yes, sir, I think—in the ICRC Report, there was one portion on Abu Ghraib ... which is what I was referencing.[24]

In this exchange, Dayton used the fact that the ICRC visited "a total of 14 detention centers or prisons" to lead General Alexander away from his claim that "what the ICRC had and what the pictures said are the event" and toward a qualified one: that a particular set of photographs might correspond to a particular portion of the ICRC report. The claim of widespread abuse in Iraq held. The meaning of that claim, however, remained open for debate.

"A VERY BRUTAL AND BLOODY EVENT": RATIONALIZING WIDESPREAD ABUSE

Alexander, having admitted that his claim was applicable to only "one portion" of the ICRC report, failed to fold the reality documented in it into that of the photographs. Meanwhile, at hearings on May 19 and July 22, Levin, Kennedy, and Byrd continued to claim that the ICRC report provided evidence of widespread abuse throughout Iraq. For instance, in his opening statement on May 19, Levin observed:

> The February 2004 report of the ICRC presents an overview of documented abuses that extend beyond the conduct of interrogations at one cell block in one detention facility ... The abuses that are alleged apparently are not limited to detention facilities. Many of the alleged violations are reported to have occurred at the time of arrest.[25]

The release of photographs taken at Abu Ghraib prison made literal denial of abuse there unfeasible. The introduction of the ICRC report did something similar: it provided evidence persuasive enough to establish that abuse had occurred throughout Iraq.

The report, however, did not force consensus on the nature of abuse. An exchange between Byrd and General John Abizaid, commander of the United States' Central Command, at the May 19 hearing, illustrates this fact. During the exchange, Abizaid attempted to make the ICRC report consistent with the claim that serious (and, thus, politically damaging) incidents of abuse were confined to Abu Ghraib prison. Abizaid did not attempt to deny, as Alexander had, that the ICRC report documented allegations of abuse in U.S. detention operations throughout Iraq. Instead, he implicitly acknowledged their findings and highlighted that many of the incidents of abuse documented by the ICRC occurred during the arrest of detainees:

BYRD: General Abizaid, the ICRC has alleged a pattern of abuse at detention cen-
    ters in Iraq. With all due respect, how can you explain the culture of abuse that
    was allowed to develop in a prison system under your ultimate command?
ABIZAID: I do not believe that a culture of abuse existed in my command . . . I be-
    lieve that we have isolated incidents that have taken place. I am aware that the
    ICRC has its view on things. A lot of its view is based upon what happens at the
    point of detention where soldiers fighting for their lives detain people, which is
    a very brutal and bloody event.[26]

In his response to Byrd, Abizaid allowed that the ICRC might have observed events throughout Iraq that the organization would call abuse; he did not challenge that those events occurred. Rather, he suggested that the conclusion that a culture of abuse existed was wrong. He suggested, first, that the ICRC evaluates detention operations through a particular "view on things" that the military does not share.[27] Abizaid then offered an alternative portrayal of the violence as "what happens at the point of detention" and added an implicit rationalization, a variation of the claim of necessity: "where soldiers [who are] are fighting for their lives detain people, which is a very brutal and bloody event."

Over the course of the committee's final three hearings, evidence emerged in support of Abizaid's claims. On July 22, General Paul Miko-lashek, inspector general of the Army, offered testimony about his office's investigation into detention operations throughout the wars in Afghanistan and Iraq. In his opening statement, he noted that "we determined that nearly half the cases [of confirmed or possible abuse], 45 out of the 94, took place at the point of capture. . . . The point of capture is the place on the battlefield that is the most uncertain, dangerous, and violent."[28]

During the committee's second hearing on September 9 (hereafter referred to as September 9 p.m.), James Schlesinger and Harold Brown, both former secretaries of defense—Schlesinger under Presidents Nixon and Ford and Brown under President Carter—testified before the committee on the findings of the Schlesinger report (officially, the *Final Report of the Independent Panel to Review DOD Operations*).[29] Their findings, as Warner described them in his opening statement, were consistent with those of General Mikolashek:

> Over the past 3 years, the U.S. has apprehended over 50,000 personnel in Iraq and Afghanistan. As of mid-August 2004, only 66 out of the 50,000 gave rise to allegations of abuse that had been substantiated with one-third to one-half of those incidents occurring at the point of capture or during transit, periods which are often in the very heat of battle and extraordinary stress.[30]

Covering U.S. detention operations in Afghanistan and Iraq, the Mikolashek report and the Schlesinger report map a terrain far more extensive than that of the ICRC report. They also provided hearing participants with a new interpretive resource: quantitative representations of abuse. These were powerful resources for denial and partial acknowledgment. I have already pointed out one: the rationalization of abuse at the point of capture, as first articulated by Abizaid. This rationalization was built into the statements of Mikolashek and Warner reproduced above. Republican Senator Jeff Sessions and two witnesses—Les Brownlee, acting secretary of the Army, and General Peter J. Schoomaker, chief of staff of the Army—also made this point at the July 22 hearing. During the committee's first hearing on September 9 (hereafter, September 9 a.m.), Warner referenced abuse at the point of capture in this way; later on the 9th, at the committee's second hearing, Session, fellow-Republican James Talent, and Schlesinger made similar statements. "The point of capture," as described by these hearing participants, is the location at which abuse is understandable, if not predictable. As Talent put it during the September 9 p.m. hearing: "People going too far in an effort to get information in an insecure environment where their friends are being shot at and they are desperate to find out what is going on, while inexcusable in one sense, in another sense is at least understandable."[31]

The availability of evidence for what occurred *outside* Abu Ghraib also allowed hearing participants to contextualize events *inside* the prison. For instance, in his opening statement, Schlesinger acknowledged that "abuses were indeed more widespread than observed on the night shift at Abu Ghraib"; however, he described the abuse at Abu Ghraib "as having its unique aspects." Schlesinger then reflected on the partiality of the photographs, suggesting that they had obscured the broader work of the U.S. Armed Forces:

> In this connection, President Kennedy said during the Cuban Missile Crisis that a picture is worth a thousand words. It clearly is if, and only if, one knows what the picture means. But if pictures are misinterpreted, they can readily become a distorting mechanism. That can easily create an inaccurate impression, hiding, indeed distorting the overall performance, as I have suggested with regard to our Armed Forces in Iraq.[32]

Brown made a similar argument, testifying that the photographed incidents displayed "a pathology not, so far as we were able to find, duplicated elsewhere."[33] Later in the hearing, Talent observed that he "would have been surprised if the kind of stuff I saw in those pictures was at all widespread because that was just sick."[34] In this way, Schlesinger, Brown, and Talent erected an interpretive wall between the abuse displayed in the photographs from Abu Ghraib and the abuse that occurred elsewhere throughout the wars in Afghanistan and Iraq.

Finally, the quantifications of detainee abuse enabled hearing participants to minimize the significance of those very incidents.[35] By interpreting the quantified instances of abuse within other numbers—the total numbers of detainees captured in the wars in Afghanistan and Iraq and, in one case, the total number of interrogations that occurred at Abu Ghraib—hearing participants downplayed abuse as a unique occurrence during detention operations. Mikolashek and Brownlee employed this form of denial on July 22; Warner and Inhofe at the September 9 a.m. hearing; and Warner, Inhofe, Lieberman, Schlesinger, and Brown at the September 9 p.m. hearing. A statement by Senator Joseph Lieberman—a Democrat at the time—that indicated that the substantiated incidents of abuse amounted to "a fraction of 1 percent of the detainees" is illustrative of this discursive tactic.[36] To build a social problem, claims-makers prefer broad definitions of problems and "big, official numbers."[37] It is not surprising, then, that to contain a problem some hearing participants built their claims about detainee abuse with relatively small, official statistics.[38]

By disaggregating quantifications of abuse so as to produce the category "abuse at the point of capture," official investigators provided themselves and hearing participants a rich, discursive resource that could be combined with taken-for-granted beliefs about combat to downplay the mistreatment of detainees. This representation of abuse also permitted hearing participants to juxtapose the photographed violence at Abu Ghraib prison with the quantified violence throughout Iraq. And, by producing quantifications of abuse based on substantiated allegations and also quantifying the number of detainees captured by U.S. soldiers, official investigators produced another resource for denial: abused detainees in the form of a "fraction of 1 percent" of all detainees.

CONCLUSION

Over the course of the Senate Armed Services Committee seven public hearings, the claim that widespread abuse occurred in the U.S. wars in Afghanistan and Iraq became undeniable. In Stanley Cohen's terms, hearing participants no longer engaged in the *literal denial* of abuse throughout Afghanistan and Iraq.[39] By the committee's final hearing, participants who spoke of the geographic extent of abuse did not offer unqualified acknowledgements of it. During the September 9 p.m. hearing, four Republicans, one Democrat, and the committee's two witnesses downplayed all incidents of abuse by contrasting substantiated incidents with the total number of detainees captured, rationalizing abuse at the point of capture, or portraying the photographed abuse at Abu Ghraib as unrepresentative of U.S. practices elsewhere. Those hearing participants who had aggressively pursued the claim that abuse was widespread during the wars in Afghanistan and Iraq—Byrd, Dayton, Kennedy, and Levin—did not present a sustained challenge to the claim that Abu Ghraib was an isolated incident. Instead, they raised other topics, such as the issue of the CIA's undocumented "ghost" detainees at Abu Ghraib, the Department of Defense's pursuit of accountability for the events at Abu Ghraib, and the failure of the department to plan for an insurgency in Iraq. These issues appeared, to critics of the administration, more potent political issues than did the geographic extent of abuse. Within the interpretive boundaries of the committee's hearings, the violence at Abu Ghraib prison had become isolated incidents among widespread, but understandable and politically inconsequential, abuse.

These developments occurred in relation to changes in the documentary record. Specifically, the publication of photographs taken at Abu Ghraib prison foreclosed literal denial, the claim that nothing—deviant, legitimate, or otherwise—occurred at Abu Ghraib prison. Hearing participants took as their point of departure that "things," in fact, happened at Abu Ghraib. The photographs enabled hearing participants to scrutinize particular events in a particular prison. They were "large-scale" representations of reality, showing a "relatively small area" of detention operations.[40] To establish the extent of abuse, participants drew on other documentary materials, such as official investigations and the ICRC report, that portray a relatively large area of detention operations. While helpful when the question is the extent of abuse, these scaled-down representations of detainee abuse facilitated other forms of denial. The reports scrutinized during the committee's final hearings provided a vantage on "widespread abuse" and, by the conclusion of the hearings, participants could speak of sixty-five instances of abuse, one-third of which happened at the point of capture. These representations, however, did not permit hearing participants to "see what [was] going on" at the point of capture.[41] Instead, they permitted officials to avoid talking about *particular* incidents of cruelty and hearing participants to engage in interpretive work around generic *types* of incidents and numerical representations.

It would be a mistake to describe the photographs taken at Abu Ghraib prison as inherently "more objective" than official investigations; it would likewise be a mistake to endow the photographs with an affective power that written narratives of violence lack.[42] In fact, effective and affective claims about problems *can* be made through narratives, such as "horror stories" of interpersonal violence.[43] Still, the photographs from Abu Ghraib, like horror stories, offer direct and immediate representations of interpersonal cruelty that are less easily rationalized and more evocative than those produced by "zooming out" of sites of violence. Indeed, "zooming out" diminishes the visibility of those very aspects of interpersonal violence that render it intolerable to liberal democracy: its ferocity, its apparent irrationality, the very excesses of cruelty that most saw in the Abu Ghraib photographs.

Accounts of abuse at the "point of capture," in contrast, fit that violence neatly into a broader framework that provided it a justification—necessity.

Finally, the competition surrounding Abu Ghraib reveals how the "ownership" of U.S. torture—as a constructed political problem—involved the ownership of the human and material resources, as well as access to the geographic sites, necessary to produce the evidentiary record that mediated Congress's debate.[44] At the time of these hearings, the documentary record of detainee abuse belonged, primarily, to the Department of Defense and the U.S. military, the organizations that established and conducted the investigations on which the committee received testimony. No doubt, the photographs and the ICRC report provided evidence in competition with those of these organizations. The Department of Defense's and the military's official investigators, however, largely outmaneuvered their competitors, making evidence available to committee members that was more extensive than those provided by the photographers at Abu Ghraib or the ICRC. By providing the "objective reality" of detainee abuse that participants in the hearings confronted, the Department of Defense and the U.S. military exerted their influence on the political debate about Abu Ghraib. Just as important, at the time of these hearings, members of the Senate Armed Services Committee were themselves relatively impoverished claims makers, at least at the level of fact; they were, in other words, dependent on the reports and investigations of others, including the very organizations whose actions committee members scrutinized.

The situation reflects dominant political relations at the time of the hearing. With the executive and legislative branches both being controlled by Republicans, the hearings served as a venue for the amplification of the Department of Defense's and the military's findings, rather than as a venue for genuine independent investigation.[45] As I argued in the previous chapter, the Senate Judiciary Committee's Chair, Orrin Hatch, excluded high-profile representatives of the executive from the Judiciary Committee's hearing on allegations of detainee abuse at Metropolitan Detention Center in New York. Doing so, Hatch effectively suppressed the symbolic importance of the committee's hearing. In considering the Senate Armed Services Committee hearings on Abu Ghraib, it is appropriate to again associate exclusionary practices and absences with the silencing of perspectives. No outside observer, human rights monitor, or legal expert appeared before the Republican Committee. The official discourse of state officials and military elites, instead, spoke to the committee on Abu Ghraib; it was only disrupted by senators who mobilized alternative discourses—that of the ICRC, for instance—circulating in media. Even then, these discourses only spoke by proxy and were often deconstructed by the committee's witnesses.

By geographically isolating Abu Ghraib, the Bush administration and its supporters in Congress contained the controversy over detainee abuse to the facility, lending weight to the claim that there were no systematic problems with U.S. detention and interrogation practices. This, however, was insufficient to resolve the scandal provoked by Abu Ghraib. Hearing participants also constructed causal claims, explanatory accounts for the violence at the prison. In so doing, they competed to assign blame for the photographed violence—to associate some actors with the violence while cordoning off others from its polluting effects. This competition is the subject of the next chapter.

CHAPTER 4

Sadism on the Night Shift

ACCOUNTING FOR ABU GHRAIB

OVER THE COURSE OF THE Senate Armed Services Committee (in this chapter, the committee) 2004 hearings on U.S. detention operations, military and civilian officials consistently stated that no policy, directive, or order permitted the photographed abuse at Abu Ghraib prison in Iraq. Against the current of this claim, a small group of senators, consisting predominantly, but not exclusively, of Democrats, argued that the abuse at Abu Ghraib prison resulted from the policy decisions of high-ranking military officials. These accounts rested on a controversial phrase and an equally controversial set of documents.

The controversial phrase was "set the conditions." It referred to a recommendation that General Geoffrey Miller made during a visit to Iraq in 2003. His recommendation that military police (MP) in Iraq facilitate military intelligence (MI) work by "setting the conditions" for interrogations came from his experience directing detention and interrogation operations at Guantánamo. The meaning of the phrase—the sort of MP behavior it implied—was the subject of considerable debate over the course of the committee's hearings. The controversial set of documents consisted of versions of the Iraq Interrogation Rules of Engagement (IROE) and, in particular, an IROE slide, allegedly from Ricardo Sanchez, the commanding general in Iraq, that listed "harsh" interrogations techniques. Who would take the blame for the violence at Abu Ghraib depended on how participants in the committee's hearings related these orders and documents to the photographed violence.

"SET THE CONDITIONS": THE CONTESTED MEANING OF
GENERAL GEOFFREY MILLER'S RECOMMENDATION

In his opening statement on May 7, Carl Levin made a provocative claim about the violence at Abu Ghraib:

> General Taguba's finding that "personnel assigned to the 372nd Military Police Company were directed to change facility procedures to set the conditions for military intelligence interrogations," is bolstered by pictures that suggest that the sadistic abuse was part of an organized and conscious process of intelligence-gathering. In other words, those abusive actions do not appear to be aberrant conduct by individuals, but part of a conscious method of extracting information.[1]

Between May 7 and May 19, the course of the committee's first four hearings, the phrase "set the conditions" came under intense scrutiny. What, though, did it mean? On May 7, Kennedy and Reed joined Levin, arguing that the recommendation was evidence that upper-level military or civilian officials had contributed to the abuse at Abu Ghraib. Contrary to this conclusion, Secretary of Defense Rumsfeld and Undersecretary of Defense Stephen A. Cambone suggested that the phrase meant something less nefarious and considerably more technical, namely the need for "coordination" (Cambone's word) or a "linkage" (Rumsfeld's) between military police at Abu Ghraib and military intelligence.[2] This coordination, Cambone and Rumsfeld believed, was intended to facilitate interrogations, not to establish an "organized and conscious process" of coercive or abusive interrogations. Rumsfeld offered his understanding of Miller's recommendation at the close of a lengthy exchange between Reed and Cambone about it:

REED: Mr. Secretary, were you aware that a specific recommendation was to use MPs to enable an interrogation process?

CAMBONE: In that precise language, no; but I knew that we were trying to get to the point where we were assuring that when they were in the general population, those that were under confinement were not undermining the interrogation process.

REED: So this was Major General Miller's own policy?

CAMBONE: No, sir, it was not a policy; it was a recommendation that he made to the command.

REED: So General Sanchez adopted this policy, making it a policy of the United States Army and the DOD, without consultation with you on any specific—

CAMBONE: Sir, I don't think that's a proper rendering of it.

REED: I don't know what the proper rendering is, but that seems to be at the core of this issue. Were you encouraging a policy that had MP officers enabling interrogations, which created the situation where these—

CAMBONE: No, sir.

RUMSFELD: May I comment? I think it is probably best put this way. They are different responsibilities, detaining and interrogating. However, they do need to be looked at together. They found, in Guantanamo, that how they are detained, in terms of the rhythm of their lives, can affect the interrogation process. . . . So it's important that there be a linkage, a relationship. The way it can be put is that it has a bad connotation. Goodness knows, that's not desirable or a policy that General Miller would have recommended.[3]

The opposing interpretations of the phrase spilled over into the committee's next hearing. On May 11, Senator Reed and Cambone engaged in another lengthy exchange about the phrase. This time, Reed explicitly rejected the notion that Miller's recommendation established a benign relationship between military police (MPs) and military intelligence (MIs):

REED: General Miller suggested that guard forces be used to "set the conditions." Based on the template at Guantanamo, those methods were coercive. Yet you did not choose to ask about this. You're completely oblivious.

CAMBONE: No, sir. Again, what I said was, we knew what the circumstances were with respect to Guantanamo. We knew what the circumstances were with respect to Iraq. We understood that the Geneva Conventions, and all of its articles, applied in Iraq. . . . The notion was that you had to have a cooperation, a cooperative attitude, team-building, call it what you will between the MPs and—

REED: Mr. Secretary, please.

CAMBONE: —the MIs.

REED: Please.

CAMBONE: Sir—

REED: This is not a cooperative attitude. This is not a guard observing the comments of a prisoner.[4]

Later in the exchange, Reed would soften his position and suggest that even if the term "set the conditions" was intended to increase cooperation between military police and interrogators, people "failed to ensure, by asking appropriate questions, that these recommendations were transmitted down to individual soldiers in a way that they would understand."[5] Still, he suggested that the term referred to something less benign, distinguishing participation "in the 'setting the conditions,' as . . . is done in Guantanamo" from mere cooperation.[6]

At the same hearing, General Taguba, whose report committee Democrats drew on to criticize Miller's recommendation, lent weight to Cambone's interpretation. In criticizing the policy, Taguba did not argue that General Miller's recommendation condoned, permitted, or encouraged abuse. On the contrary, Taguba testified that his investigation "did not find any evidence of a policy or a direct order given to these soldiers to conduct what they did."[7] In his report and testimony, Taguba argued that Miller's recommendation effectively put a military intelligence commander in charge of military police. Military regulations, Taguba believed, expressly prohibited this arrangement, as they bar military police from participating in interrogations. This criticism was not identical to that of Reed and Levin, who described the policy as establishing the use of coercive practices at Abu Ghraib.

Members of the committee continued to debate Miller's recommendation over the next two hearings. In these hearings, the technical and benign meaning of the phrase stood and, notably, no Democrat referenced the phrase when speaking of an intentional process of coercive interrogation. Indeed, hearing participants described the policy recommendation in increasingly commonsensical terms. At the committee's hearing on the afternoon of May 11, General Keith Alexander suggested, in his opening statement, that Miller's recommendation was meant to simply increase communication between MPs and MIs:

> The people who understand the environment that those prisoners are in day in and day out . . . are the MPs, and the best way to understand that interrogation plan and the methods that the interrogator will use is the MP . . . and that is one of the things that we need to have MP and MI talk about. Is this detainee . . . having a good day or bad? Has he been quiet, or has he been talking? What is the way to discuss this with him?[8]

When questioning Miller on May 19, Lindsey Graham also portrayed the recommendation as commonsensical:

GRAHAM: It is stupid to not be able to talk to the people who are running the jail about how the prisoner is doing that day before you interrogate him, right?
MILLER: Yes, sir, that is exactly right.[9]

Still, it remained possible to criticize Miller's recommendation, and hearing participants questioned whether it was advisable, consistent with military regulations, and well-understood by soldiers at Abu Ghraib. Those critical of the recommendation, however, no longer treated it as a euphemism for coercive practices. Instead, its relation to the abuse at Abu Ghraib became less direct. Kennedy and McCain suggested that the recommendation was likely misunderstood by those who implemented it. In an exchange with Miller, McCain pushed this claim particularly hard, arguing that it appeared that military police received orders from military intelligence to abuse detainees at Abu Ghraib. Miller, for his part, maintained that "leadership that received the recommendations . . . had a clear understanding of the recommendations."[10] McCain's followed up by noting, "there must have been a breakdown somewhere."[11] To this, Miller responded that, if a breakdown had occurred, it did so after his visit.

Critics in the committee no longer argued that Miller's recommendation—that military police "set the conditions" for interrogations—established an abusive detention and interrogation program. Instead, they argued that a *misinterpretation* of Miller's recommendation may have *contributed* to detainee abuse at Abu Ghraib. The causal link between the recommendation and the abuse had weakened. It was no longer direct; it did not lead from Miller through the recommendation through military intelligence to the military police whose actions were photographed at Abu Ghraib. Instead, this explanation suggested that the recommendation had, in fact, veered dramatically off its intended course and only resulted in abuse because of relatively low-level and local failures at Abu Ghraib prison.

Several committee Republicans (Graham, John Cornyn, James Inhofe, Pat Roberts, and Saxby Chambliss), Democrat Bill Nelson, and General Alexander further weakened the link between Miller's recommendation and the photographed abuse. They did this by consistently praising Miller for his work at Guantánamo. The implication was obvious. At

Guantánamo, the military effectively interrogated detainees without abusing them. Polices developed at the facility, then, could not be the source of the abusive practices photographed at Abu Ghraib.

This tactic was most apparent on May 19, when Miller testified before the committee. At that hearing, Senator Roberts asked Miller whether "the abuse evidenced in the photos [would] be permitted or condoned at any of the practices or policies at Guantanamo Bay." Miller responded simply, "Senator, they would not." [12] Later in the hearing, Chambliss spoke of his visit to Guantánamo and asked Miller to address abuse at the facility:

CHAMBLISS: I had the opportunity to visit [Guantánamo], both before the new camp was built as well as afterwards, and I saw the interrogation of prisoners down there. From what I saw, and from what I have heard, there has been no systemic prisoner abuse . . . at Guantanamo, and I just wish you would address that very quickly.

MILLER: Sir, there was no systemic abuse of prisoners at Guantanamo at any time. I believe that there were three or four events.[13] . . . It was the effect of strong, dynamic leadership by the chain of command 24 hours a day, 7 days a week, that did not allow the abuse to happen. We walked the cell blocks and the interrogation booths of Guantanamo around the clock—not because we did not trust our people, but this is a very difficult mission, and it takes active engagement by leadership to ensure that it is done correctly.[14]

Earlier, I discussed Senator Reed's statement that coercive methods were available at Guantánamo and that the phrase "set the conditions" referred to such practices. While Reed did not explicitly contest the propriety of these practices at Guantánamo, he did suggest that they were actively brought to Abu Ghraib prison in Iraq, a place where the Geneva Conventions applied and where such practices would be inappropriate. Miller's testimony, however, implicitly countered such an account. His policies, he claimed, did not permit anything shown in the Abu Ghraib photographs; further, the abuses that had occurred at Guantánamo under his leadership were less prevalent and far less severe than those at Abu Ghraib.

After the May 19 hearing, Miller's recommendation did not appear in any significant account of abuse at Abu Ghraib prison in the committee.[15] To be sure, it remained a feature of media accounts of Abu Ghraib; the phrase appeared—its opaque meaning still casting a shadow over Abu

Ghraib—in the writing of both the *Washington Post* and *New York Times* around this time. The *Post*, for instance, reported that

> military intelligence officers ... were using MPs to help "set the conditions" for interrogations, according to an investigative report compiled by Maj. Gen. Antonio M. Taguba. Several MPs have since said in statements and through their attorneys that they were roughing up detainees at the direction of U.S. military intelligence officers.[16]

For members of the committee, however, the phrase had lost much of its discursive potency, as well as its explanatory power. On July 22, Jeff Sessions, went so far as to insinuate that the recommendation was a "minor nothing."[17] There was, however, another way to explain the abuse at Abu Ghraib; this second explanation also linked high-ranking officials in the military chain of command to the violence at the facility.

"A SMOKING GUN OF ILLEGALITY AND IMPROPRIETY": THE CONTESTED MEANINGS OF THE INTERROGATION RULES OF ENGAGEMENT

The second debate over military policy and accountability for Abu Ghraib concerned the set of IROE documents that the military chain of command in Iraq provided military interrogators. To some, these documents suggested that high-level officials—notably, the Commanding General Ricardo Sanchez—had made harsh interrogation techniques, including sleep management, sensory deprivation, isolation, and the use of dogs, stress positions, and dietary manipulation—available for use in Iraq. In the debate about the IROE, members of the committee employed what the sociologists Michael Lynch and David Bogen refer to as the documentary method of interrogation, the use of material documents as "resources for questioning a witness."[18] Committee members closely examined the IROE documents, competing with each other and witnesses to define what precisely they meant and how they related to the photographed violence at Abu Ghraib.

On May 11, Senator Levin first raised the IROE, reading to Secretary Cambone a sentence from an annex of the Taguba report: "The interrogation officer in charge will submit memoranda for the record

INTERROGATION RULES OF ENGAGEMENT

Approved approaches for
All detainees:

Direct
Incentive
Incentive Removal
Emotional Love / Hate
Fear Up Harsh
Fear Up Mild
Reduced Fear
Pride & Ego Up
Futility
We Know All
Establish Your Identity
Repetition
File & Dossier
Rapid Fire
Silence

Require CG's Approval:

Change of scenery down
Dietary Manip (monitored by med)
Environmental Manipulation
Sleep Adjustment (reverse sched)
Isolation for longer than 30 days
Presence of Mil Working Dogs
Sleep Management (72 hrs max)
Sensory Deprivation (72 hrs max)
Stress Positions (no longer than 45 min)

Safeguards:

~ Techniques must be annotated in questioning strategy
~ Approaches must always be humane and lawful
~ Detainees will NEVER be touched in a malicious
   or unwanted manner
~ Wounded or medically burdened detainees must be
   medically cleared prior to interrogation
~ The Geneva Conventions apply within CJTF-7

EVERYONE IS RESPONSIBLE FOR ENSURING COMPLIANCE TO THE IROE.
VIOLATIONS MUST BE REPORTED IMMEDIATELY TO THE OIC.

The use of the techniques are subject to the general safeguards as provided as well as specific guidelines
implemented by the 205th MI Cdr. FM 34-52 and the Commanding General, CJTF-7

FIGURE 4.1. Re-creation of the Interrogation Rules of Engagement slide that listed
"harsh" interrogations techniques available for use in Iraq.

Source: Author. Also see note 20.

requesting harsh approaches for the commanding general's approval prior
to employment—sleep management, sensory deprivation, isolation longer
than 30 days, and dogs."[19]

Over the course of the next four hearings, debate focused on the techniques that Sanchez had authorized for use in Iraq and, especially, on a
slide (see figure 4.1) that seemed to suggest that Sanchez had given U.S.
interrogators in Iraq permission to use harsh interrogation approaches.[20]
This debate unfolded over the course of the committee's two May 11 hearings and its May 19 hearing. On May 11, during the committee's first hearing that day, statements and exchanges on these documents were rather
general. Levin questioned Cambone about his awareness of the availability of harsh interrogation techniques in Iraq; Cambone testified that he
was unaware that such techniques were permitted. Kennedy asked Cambone whether Secretary Rumsfeld had permitted harsh interrogation

techniques to be used in Iraq; Cambone testified that Rumsfeld had not. In these exchanges, Cambone testified that General Sanchez (as opposed to Rumsfeld or Cambone) had developed the Interrogation Rules of Engagement and could approve their use by interrogators in Iraq. At the second of the two May 11 hearings, Senator Levin questioned two witnesses, Generals Alexander and Ronald Burgess, about the legality of the interrogation techniques; both Senators Levin and John Warner, the Republican committee chair, asked whether Sanchez had approved any harsh interrogations.

On May 19, with Generals Sanchez, Miller, and John Abizaid testifying to the committee, a broader group of senators posed related questions to the witnesses. Senators Levin, Byrd, Reed, Dayton, and Clinton (Democrats) and Collins (a Republican) questioned General Sanchez about whether he had approved the document; Senators Dayton, Reed, and Collins also asked Sanchez whether he had granted permission for the use of any aggressive interrogation techniques in Iraq. Reed and Clinton questioned General Miller about whether he was aware or had been briefed on the content of the documents when he visited Iraq in 2003. And Senators Reed and Lieberman questioned witnesses about the legality of the interrogation techniques listed on the slide. On that day, questions and statements on this document were more frequent than they had been previously. They were also relatively dramatic, with senators holding up, gesturing at, and reading from the rules of engagement slide, employing it as a prop for the performance of congressional oversight (see figure 4.2).

These questions constituted the interpretive boundaries of the debate about the Interrogation Rules of Engagement in Iraq. And, as with the phrase "set the conditions," official responses to these questions downplayed, if not outright denied, the link between the military chain of command and the document, disowning the IROE in Iraq and the specific IROE slide. In doing so, they denied responsibility for the IROE's creation and adaption in Iraq. As noted above, Cambone, in his testimony to the committee on the morning of May 11, attributed the slide to Sanchez and denied that either he or Rumsfeld had approved additional interrogation techniques for use in Iraq. In a second hearing on May 11, General Alexander attributed, as Cambone had, the slide to General Sanchez. When, on

FIGURE 4.2. Senator Jack Reed uses the Interrogation Rules of Engagement slide, which purportedly shows "harsh" interrogations techniques that could be used with detainees in Iraq, while questioning Colonel Marc Warren.

Source: Getty Images. Photograph by Alex Wong.

May 19, Sanchez appeared before the committee, the general testified that he had first seen the document when it was discussed in an earlier committee hearing. During this hearing, Colonel Marc Warren, then the staff judge advocate for the Army in Iraq, revealed to Clinton that the slide had been drafted by Captain Carolyn Wood, a lower-ranking, military intelligence battalion commander, not Sanchez. In a follow-up question to General Miller, Clinton challenged the claim that the document had been "developed at a relatively low level" by citing a finding from an annex in the Taguba report that suggested the document had been briefed to Miller when he visited Abu Ghraib prison in 2003.[21] Miller, however, denied this.

The disavowal of the document was not, on its own, sufficient to sever its link to the abuses at Abu Ghraib prison. On May 19, Sanchez testified to Senator Byrd that he had approved Interrogation Rules of Engagement (on September 12, 2003, and "again in the October time frame") but that he had not "seen the specific slide that was referred to."[22] Although not publicly available at the time, the September 14, 2003, memorandum on "interrogation and counter-resistance policy" permitted the very same techniques, with Sanchez's approval, listed on the controversial right side of the slide.[23] The October memorandum, which was acquired and reported on by the *Washington Post* in late May and early June 2004 did not list all of these interrogation techniques.[24] However, it permitted (with Sanchez's approval) the presence of military dogs in interrogations and suggested that interrogators could seek approval for interrogation techniques *not* described in the memoranda.

Sanchez, in other words, denied approving a document and its presentation of techniques that were, at least in September 2003 when the abuse of detainees at Abu Ghraib was ongoing, the very interrogation practices that he approved for use in Iraq. This issue, however, was not raised. Had it been, it would still have been difficult to directly link Sanchez to the abuse at Abu Ghraib. As hearing participants recognized, the IROE established a route by which Sanchez's influence might end up at Abu Ghraib. But the slide withheld as much as it permitted. By requiring that interrogators seek Sanchez's approval for the use of the controversial interrogation practices, the IROE slide left that influence dormant—only further requests for authorizations could activate it. During the hearings, it emerged that Sanchez had only granted approval for one additional interrogation technique: the use of segregation, the isolation of a detainee, in excess of thirty days. This claim is important. It distances Sanchez from the particularly controversial photographed violence at Abu Ghraib—the use of dogs, stress positions, and forced nudity. The IROE slide could be said to inform U.S. interrogators of the scope of practices that their commanding general permitted in Iraq. These practices included some—such as the use of stress positions and dogs—that were caught up in the controversy surrounding the Abu Ghraib photographs. But the IROE did not, Sanchez credibly argued, *authorize* interrogators to use those practices. Instead, it required them to seek Sanchez's permission to do so. It required interrogators, in other words, to instigate further organizational exchanges. Such exchanges had occurred; however, they had only resulted in Sanchez authorizing interrogators to keep detainees in isolation. Sanchez, in the words of Sessions, had only permitted military interrogators to do what "is done in American prisons every day."[25]

There were other claims about what the IROE slide did and did not do. On May 19, Sessions and Warren highlighted "safeguards" that the slide included. These, they argued, would keep U.S. interrogators within the bounds of the Geneva Conventions. Sessions's exchange with Sanchez is illustrative:

SESSIONS: I am troubled by this suggestion that the interrogation rules are some sort of a smoking gun of illegality and impropriety. . . . As I read this document—this is a restrictive document that says such an action must have the direct approval of the commanding general. Is that the way you understand it, General Sanchez?

SANCHEZ: Sir, that is the way I read that document also. . . .

SESSIONS: I would like to note that, in big print here, it says, "Safeguards. Approaches must always be humane and lawful. Detainees will NEVER"—in capital letters—"be touched in a malicious or unwanted manner." Were the actions in this prison in violation of that directive? The allegations and the pictures we have seen, those would be in violation of that directive, would they not?

SANCHEZ: Sir, if those allegations are proved in the investigative process to be true, those would be violations.[26]

Even as the slide suggested that U.S. interrogators had permission to use harsh interrogation techniques, so long as they seek approval from General Sanchez, the slide also demanded that U.S. interrogators treat detainees humanely and in ways consistent with the Geneva Convention. It seemingly permitted and prohibited what some of the Abu Ghraib photographs showed.

Finally, military officials argued that the use of the "harsh" interrogation techniques listed on the slide would not, in and of themselves, violate the Geneva Conventions or military regulations. Instead, the legality of the techniques would depend on how interrogators specifically interpreted and implemented the slide. This argument is important, as it minimized the military chain of command's responsibility for the abuse of detainees at Abu Ghraib. And, in the next chapter, we will see military officials make a comparable claim about detainee abuse at Guantánamo. This argument also resonates with the dynamics of organizational behavior. "Superiors do not like to give detailed instructions to subordinates . . . Pushing down details relieves superiors of the burden of too much knowledge, particularly guilty knowledge."[27]

Warren made this point, in response to a question posed by Lieberman, to downplay the notoriety that had attached itself to the slide:

LIEBERMAN: But again, you would say that of the group on the right, which has attracted the attention of the committee, the media, and the public, none of these are inherently or automatically in violation of the Geneva Conventions?

WARREN: . . . To use a term I have learned in the past week in Washington, the optics are bad on that chart. But if you read the actual definitions you will find, for example, with regard to environmental manipulation, it sounds horrible. But the fact is that environmental manipulation can be as simple as, while at all times maintaining the minimum requirements of the Geneva Conventions, that a person who cooperates in interrogations would get an air conditioned room. A person who is not cooperating gets the minimum, non-air conditioned room.[28]

The IROE slide met a fate similar to that of the phrase "set the conditions." Its capacity to link high-ranking officials to the violence at Abu Ghraib weakened over the course of the hearings. The slide had not, in fact, been created or approved by a high-ranking military official. It included safeguards that prohibited the behavior depicted in the Abu Ghraib photographs. And, while it did seem to make controversial practices available to U.S. interrogators at Abu Ghraib, some of those controversial practices were not, according to at least one military lawyer, all that controversial. Besides, those practices required Sanchez's approval for use; Sanchez had granted approval only for detainees to be kept in isolation. Over the course of the hearings, the slide revealed itself to be no smoking gun. No line of causality could be traced from it to Sanchez.

MIGRATING POLICY

On September 9, 2004, the Senate Armed Services Committee held the final two of its seven hearings on Abu Ghraib. The first hearing focused on the findings of the Fay-Jones reports, the military's two investigations of intelligence activities at Abu Ghraib prison. Generals George R. Fay and Anthony R. Jones, the lead investigators for the reports, and General Paul J. Kerns, the Army's appointing authority, gave testimony about their reports. The second hearing involved James Schlesinger and

Harold Brown, who gave testimony on the findings of their independent investigation.

Over the course of these hearings, a specific and fairly well-defined explanation of the abuses at Abu Ghraib emerged. This explanation emphasized two things. First, it emphasized that policies designed for Guantánamo and Afghanistan "migrated" to Abu Ghraib. Second, this explanation emphasized that this migration of policy, as well as shifting rules of engagement in Iraq, contributed to confusion at Abu Ghraib that, in turn, led to detainee abuse. It is important to note that this explanation highlighted that it was this confusion over policies, not the policies themselves, that accounted for the abuse of detainees at the facility.

This account had a well-established chronological dimension. It began with the Bush administration's decision after the September 11 terrorist attacks to deny alleged members of al-Qaeda and the Taliban prisoner of war status under the Geneva Conventions and to declare that detainees would be treated "humanely, and to the extent appropriate and consistent with military necessity, in a manner consistent with the principles of the Geneva Conventions."[29] This led to, in the words of Brown,

> a series of determinations about allowed interrogation methods beyond those long customary. . . . The Secretary of Defense authorized and then rescinded a list of such methods for Guantanamo. After study by a working group that was headed by the Air Force General Counsel, he promulgated a narrowed-approved list, again limited to interrogations of unlawful combatants held at Guantanamo.[30]

This process involved, as Senator Levin pointed out, Office of Legal Counsel opinions, including "one dated August 1, 2002 that . . . 'held that in order to constitute torture, an act must be specifically intended to inflict severe physical pain and suffering that is difficult to endure.' "[31]

These decisions and opinions led, according to this account, to the development of interrogation policies that were, as Levin read from the Fay-Jones report during the a.m. hearing, "not completely consistent with Army doctrine concerning detainee treatment or interrogation tactics."[32] These new, unconventional policies were meant for use in Guantánamo, where the administration had decided the Geneva Conventions did not protect detainees; however, according to Brown, various versions of expanded lists migrated, unauthorized, to Afghanistan and to Iraq where the Geneva Conventions continued to apply. . . . That migration of rules and of personnel led to confusion about what interrogation practices were authorized and to several changes in directions to interrogators. I believe that was a contributing factor in the abuse of detainees.[33]

Compared with the claim that no policy permitted torture, the "migrating policy" account is something of a compromise, a nod of official acknowledgment. It integrates revelations about Office of the Legal Counsel and Department of Defense interrogation policies that were not known to the public when the Abu Ghraib photographs were first released. It accommodates, for instance, the revelation that Secretary Rumsfeld had personally authorized interrogation practices beyond those listed in the Army's field manual for interrogation for use at Guantánamo. In December 2002, Rumsfeld signed a memorandum granting approval for the use of stress positions, isolation, hooding, sensory deprivation, removal of clothing, and "mild, non-injurious contact." The explanation also implicitly recognized, in the acknowledgment of "confusion," the influence of the social psychological context on U.S. soldiers and interrogators. Indeed, the Schlesinger report included an annex that drew on the findings of the Stanford prison experiment.[34] The emergence of this account is an important moment in the debate about torture. On the one hand, it was an early recognition, among political elites, that high-ranking administration officials, if not the president himself, were caught up in the making of policies that promoted torture. On the other hand, the account did not yet go that far. The specific content of the policies was not the primary focus of congressional concern; again, it was the confusion over policies, not what the policies allowed, that seemed to explain the abuse and torture of detainees.

While some of these policies are described by Schlesinger as "over the top," they are not, in and of themselves, condemned or described as "abusive" or "torture" policies. In fact, the policies that hearing participants described as migrating—that is, the policies at Guantánamo—were also described, as the IROE slide was, as prohibiting the photographed abuses. General Kern, for instance, pointed out that some actions at Abu Ghraib, such as the use of a muzzled dog during interrogations, was "not even possible in Guantanamo."[35] Brown and Schlesinger, in an exchange with Senator Sessions, stated that the policies actually prohibited the photographed violence. It was, fully, the confusion caused by the migration of policies and the frequent changes to interrogation rules of engagement in Iraq, rather than what the policies permitted, that resulted in the abuse at Abu Ghraib prison.

The explanation, then, emphasized Abu Ghraib's uniqueness—the local conditions there that did not exist at other U.S. facilities, especially Guantánamo, that led to the photographed abuse. Schlesinger went so far to "characterize those activities by the night shift on Tier 1 as an '*Animal House*.'"[36] This was an image that Schlesinger earlier tested when, in late August, he discussed his panel's report with the media. Then, he was more evocative: "There was sadism on the night shift at Abu Ghraib, sadism that was certainly not authorized . . . It was kind of '*Animal House*' on the night shift."[37] The comparison is stunning for its audacity, cleverness, and datedness. Audacious, for Schlesinger refers to an entirely unserious movie—one iconic for being unserious—to account for the physical and sexual abuse and torture of unarmed and often innocent detainees in U.S. custody. Clever, for Schlesinger effectively condensed four months of controversy about Miller's recommendations, Sanchez's IROE, and Rumsfeld's authorizations into five words. "*Animal House* on the night shift" was somehow clearer in its message than any of the other explanations offered to the committee. Dated, because *Animal House* was released during the Carter administration, when Schlesinger's panel member, Harold Brown, served as secretary of defense.

Schlesinger's August statement on Abu Ghraib preempted his appearance before the committee in September. Media coverage of the release of his report and his briefing was substantial; the *New York Times*, *Washington Post*, and *USA Today* all ran front-page stories referring to Schlesinger's report and citing his reference to *Animal House*.[38] This coverage implicated Rumsfeld for the abuse at Abu Ghraib, but in the way that I have described above. The articles emphasize that Schlesinger's report did not claim that Rumsfeld or other high-ranking officials set policies that contributed to abuse or torture; instead, they focus on Rumsfeld's contributions to local confusion that confounded military police at Abu Ghraib. No reporting on the committee's final 2004 hearing on Abu Ghraib refers to *Animal House*. The day after, both the *Post* and the *Times* published scathing editorials about the Bush administration's handling of Abu Ghraib.[39] Both editorials credit Congress for questioning the military's and Schlesinger's refusal to meaningfully hold any high-ranking official accountable for Abu Ghraib; both, though, also lament that the committee was itself unable to pursue meaningful accountability for Abu Ghraib.

CONCLUSION

The geographic and causal dimensions collide in the "policy migration" account. In September 2004, the Senate Armed Services Committee did not recognize that the widespread abuse that the ICRC and others had documented in Iraq and elsewhere was consequential and serious. As noted in the previous chapter, the "widespread abuse" that occurred around Abu Ghraib prison was politically nonproblematic and, at Guantánamo, the facility for which the migrating policies were designed, only nonsystematic and "minor" instances of abuse were publicly recognized by U.S. politicians. It was at Abu Ghraib prison and only there that Rumsfeld's authorization of pain-inducing interrogation practices and Office of Legal Counsel opinions on the treatment of detainees bore any relation to abuse. The abuse at Abu Ghraib was portrayed as an anomaly, and local conditions, including the confusion caused by policy, local leadership breakdowns, and the pathology of a few soldiers, purportedly accounted for the abuse there.

This situation would begin to change in December 2004 when memos and e-mails from FBI agents who had been posted at Guantánamo were publicly released. These materials documented abuse at Guantánamo that an FBI agent described, in one e-mail, as torture. One account was particularly troubling. An FBI agent had witnessed: "On a couple of occasions, . . . a detainee chained hand and foot in a fetal position to the floor, with no chair, food or water. Most times they had urinated or defecated on themselves and had been left there for 18, 24 hours, or more."[40]

Soon after, another official investigation, headed by Generals Randall Schmidt and John Furlow, would be launched. On June 12, 2005, about a month before the Senate Armed Services Committee would invite the generals to testify about their investigation, *Time* published an article based on the interrogation log of Detainee 0-63, Mohammed al-Qahtani. The article recounted how, at Guantánamo, al-Qahtani was strip-searched and made to "stand nude"; how he was told "to bark like a dog and growl at pictures of interrogations"; how Army interrogators hanged "pictures of scantily clad women around his neck"; and how "a female interrogator so annoy[ed] al-Qahtani that he [told] his captors he [wanted] to commit suicide."[41] During a 2005 Senate Armed Services' Committee hearing on Guantánamo, which is the focus of the next chapter, Senator Reed scrutinized the abuses that had occurred there and observed, "That sounds remarkably similar to what occurred at Abu Ghraib, people being led around in chains, people being forced to wear lingerie. Perhaps a coincidence, perhaps not."[42]

The "isolated" incident was becoming emblematic.

CHAPTER 5

"Honor Bound"

THE POLITICAL LEGACY OF GUANTÁNAMO

OVER THE COURSE OF THE Senate Armed Services Committee's seven hearings on Abu Ghraib, a core group of Republican Senators, Democrat Bill Nelson, and several military witnesses (Generals Smith, Alexander, and Miller) praised General Geoffrey Miller for having "straightened out," in Senator Pat Roberts's words, Guantánamo.[1] As Saxby Chambliss put it:

> I think I was [at Guantánamo] the day that General Miller first arrived, as a matter of fact. I observed random interrogations down there. General Miller did correct a problem that existed. There were charges of abuse that were much slighter than these charges of abuse [at Abu Ghraib prison], and General Miller dealt with those swiftly and directly.[2]

This praise of Miller rebounded onto Guantánamo. Having been "cleaned up" by the general, detention and interrogation practices at Guantánamo were political nonissues. If Abu Ghraib was an "*Animal House*," as James Schlesinger described it, the soldiers at Guantánamo were "honor bound to defend freedom," a phrase Miller institutionalized at the facility. In Congress, this portrayal of Guantánamo was empirically credible, based, as it was, on the fact that no major incidents of abuse had been publicly documented by official, government sources.

This characterization of Guantánamo may strike the reader as peculiar. That the prison harms the global image of the United States is a truism of media coverage of the facility.[3] Political consensus about the wisdom of the policies and practices at Guantánamo, as well as about the continued use of detention facilities there, does not yet exist. However, many U.S. politicians, Republicans and Democrats alike, publicly recognize Guantánamo as a symbol of U.S. human rights violations. During the 2008 U.S. presidential campaign, both Senators Barack Obama and John McCain argued that the detention facility at Guantánamo Bay should be closed.[4] As president, Obama took immediate action toward realizing this goal, signing an executive order that would close the detention facilities at Guantánamo "no later than 1 year from the date of this order."[5] Midway through Obama's second term, Guantánamo remained in operation; meanwhile, the symbolic harm of the prison idled:

> Even if the administration concludes that it will never close the prison, it cannot acknowledge that because it would revive Guantanamo as America's image in the Muslim world. "Guantanamo is a negative symbol, but it is much diminished because we are seen as trying to close it," the official said. "Closing Guantanamo is good, but fighting to close Guantanamo is O.K. Admitting you failed would be the worst."[6]

This chapter takes this transition as its puzzle. How did Guantánamo become a mark on the collective visage of the United States? Why did this transition in political discourse occur? The answers to these questions concern both changes in the documentary record surrounding Guantánamo and the political context in which members of Congress debated the facility. Specifically, the public release of FBI e-mails and a military interrogation log provided, much as the Abu Ghraib photographs had, credible evidence of detainee abuse and torture. These documents portrayed a very different reality of detainee abuse at Guantánamo than did Miller's testimony to the committee that "three or four minor events" had occurred at the facility. This chapter discusses this development, showing how it affected Congress's debate. This chapter also shows how developments in the political context—specifically the Supreme Court's ruling in *Hamdan v. Rumsfeld* and the 2006 midterm elections—altered the debate; these changes did so by elevating the rule of law and human rights as interpretive frames for making sense of allegations of abuse at Guantánamo.

BACKGROUND

The U.S. presence at Guantánamo Bay dates to 1903, when, following the Spanish-American War, the United States leased land and water around the bay from Cuba and established a fueling station there.[7] A 1934 treaty reaffirmed the lease and provided that it would continue perpetually.[8] Until President Obama reestablished diplomatic relations with Cuba, Guantánamo was the only naval base that the United States operated "in a country with which the U.S. does not maintain diplomatic relations."[9] In 1991, the George H. W. Bush administration began using Guantánamo to hold asylum seekers from Haiti; in 1994, the United States started holding Cuban refugees there.[10] While Guantánamo has not been an integral part of U.S. immigration policy since 1996, when the final Cuban refugees held there were allowed to enter the United States,[11] "normally, Guantanamo houses around 30 migrants at any given time," according to the U.S. military.[12] In 2007, the U.S. military began building facilities to "temporarily house not only political and economic asylum seekers, but victims of natural disasters and other unforeseen events."[13] The earliest print media references that I have found to Guantánamo in the context of the war on terror came on October 2, 2001, in the *Guardian* and the *Washington Times*.[14] These foreshadowed the complicated legacy of the facility and the U.S war in Afghanistan. In the *Guardian*, George Monbiot argued against a military response to terrorism and for a diplomatic and humanitarian one. He cited the U.S. experience in Cuba as evidence of how *not* to confront a political enemy:

> There are many in Washington who privately acknowledge that Fidel Castro's tenure has been sustained by US hostilities and embargos. Had the US withdrawn its forces from Guantanamo Bay, opened its markets and invested in Cuba, it would have achieved with generosity what it has never achieved with antagonism."[15]

In the *Washington Times*, Bruce Fein took the opposite position, celebrating the fact that "nation-building is off the table" in Afghanistan; Fein advocated "creating a United States antiterrorism defense base [in Afghanistan] like our Guantanamo naval base in Cuba."[16]

Hints of the Bush administration's decision to create a detention facility at Guantánamo came on November 25, 2001, when the *New York Times* reported that "Pentagon officials designing military tribunals for suspected terrorists are considering the possibility of swift, secretive trials on ships at sea or on United States installations, like the naval base in Guantánamo Bay, Cuba."[17] A month later, at a December 27, 2001, press briefing, Secretary of Defense Donald Rumsfeld detailed the Defense Department's plans to create a detention facility at Guantánamo.[18] On January 6, 2002, American soldiers began arriving there to build maximum-security detention facilities.[19] Five days later, the first detainees, twenty in total, arrived at Guantánamo.[20]

The conditions of detainment at Guantánamo immediately raised concerns among human rights organizations. The International Committee of the Red Cross (ICRC) publicly stated that it regarded the twenty detainees transported to Guantánamo as prisoners of war, protected by the Geneva Conventions, rather than, as the Bush administration labeled the detainees, "unlawful combatants."[21] The ICRC and Amnesty International (AI) both expressed concerns about the handling of the detainees. The ICRC characterized the decision to shave the beards of the detainees as a possible violation of the detainees' human dignity. AI released a press release condemning the United States for its plans to drug, hood, and shackle the detainees on the flight from Afghanistan to Guantánamo; the organization also criticized the administration's plans to hold detainees in "6 × 8 feet chain-link 'cages' at least partially open to the elements."[22] All of these practices, according to Amnesty, fell below or violated international human rights standards.

The criticisms, however, barely registered in Congress. In late January 2002, a group of twenty members of Congress visited Guantánamo. Several members of the group downplayed human rights reports of abuse at the prison and described the trip as motivated by a concern over interrogation and intelligence, rather than detention conditions.[23] Republican Representative Bob Stump, who participated in the visit and was, at the time, chair of the House Armed Services Committee, referred to the criticisms of Guantánamo as "anti-American."[24] Republican Ileana Ros-Lehtinen described the criticism as ironic, given the concern that human rights organizations were showing for "these assassins, these terrorists, these sworn enemies of America and the principles of freedom and democracy when right outside the barbed-wire fence from Gitmo, 11 [million] Cubans are literally ready and willing to die to get to the freedom of our shores."[25] Senator Bill Nelson, a Democrat from Florida and a member of Senate Armed Services Committee, was more generous to critics than his Republican colleagues were, recognizing human rights concerns as legitimate. However, he, too, downplayed these concerns and, instead, emphasized the importance of intelligence-gathering, saying, "the question of humane treatment is certainly a legitimate question, but I can't imagine . . . that the United States is not giving anything but humane treatment. That is the character, that is the nature of our people. . . . What I want to find out is, are we getting information? We are in a war against terrorists."[26]

In fact, in 2002, there is only one critique of Guantánamo in the congressional record, and it is an indirect one. On March 20, 2002, Democrat House member Dennis Kucinich offered a "prayer for America." In it, he observed that the American people, through their elected representatives, had not authorized "permanent detainees in Guantanamo Bay."[27] Similarly, in 2003, there are, again, few critical references to Guantánamo in the congressional record and those that do appear are generally ambiguous or refer not to the treatment of detainees at the prison, but the legal processes by which the executive branch determined the category to which a detainee belongs (and, thus, establishes what legal protections a detainee receives).[28] Among U.S. politicians, Guantánamo was a nonproblem for its first few years of existence. This began to change, however, in late 2004, when a flurry of reporting weakened the credibility of claims that Guantánamo had avoided the detainee abuse problem that Abu Ghraib housed.

THE REALITY OF TORTURE AT GUANTÁNAMO

In 2004, the release of the Abu Ghraib photographs drew public attention to the treatment of detainees in U.S. custody. Public scrutiny of Guantánamo increased, too, but this scrutiny barely registered with members of the Senate Armed Services Committee when they investigated Abu Ghraib in 2004.[29] When the committee's hearings ended in September 2004, Guantánamo had effectively been excluded from the committee's narrative of detainee abuse. In the months following the completion of these hearings and the 2004 U.S. presidential election, revelations about detention practices at Guantánamo proliferated. What emerged was a disturbing picture of the detainees' everyday life at Guantánamo and the practices that the U.S. military employed there. That official sources, FBI and military interrogators, had documented these practices, that these sources had directly observed detention and interrogation operations, and that these sources evocatively recorded these operations made these accounts particularly problematic for those who would portray Guantánamo as a model prison.

In a front-page article in the October 17, 2004, edition of the *New York Times*, Neil A. Lewis, citing interviews with unnamed "military guards, military intelligence agents, and others," alleged that detainees at Guantánamo were regularly subjected to "harsh and coercive treatment."[30] The article claimed that one "regular procedure" was

> making uncooperative prisoners strip to their underwear, having them sit in a chair while shackled hand and foot to a bolt in the floor, and forcing them to endure strobe lights and screamingly loud rock and rap music played through two close loudspeakers, while the air-conditioning was turned up to maximum levels.

Lewis's article juxtaposed these allegations with the military's and the Schlesinger panel's claims that the interrogation techniques approved by Secretary Rumsfeld were "used only on two occasions" and that there "were about eight abuses" at Guantánamo. On November 30, in another front-page article, Lewis reported on a classified ICRC report, based on the ICRC's June 2004 visit to Guantánamo, that contained similar allegations.[31] Specifically, the report found "that the American military has intentionally used psychological and sometimes physical coercion 'tantamount to torture.'"

In December 2004, the ACLU acquired and released e-mails and memoranda documenting FBI agents' experiences at Guantánamo as part of a Freedom of Information suit. The materials were consistent with Lewis's reporting for the *New York Times* and provided firsthand accounts of detention and interrogation practices at the facility. In one particularly troubling e-mail, an FBI agent described witnessing a detainee in an "unventilated room well over 100 degrees. The detainee was almost unconscious on the floor, with a pile of hair next to him. He had apparently been literally pulling his hair out throughout the night."[32] Other documents alleged military dogs had been used during interrogations at Guantánamo.

As Dan Eggen and R. Jeffrey Smith reported in the *Washington Post*, this conflicted with General Geoffrey Miller's account of what went on at the facility he ran: "Miller has acknowledged urging in September 2003 that military dogs be sent to Iraq to help deter prison violence, but he told a team of Defense Department investigators in June—and many reporters—that 'we never used the dogs for interrogations while I was in command' of Guantánamo Bay."[33]

The FBI's allegations led General Bantz J. Craddock to open an investigation into interrogations at Guantánamo. Craddock named Brigadier General John T. Furlow the investigating officer. In February 2005, Craddock appointed Lieutenant General Randall M. Schmidt the senior investigating officer of the investigation. Schmidt's appointment permitted the investigation to interview officers outranking General Furlow.

In March 2005, while Generals Furlow and Schmidt's investigation was ongoing, the Department of Defense released the executive summary of the Church report. The report, led by Vice-Admiral Albert T. Church III, was the Department of Defense's final major review of U.S. detention practices spurred by the revelations from Abu Ghraib. On March 10, 2005, Church appeared before the Senate Armed Services Committee to give testimony on the findings of his investigation. In that testimony, he characterized abuse at Guantánamo as on being on "the low end"; there were "incidents of slapping or what we call minor abuse cases."[34]

Church's account was consistent with those that Miller and the Schlesinger panel offered in 2004. Despite it, another image of Guantánamo began to take shape. In his opening statement, Carl Levin cited revelations from the FBI's e-mails and told a very different story than had Church:

> Just in the past few months, we have learned of FBI agents' strong objections to aggressive and coercive interrogation techniques at Gitmo, which FBI agents in one e-mail labeled "torture" and in a number of e-mails deemed so disturbing that agents had guidance to "step out of the picture" when the military were carrying out interrogations.[35]

As I noted in chapter 3, the official investigations of abuse in Iraq largely suppressed the "distinctive local . . . character" of violence done against detainees in U.S. custody.[36] While the reports acknowledged incidents of violence, such as those at the point of capture, they obscured the nature of those events and facilitated official denial of them. In his testimony, Church provided a similarly obscured view on acknowledged abuse at Guantánamo, describing each instance with only the phrases "instances of slapping" and "minor abuse cases." The FBI's e-mails provided a different vantage on abuse at Guantánamo. Like the Abu Ghraib photographs, the FBI's e-mails richly and evocatively portrayed the disorders and excesses of U.S. detention and interrogation practices. Their portrayals, again like the Abu Ghraib photographs, were difficult to fit to the interpretive contours of legitimate democratic force, which should appear restrained and instrumentally organized. They also were difficult to square with the claim that minor abuses had occurred at Guantánamo. Here, in the FBI's e-mails, are the vulnerabilities of the suffering human body. Here are detainees in the fetal position; here is urination, defecation, and, in one case, a detainee, nearly unconscious, lying amid his own hair.

THE INTERROGATION OF MOHAMMED AL-QAHTANI

From October to December 2004, the three months that followed the Senate Armed Services Committee's final hearing on Abu Ghraib, a vast documentary record of abuse and torture replaced the assertions, emanating from the Department of Defense, that a few, minor abuses occurred at the Guantánamo. On June 12, 2005, another influential report, based on the Army's own interrogation log of a single, high-value detainee, entered the public domain. The report, published by *Time* magazine and featured as its January 20 cover story, was based on the military's interrogation log of Detainee o-63, Mohammed al-Qahtani, at Guantánamo. Al-Qahtani is (one of the people) suspected to be the twentieth hijacker, who was meant to participate in the September 11 terrorist attacks as the fifth hijacker of Flight 93.[37] In August 2001, al-Qahtani had been denied entry into the United States; he was subsequently deported and then captured in Afghanistan in 2001.[38] (*Time* released extracts of the log with the article; they would release the full log in March 2006.) The article and the publicly available extracts revealed that al-Qahtani's interrogation involved sleep deprivation, sensory bombardment through exposure to noise, isolation, forced nudity, a military dog, and prolonged interrogations (which lasted up to twelve hours). Female interrogators and "pictures of scantily clad women" were also used to harass al-Qahtani.[39]

Like the FBI's e-mails before it, al-Qahtani's interrogation log provides an immediate, seemingly direct vantage on Guantánamo. Writing for *Time*, Adam Zagorin and Michael Duffy aptly characterize the log as

> like a night watchman's diary. It is a sometimes shocking and often mundane hour-by-hour, even minute-by-minute account of a campaign to extract information. The log records every time al-Qahtani eats, sleeps, exercises or goes to the bathroom and every time he complies with or refuses his interrogators' requests.[40]

The *Time* report did not challenge the propriety of al-Qahtani's interrogation. Al-Qahtani's status as the "so-called 20th hijacker" frames the article, his possession of vital information about al-Qaeda is frequently cited, and the report closes with the authors' admission that "in the war on terrorism, the personal dignity of a fanatic trained for mass murder may be an inevitable casualty."[41] Still, the report, drawing on al-Qahtani's interrogation log, documents the descent of the interrogation into absurd types of harassment, cruelty and torture. Frustrated by al-Qahtani's apparent capacity to resist interrogation and emboldened by Secretary of Defense Donald Rumsfeld's December 2002 authorization of "stronger coercive methods," military interrogators began to innovate. They prevented al-Qahtani from sleeping during lengthy interrogations by "dripping water on his head or playing Christina Aguilera music."[42] The report also revealed that

> his handlers at one point perform a puppet show "satirizing the detainee's involvement with al-Qaeda." He is taken to a new interrogation booth, which is decorated with pictures of 9/11 victims, American flags and red lights. He has to stand for the playing of the U.S. national anthem. His head and beard are shaved. He is returned to his original interrogation booth. A picture of a 9/11 victim is taped to his trousers. Al-Qahtani repeats that he will "not talk until he is interrogated the proper way." Over the next few days, al-Qahtani is subjected to a drill known as Invasion of Space by a Female, and he becomes especially agitated by the close physical presence of a woman.[43]

Like detainees at Abu Ghraib, al-Qahtani was interrogated in the presence of a military dog and stripped and forced to stand nude. He was told to "bark like a dog and growl at pictures of terrorists." Interrogators hung "pictures of scantily clad women around his neck." These, apparently, are some of the "minor abuses" to which Church, in his earlier testimony to the Senate Armed Services Committee, referred.

Time's report also documents the consequences of these practices, particularly sleep deprivation and stress, on al-Qahtani, who, intermittently, refused food and drink. On December 7, 2002, al-Qahtani's interrogation ceased for twenty-four hours—although he was still denied sleep—after the detainee became "seriously dehydrated." A doctor monitored al-Qahtani's condition and, later on the seventh, al-Qahtani's pulse slowed:

> An electrocardiogram is administered by a doctor, and after al-Qahtani is transferred to a hospital, a CT scan is performed. A second doctor is consulted. Al-Qahtani's heartbeat is regular but slow: thirty-five beats a minute. He is placed in isolation and hooked up to a heart monitor. The next day, a radiologist is flown in from Roosevelt Roads Naval Air Station in Puerto Rico, 600 miles away, to read the CT scan. The log reports, "No anomalies were found." Nonetheless, al-Qahtani is given an ultrasound for blood clots. For the first time since the log began, al-Qahtani is given an entire day to sleep. The next evening, the log reports that his medical "checks are all good." Al-Qahtani is "hooded, shackled and restrained in a litter" and transported back to Camp X-Ray in an ambulance.[44]

The description of al-Qahtani's condition is notable for a number of reasons. On the one hand, it provides evidence that medical professionals at Guantánamo were complicit in al-Qahtani's mistreatment.[45] On the other, *Time*'s initial report downplays the physical consequences of al-Qahtani's treatment, including al-Qahtani's sustained pulmonary problems while in detention. Indeed, the report seems to suggest, as proponents of "enhanced interrogation" often do, that such practices have no lasting, physical consequences. Both the report and log also attempt to bolster the prevailing image of U.S. interrogation as well regulated by documenting the frequency with which military doctors evaluated al-Qahtani as fit to undergo interrogation. And yet, the report, like the log, permits a reading against its grain. Against the image of a well-regulated interrogation, one finds interrogators experimenting with practices that appear far from professional or scientific—the puppet show, the images of "scantily clad women," and the use of women to "agitate" al-Qahtani. Against the image of precise, surgical practices, one finds al-Qahtani's suffering—his heart rate slows; he suffers from chest pain, kidney pain, and head pain. He develops a boil on his legs; he is constantly exercised to prevent swelling in his feet from prolonged standing.[46]

The week following the release of *Time*'s report was an especially fraught one for Guantánamo. In response to the report, the Department of Defense released details about al-Qahtani's interrogation, emphasizing the value of the information gained.[47] Vice President Cheney and Secretary of Defense Donald Rumsfeld also spoke publicly about the facility, defending the treatment of detainees there and its continued use in the face of increasing congressional resistance.[48] In a series of statements made in mid-June, members of the president's party, however, indicated that they were split on the continuing use of the prison. On June 10, Florida Senator Mel Martinez became the first Republican to advocate the closing of Guantánamo, calling the facility "an icon for bad stories."[49] After the release of the log, Senator Chuck Hagel of Nebraska, also a Republican, joined Martinez, citing Guantánamo as a reason that America is "losing the image war around the world" and argued that closing the facilities there would improve the U.S.'s global standing.[50] Senator Bill Frist, the Republican Senate Majority Leader, acknowledged the political peril of Guantánamo, but argued against closing it: "To cut and run because of image problems . . . is the wrong, wrong thing to do."[51]

Amid these developments, the Senate Judiciary Committee held a hearing, entitled "Detainees." The chairman of the committee at that time, Republican Arlen Specter, narrowly defined the committee's agenda in his opening statement: "The focus of today's hearing is going to be on the procedures used with detainees. We do not have within the scope of this hearing the issues of torture or mistreatment."[52] Committee Democrats, however, aggressively criticized the ongoing use of Guantánamo. Patrick Leahy, the committee's ranking Democrat, referred to the facility as "an international embarrassment" that "undermined our leadership and damaged our credibility. It has drained the world's good will for America at alarming rates."[53] Joseph Biden and Russ Feingold echoed Levin's critique; both noted that the facility had harmed the U.S. reputation in the "Muslim world." Ted Kennedy was more oratorical, using the duration of his question-and-answer period to make a lengthy statement on Guantánamo. In it, Kennedy referred to the country's Founding

Fathers, described the violence at Guantánamo as torture, and cited the FBI's allegations:

> In many parts of the world, we are no longer viewed as the Nation of Jefferson, Hamilton, and Madison. Instead, we are seen as a country that imprisons people without trial and degrades and tortures them. Our moral authority went into a free fall. The FBI has reported the use of torture as an interrogation tool at Guantanamo and complained to the Justice Department and the Defense Department about its use. And the Red Cross has documented scores of abuses at Guantanamo and elsewhere. Top officials in the administration have endorsed and defended interrogation that we have condemned in other countries, including forcing prisoners into painful stress positions for hours, threatening them with dogs, depriving them of sleep, using so-called water-boarding to simulate drowning. We have degraded and exploited our own female military personnel by encouraging them to use sexually degrading methods of interrogation. . . . There is no question that Guantanamo has undermined our efforts in the war on terrorism. It has stained our reputation on human rights. It has inflamed the Muslim world, and it became a powerful recruiting tool for terrorists.[54]

The summer of 2005 was a critical moment in the political contest over Guantánamo. In 2004, the prison's positive and credible image (at least among U.S. senators) had served Republicans and military officials well. Now, however, Guantánamo required accounting. The Senate Armed Services Committee's July 13 hearing on the Schmidt-Furlow report provided a stage for just that.

SUSTAINING "HONOR BOUND"

The committee's hearing on the Schmidt-Furlow report opened with John Warner, who maintained his chairmanship after the Republicans held the Senate in the 2004 election, applauding the Department of Defense. "This is the 12th major senior-level review of detainee operations and allegations of detainee abuse that has completed by various elements of the Department of Defense," Warner announced, before adding, "In my judgment, the Department has performed credibly in investigating allegations of abuse and failure to follow professional standards and the law and regulation in

these instances."[55] Warner went on to highlight some of Schmidt and Furlow's major findings, downplaying concerns about Guantánamo by noting
that the generals' report indicated, "in three instances, just three instances,
interrogations . . . at Gitmo used techniques that violated Army doctrine
and guidance from DOD. Now, this apparently is three out of some 24,000
interrogations that were conducted at Gitmo."[56]

The Democrats' ranking member, Carl Levin, responded by describing the FBI's allegations of abuse and torture at Guantánamo, just as he
had in his opening statement to the committee's earlier hearing on the
Church report:

> These FBI e-mails, which came to light in December of last year following a
> FOIA request, spoke of DOD interrogators' "torture techniques" and "co-
> ercive techniques in the military's interviewing toolkit." One FBI agent at
> the time expressed alarm over DOD interrogation plans for one Gitmo de-
> tainee, saying, "You won't believe it." Subsequent e-mails described abuses
> that FBI agents had witnessed, including detainees being chained in a fetal
> position on the floor for 18 to 24 hours at a time, having urinated and def-
> ecated on themselves, and being subjected to extreme cold.[57]

"The Schmidt-Furlow report," Levin continued, "confirms that detainees
were subjected to 'degrading and abusive' treatment."[58] He then added,
"the report finds the use of techniques such as "short-shackling" in a fetal
position for hours at a time, or using military working dogs to intimidate
detainees during interrogation sessions, or a female interrogator rubbing up
against a detainee's back and running her fingers through his hair as a form
of 'gender coercion.'"[59]

Levin then explicitly referred to Abu Ghraib, directly challenging the
claim that U.S. detainee abuse was the result of the actions of a few "rogue
military police on a night shift."[60] Already, two competing and fully incompatible images of Guantánamo had emerged. Much of the subsequent
testimony was dedicated to making sense of this doubled Guantánamo—
Warmer's facility, where only three of 24,000 interrogations involved a violation of Army doctrine, and Levin's, where detainees were systematically
abused and tortured.

After Levin finished his opening statement, Craddock and Schmidt
summarized the investigation's major findings. Schmidt gave the bulk of this

testimony, noting that the investigation had confirmed several of the FBI's allegations. Specifically, the investigation documented, as FBI agents had, that the following had occurred:

- Detainees had been "short shackled" to the floor of the interrogation room
- An interrogator had ordered that a detainee's mouth be duct taped to quiet the detainee
- Interrogators subjected detainees to noise—yelling and loud music—during interrogations
- Interrogators used "air conditioners to make rooms uncomfortable"
- Interrogators ordered that detainees be moved "from cell to cell to disrupt sleep patterns"
- A female interrogator "approached a detainee from behind, rubbed against his back, whispered in his ear, & ran fingers through his hair"
- A female interrogator "put perfume on a detainee's arm"
- A female interrogator "told a detainee that a red marking on her hand was menstrual blood and then wiped her hand on the detainee"[61]

Schmidt's testimony on Detainee 0-63, Mohammed al-Qahtani, involved five slides, three of which described fourteen "substantiated findings" about his treatment. These ranged from forms of "gender coercion" similar to those listed above: "Twice, MPs held down [al-Qahtani] while a female interrogator straddled the detainee without placing weight on the detainee"; once, a female interrogator "massaged the back and neck of [al-Qahtani] over his clothing"; and, "on numerous occasions," female interrogators "invaded the personal space of [al-Qahtani] to disrupt his concentration."[62] Other techniques similarly played on issues of gender and sexuality: al-Qahtani's mother and sister were called whores; he had a "woman's bra and thong placed on his head"; and interrogators "told him he was a homosexual . . . and that other detainees knew." Al-Qahtani was also forced "to dance with a male interrogator" and subjected "to several strip searches as a control measure"; on one occasion, an interrogator tied a leash to al-Qahtani's hand chains and "led him around the room through a series of dog tricks."[63] Schmidt and Furlow also found that al-Qahtani was subjected to noise, kept in an air-conditioned room manipulated to make it "uncomfortable," exposed to a military dog that was directed to "growl, bark, and show teeth," kept in isolation for 160 days, and subject to eighteen- to twenty-hour interrogations for forty-eight out of fifty-four days.[64]

While Schmidt and Furlow concluded that each individual practice employed on al-Qahtani was legal and authorized and that these practices did not constitute torture, they held that the "cumulative effect" of al-Qahtani's treatment had an "abusive and degrading impact on the detainee."[65]

At the committee's March 2005 hearing with Vice-Admiral Church, divergent claims about detainee abuse at Guantánamo existed side-by-side. This trend persisted into July. Despite the findings of the Schmidt-Furlow report, General Craddock, the highest ranking military witness to appear before the committee that day, and Roberts and Chambliss all offered lengthy statements of praise for Guantánamo. Roberts used his question-and-answer period to offer a particularly impassioned and lengthy monologue on the prison that took him, as he put it at the close of his statement, "way over my time, but I really do not give a damn."[66]

Roberts's statement includes several of the major forms of denial employed by other committee Republicans, as well as General Craddock. For this reason, it is worth discussing in depth. Roberts downplayed the substantiated instances of abuse—three (the treatment of al-Qahtani, the use of short shackling, and the use of duct tape)—by contextualizing them within the total number of interrogations at Guantánamo as Warner earlier had. Roberts also, as Joseph Lieberman had when addressing Abu Ghraib in 2004, emphasized the rarity of abuse by highlighting the "incident rate" of detainee abuse at Guantánamo:

> 24,000 total interrogations that have been conducted at Gitmo. So out of 24,000 interrogations, 3 total incidents. My math, that makes for an incident rate of .000125. . . . Is this what this has come down to, 3 misdemeanors out of 24,000 interrogations, 3 misdemeanors that occurred 2 or 3 years ago, not today, not to practices that are being conducted today under your command and under the commander down there?[67]

(Over the course of the hearing, Warner, Roberts, Chambliss, and Inhofe, all Republicans, each cited these statistics to downplay the problem of abuse at Guantánamo.)

Roberts also employed several other, familiar forms of denial. He denied the victims of U.S. abuse, quite literally, claiming that those who had been abused are "not 'detainees'; they are terrorists and they are very bad people."[68] Roberts also offered an opaque advantageous comparison, arguing that U.S. detention practices were, by historical standards (that he did not articulate), highly impressive: "Never before in history has any country faced with a barbaric terrorism implemented a policy of terrorist detention so unique, so unprecedented, and so humane, in my personal view."[69] (Senator Inhofe made a similar statement.) Roberts also employed the claim of necessity, arguing that the information that the U.S. gathered at Guantánamo "is current and can save lives, more especially in events like Casablanca and Madrid and, yes, London, and yes, plots against the United States."[70] Roberts further positioned himself as a privileged spokesperson for Guantánamo, having visited it and not having seen "any perfume . . . any straddling . . . any sleep deprivation, because that does not work."[71] He also cited Miller's slogan for Guantánamo to suggest the level of professionalism at the facility: "Their motto on the back of their cover says 'Honor Bound.' When you went through that facility, everybody saluted you and said 'Honor Bound,' and you said 'Honor Bound' back to them."[72] Finally, Roberts referred to a range of privileges that he claimed detainees at the detention facility enjoy, ranging from choices of "113 Muslim dishes" that outdo the choice of food given American soldiers, "better health care and better facilities than many of my rural small communities [in Kansas]," "ice cream on Sunday," soccer, volleyball, and ping pong facilities, and the freedom to pray.[73]

RECONCILING "HONOR BOUND" AND THE FBI'S GUANTÁNAMO

In Roberts's portrayal of Guantánamo, the abuse of detainees is a statistical anomaly; the detainees imprisoned there are barbaric terrorists; and U.S. treatment of those barbaric terrorists is, by historic and commonsensical standards, impressive and humane. This Guantánamo stands as an alternative to the nightmarish one described by the FBI and critics who fixated on the interrogation log of a single detainee. The portrayal also begs a question: If Roberts' description of Guantánamo was accurate, why had FBI agents posted at Guantánamo found the military's practices at the facility so troubling? And why had those agents been told to "step out of the picture," as Levin said they had?

Warner raised this issue with the hearing's witnesses, and an explanation quickly emerged: FBI agents view detention and interrogation operations through a qualitatively different lens than does the military. The FBI's lens was a legal one, and the bureau viewed the treatment of detainees through its concern for the collection of information that could be used against the detainees in federal courts. This was the gist of an exchange between Warner and General Furlow:

WARNER: The findings by and large . . . indicate that the interrogating procedures were conducted in accordance with directives from the [Secretary of Defense], even though from time to time they were changed. Now, the Bureau people were looking at this same set of facts coming from these detainees and the procedures from the perspective of future criminal operations in the United States; am I correct on that?

FURLOW: Mr. Chairman, that is correct. The FBI agent went down there with the idea of conducting a prosecutable case in a court of law.

WARNER: The standards by which they collect evidence for prosecutions, presumably for Federal courts as opposed to State, were quite different than the standards promulgated by [Rumsfeld]; am I correct in that observation?

FURLOW: Yes, sir, that is correct.[74]

While neither Warner nor Furlow explicitly described the objective of Department of Defense interrogations, both men likely understood that the aim of a military interrogation at Guantánamo is to produce "actionable intelligence" that could be used for national security purpose.[75] The standards by which the military and FBI collected evidence were different and so, too, were the interrogation practices both used to collect that evidence. This was the implicit reasoning that Warner and Furlow used here.

There are three things of note about this explanation of the divergent accounts that FBI agents and military investigators offered of U.S. practices in Guantánamo. First, when confronting incompatible accounts of events, people will often attribute different interpretive lenses to those giving the competing accounts.[76] As I documented in chapter 3, General Abizaid used a similar tactic in May 2004 to resolve the divergent accounts of U.S. detainee abuse in Iraq that the ICRC and military officials offered.

Second, this argument assumes a legal dichotomy between criminal investigations and military intelligence that would dissolve, at least temporarily, in 2006 when the Supreme Court rejected the Bush administration's paradigm for trying terrorists in its *Hamdan v. Rumsfeld* decision.

I deal with this development in greater detail below; for the sake of this discussion it is important that the court's decision required that U.S. military commissions have standards of evidence comparable to those used in military and civilian courts. This requirement forced Congress, who was charged with crafting legislation establishing the commissions, to confront the problem of evidence gathered through coercion or torture.

Finally, the argument that the FBI and the U.S. military have qualitatively different standards of interrogation—and that the practices used at Guantánamo were consistent with military standards—required discursive work to render what happened at Guantánamo consistent with those standards. The military's investigators did this by describing specific events at Guantánamo as expressions of categories of authorized interrogation practices. For some incidents, this effort was relatively straightforward. General Schmidt observed that the "impersonation of FBI and Department of State agents was authorized under the Secretary of Defense action memo in December 2002 under category 1, deception."[77] The use of air conditioners, similarly, "was authorized under the [secretary of defense's] 16 April 2003 memo. Environmental manipulation was approved as an appropriate and humane interrogation technique."[78] In these instances, Schmidt simply asserted that certain practices—and relatively noncontroversial ones at that—used at Guantánamo were consistent with the techniques that Rumsfeld authorized.

To construe other practices, particularly the controversial use of "gender coercion," consistent with military standards was more difficult. To do this, General Schmidt first introduced a type of interrogation practice—a specific "approach" from the Army's field manual for interrogation. He then offered a definition of the approach, rephrasing the definition inscribed in the manual. He further developed the type by providing a hypothetical application of the approach to the war on terror; in so doing, he reconstructed the ideal form of the technique to the particulars of the debate about Guantánamo. Finally, Schmidt asserted that a specific, documented behavior at Guantánamo was consistent with that category.

In General Schmidt's rendering, "gender coercion" was the outcome of the translation of a "high-order, fairly benign looking technique" into "an application . . . that got very specific."[79] One relevant technique that Schmidt cited to account for "gender coercion" is "futility." The general began his account of "gender coercion" by defining the goal of the "futility" as "to convince the source that resistance to questioning is futile."[80] He then listed ways that this technique might, hypothetically, be applied at the war on terror: "Tell the detainee about how al Qaeda is falling apart, talk about how everyone has been killed or captured, and tell him what we know about him so that he feels that he has already been exploited at some point and it is futile to withhold information."[81]

Schmidt's hypothetical scenario is consistent with the field manual's portrayal of futility as "effective when the interrogator can play on doubts that already exist in the source's mind."[82] The manual suggests the following hypothetical applications of the technique:

> If the source's unit had run out of supplies . . . it would be somewhat easy to convince him all of his forces are having the same logistical problems. A soldier who has been ambushed may have doubts as to how he was attacked so suddenly. The interrogator should be able to talk him into believing that the interrogator's forces knew of the EPW's [Enemy Prisoner of War's] unit location, as well as many more units.[83]

Yet Schmidt claimed, "as it gets down to the interrogation room," futility may take a very different form:

> It may involve gender coercion via some form of domination. The detainee does not want to hear this and he does not want to hear it from a woman. You will see that being straddled, not touched, massaged, or possibly mild non-injurious touching, such as putting perfume on the arm and that sort of thing, invades a detainees [sic] personal space. This is part of how they make the futility element work, with this more aggressive technique.[84]

A second, similar account of "gender coercion" employed the same argument, presented only in a simplified form. To further account for "gender coercion," Schmidt cited the interrogation approach of "ego down," an approach that permits the interrogator to attack, as Schmidt told the committee, "the source's sense of personal worth."[85] The field manual describes the goal of the technique:

> To pounce on the source's sense of pride by attacking his loyalty, intelligence, abilities, leadership qualities, slovenly appearance, or any other perceived

weakness. This will usually goad the source into becoming defensive, and he will try to convince the interrogator he is wrong. In his attempt to redeem his pride, the source will usually involuntarily provide pertinent information in attempting to vindicate himself.[86]

As with futility, Schmidt argued ego down must be translated into a specific application. In this case, its application involved interrogators making statements to al-Qahtani that his mother and sister were whores and that he was a homosexual; the use of unnecessary strip searches on al-Qahtani; forcing al-Qahtani to wear women's clothing; forcing al-Qahtani to dance with a male interrogator; and putting al-Qahtani on a leash and forcing him to act like a dog.

Schmidt's method of accounting for "gender coercion" is significant for several reasons. First, it set the stage for a contentious debate about accountability for al-Qahtani's treatment. Schmidt and Furlow recommended that General Miller be held accountable and admonished for failing to supervise the interrogation of al-Qahtani. This recommendation rested on the argument that, while no specific technique used on al-Qahtani violated U.S. military standards of interrogation, the cumulative effects of the interrogation were degrading and abusive.[87] Craddock, however, decided against taking action this recommendation; he reasoned that, because each individual interrogation practice was authorized and legal (as Schmidt and Furlow had found), he did not believe that any wrongdoing had occurred. There was simply "nothing for which to hold" Miller accountable," Craddock told the committee.[88]

From a human rights perspective, this account is significant because it suggests that the military's field manual for human intelligence permits— or may effectively be *presented* as permitting—a range of interrogation practices that violate international standards for the humane treatment of detainees. This, however, is not the prevailing view of the military's field manual, particularly among U.S. politicians. McCain, for instance, argued that the manual provides a workable standard for U.S. interrogations; he also argued that it was Secretary Rumsfeld's decision to approve techniques beyond those permitted in the field manual—not the manual itself—that contributed to the abuse at Guantánamo. This belief about the manual is consequential. In December 2005, Congress passed the Detainee Treatment Act, which included the "McCain Amendment" that constrained military interrogators to the techniques listed in the manual. In 2006, the military revised and published a new version of the field manual that explicitly prohibits a number of practices employed during the war on terror. These include forcing detainees to remove their clothing or perform or pose in sexual ways, hooding detainees, using duct tape on detainees, beating detainees, "waterboarding" detainees, subjecting detainees to military dogs, exposing detainees to extreme temperatures, "conducting mock executions," and depriving detainees of necessities, such as "food, water, or medical care."[89] While legislative efforts to constrain all U.S. intelligence agencies to the revised field manual failed in 2008, President Barack Obama signed an executive order establishing the military's field manual as the standard for all U.S. interrogations.

These developments represent a positive step toward standardizing U.S. interrogation practices and limiting interrogators to practices designed to be consistent with international obligations. At the same time, the revised manual permits the isolation of detainees and forms of sensory deprivation and sleep deprivation; these practices are enumerated in "Appendix M" of the manual. It is also of note that the various interrogation approaches that Army investigators cited in their testimony to the Senate Armed Services Committee—ego down and futility—also remain part of the military's approved method of interrogation. It is unclear whether the explicit prohibition on forced nudity and forced sexual performances or poses would interfere with official efforts to justify many of the practices used on al-Qahtani. It is not clear, in other words, whether the interpretive flexibility that military officials seized to align various forms of "gender coercion" with the military's approved interrogation practices has been relinquished.

Finally, this account begs a question. Military officials used different forms of denial to account for the violence at Abu Ghraib and Guantánamo. Discursively, military officials expelled the violence at Abu Ghraib from military policy. They did so by arguing that the violence violated imperatives to treat detainees humanely. Even the use of techniques, such as stress positions, permitted to U.S. interrogators in the Interrogation Rules of Engagement in Iraq violated those very standards, since the proper requests for use of those techniques were neither asked for nor granted. At no time did military officials argue that stripping detainees or placing them on a leash was a legitimate interrogation practice, an "application" of "ego down" or "futility" that "got very specific." This was so, despite the fact that the field manual guided interrogations in Iraq, just as it had at Guantánamo.

The violence at Guantánamo was not identical to that practiced at Abu Ghraib. Lacking photographs of this violence, one may only point to superficial similarities between the descriptions of violence there and the digital images taken at Abu Ghraib. But the superficial similarities are striking. U.S. interrogators stripped al-Qahtani, placed women's underwear on his head, harassed him with military work dogs, leashed him, and denied him sleep. Similar practices were also used and photographed at Abu Ghraib. Military officials, though, did not deny the connection between the violence at Guantánamo and military policy, as they had between the violence at Abu Ghraib and military policies. Instead, they characterized it as applications of officially sanctioned interrogation techniques. "Futility" appeared at Guantánamo as "gender coercion." "Ego down" involved stripping al-Qahtani and forcing him to wear women's clothing and perform dog tricks. As the legal scholar David Luban has wryly observed, "Apparently, the Army no longer regards many of the Abu Ghraib techniques as inhumane."[90]

Why did military officials respond so differently to Abu Ghraib and Guantánamo? Like the violence at Abu Ghraib, the violence at Guantánamo arrived on the political scene in evocative, localized representations produced by U.S. citizens. The FBI's accounts and the military's interrogation log offered glimpses of the leaky, suffering body, which dominant constructions of democratic violence tend to repress. Recall, from the opening of this chapter, the unconscious detainee lying next to a pile of his own hair. This helps account for why, after years of bipartisan consensus about or inattention to Guantánamo, the practices at the facility became a matter of public concern in late 2004 and 2005. At the same time, it is likely that the visuality of Abu Ghraib contributed to the sustained and intensive public attention the case received. The photographs are powerful illustrations that could be paired with reporting on Abu Ghraib in ways that the FBI's e-mails or the military's interrogation log could not be. The photographs are also better props for protest, art, and documentary making than are the more literary e-mails and interrogation log.

There are other reasons, I think, why different forms of denial were employed in these two cases. The violence at Guantánamo occurred in the Bush administration's pet prison. It also occurred against a detainee, al-Qahtani, whose interrogation was publicly linked to General Miller and Secretary of Defense Donald Rumsfeld. *Time*'s initial reporting noted that al-Qahtani's interrogation log "spans 50 days in the winter of 2002–03 . . . during which 16 additional interrogation techniques were approved by Defense Secretary Donald Rumsfeld for use on a select few detainees, including al-Qahtani."[91] Schmidt and Furlow's report similarly noted that Rumsfeld's 2002 memo authorized the use of interrogation techniques designed to "counter resistance techniques" of al-Qahtani.[92] What was at stake in the military's and the committee's evaluation of al-Qahtani's treatment was not, as it was at Abu Ghraib, *whether* high-ranking military and Bush administration officials were responsible for the use of particular detention and interrogation practices, but *what sort* of practices these men had permitted. Rendering the practices consistent with military standards drained al-Qahtani's treatment of its illegality and undercut demands for accountability. Moreover, U.S. politicians largely viewed Guantánamo, at least at the moment examined here, as a tool of national security; the interrogations aimed at extracting much needed intelligence from allegedly high-value detainees. This meant that al-Qahtani's treatment was understood within a more durable interpretive frame than was the violence at Abu Ghraib. This framing is obvious in distinctions that military officials drew between FBI interrogations, which aim to gather evidence for civilian trials, and military interrogations at Guantánamo, which are primarily aimed at collecting information that can be used in the war on terror.

Though different in form and communicating contradictory information about the meaning of U.S. interrogation policy, the accounts of Abu Ghraib and Guantánamo ultimately seek the same thing: the discursive absolution of high-ranking civilian and military officials and the preservation of the legitimacy of U.S. interrogation policies. This is obvious in the accounts of Abu Ghraib, which portrayed the violence there as a spatially and causally isolated events. It is less so in the accounts of Guantánamo. In the latter case, the military's account of al-Qahtani's treatment integrates the violence of U.S. soldiers into official policies, either those of Secretary Rumsfeld or what was then a thirteen year-old interrogation manual. Yet the integration of the controversial behaviors of interrogators into approved policy also offered an account of the interrogators *interpreting* and creatively *applying* those policies. If the violence practiced at Guantánamo resides in the directives of policy makers and the standards of the

U.S. military, it does so only latently, as the negative, organizational space in which interrogators acted.

FROM "HONOR BOUND" TO GLOBAL STAIN: THE TRANSFORMATION OF GUANTÁNAMO

Though portraying the interrogation techniques used at Guantánamo as legal and authorized, Schmidt and Furlow's report and testimony, coupled with the FBI's allegations of "torture," permitted the construction of alternative, critical claims about Guantánamo. We already saw how Levin rejected the claim that detainee abuse resulted from the actions of "a few rogue military police on a night shift" and, instead, blamed "aggressive interrogation techniques."[93] Similarly, Jack Reed compared al-Qahtani's treatment at Guantánamo to what the photographs at Abu Ghraib showed: "mother and sister were whores, dancing with male interrogators, homosexuality allegations, et cetera . . . That sounds remarkably similar to what occurred at Abu Ghraib, people being led around in chains, people being forced to wear lingerie. Perhaps a coincidence, perhaps not."[94] The following day, when the committee's Subcommittee on the Personnel convened to discuss Guantánamo, Kennedy echoed Levin and Reed, comparing the treatment of detainees at Guantánamo to the violence at Abu Ghraib:

> The interrogation techniques that were described by the FBI and again yesterday in graphic detail to this committee, were eerily reminiscent of the abhorrent practices that took place at Abu Ghraib: forcing a detainee to wear women's underwear on his head, leashing the detainee like a dog and forcing him to do dog tricks, intimidating detainees with military dogs, and stripping detainees.[95]

In chapter 4, I argued that Senator Levin and other Democrats failed to sustain an account of Abu Ghraib that linked the violence there to official policies in part because there were no significant cases of officially documented abuse in the places where those policies originated. We see in these statements by Levin, Reed, and Kennedy how revelations about abuse at Guantánamo—inscribed in official documents that provided local vantages on the facility—permitted the sort of critiques that members of the Senate Armed Services Committee were unable to make in 2004. These sort of claims also resonated in the media. Following the committee's June 12 hearing and the release of the executive summary of the Schmidt-Furlow report, the *Washington Post* published a 1,200 word, front page story on Guantánamo. Early in the article, the author, Josh White, acknowledged that Schmidt and Furlow found that the practices used on al-Qahtani did not constitute torture. Then, White wrote, "The report's findings are the strongest indication yet that the abusive practices seen in photographs at Abu Ghraib were not the invention of a small group of thrill-seeking military police officers. The report shows that they were used on Qahtani several months before the United States invaded Iraq."[96]

The initial *New York Times* reporting on the committee's hearing largely summarized Schmidt and Furlow's conclusions.[97] However, a subsequent editorial described the practices that Schmidt and Furlow documented as a violation of "American moral values" and pointless; these techniques, the editorial continued, "were later exported to the Abu Ghraib prison."[98] The editorial concluded by admonishing the Bush administration for not offering and Republicans in Congress for not demanding "a real reckoning on the prisoner abuse."

The FBI's e-mail, the interrogation log of al-Qahtani, and even the Schmidt-Furlow report all provided evocative, rich, and detailed evidence of what occurred at Guantánamo. Clearly, none of the documents forced consensus on the causes and seriousness of detainee abuse and torture at Guantánamo; supporters and opponents of the prison alike found support for their claims in this set of documents. But what is obvious is that political support for Guantánamo had splintered since 2004; meaningful congressional opposition to the prison had emerged and an account that linked the politically toxic abuse at Abu Ghraib back to, at least, the secretary of defense through his policies for Guantánamo had emerged. It was no longer that the additional techniques that Rumsfeld had approved for use at Guantánamo had "migrated" and created "confusion" at Abu Ghraib. Now, it seemed, wherever those policies went, one found degraded, humiliated, and tortured detainees.

But the development of a documentary record that portrayed the disorders and excesses of Guantánamo are only part of the story of its transformation from model prison to a global stain. Changes in the political context further emboldened critics of Guantánamo. Two are of particular note: the Supreme Court's ruling in *Hamdan v. Rumsfeld* and the Democrats' decisive electoral victory in 2006.

HAMDAN V. RUMSFELD AND THE EMERGENCE OF THE RULE OF LAW

In 2003, when the Senate Judiciary Committee received testimony on the abuse of detainees at Metropolitan Detention Center in Brooklyn, the September 11 terrorist attacks, the threat of terrorism, and national security were the dominant, interpretive frames through which U.S. officials considered detainee abuse. All participants in the committee's hearings acknowledged the terrorist attacks and the uncertainty that they engendered. The war in Iraq forced open this frame, as the protection of human rights emerged as the primary legitimating claim for the war. Within this political and interpretive context, the abuse of detainees in Iraq appeared a pressing political problem. This, however, left a dichotomy in place between the U.S. war in Iraq, where the protection of human rights and the rule of law politically mattered, and the broader U.S. war on terror. As I argued above, when FBI complaints about the treatment of detainees at Guantánamo became public, the administration's supporters in the Senate Armed Services Committee drew on the distinction between criminal investigations, which the FBI aimed to carry out, and intelligence investigations, which were necessary to combat terrorism, to downplay FBI concerns.

One particularly potent change in the political context surrounding Guantánamo came about a year after Congress considered the Schmidt-Furlow report. In June 2006, the Supreme Court issued a ruling in *Hamdan v. Rumsfeld*.[99] The case, brought on behalf of Salim Ahmed Hamdan, a Yemeni detainee at Guantánamo, challenged the Bush administration's use of military commissions, rather than federal courts, to try alleged terrorists held at Guantánamo.[100]

The court ruled, 5–3, against the administration's military commissions.[101] The court, however, did not outright reject military commissions. Rather, they rejected the commissions in part because the administration had failed to seek legislative authorization for them. The court's ruling also found that the commissions, as constituted by the Bush administration, failed to satisfy the minimum requirements of military law and the Geneva Conventions. The court specifically noted the commissions' "failure to guarantee the defendant the right to attend the trial and the prosecution's ability under the rules to introduce hearsay evidence, unsworn testimony, and evidence obtained through coercion."[102]

The ruling that Congress must authorize the use of military commissions altered the relationship between the two branches. Prior to the court's decision, Congress had largely deferred to the administration's detention and interrogation agenda. Congress's hearings on these issues generally followed the release of a major investigation; because they were dominated by witnesses from the executive, these hearings also amplified the executive's positions on them. The two were now becoming collaborators, although certainly not equal ones, in policy making. Between the ruling in *Hamdan* in June 2006 and September 2006, the Senate and House Armed Services Committees and the Senate and House Judiciary Committees held series of hearings on military commissions, the prosecution of detainees, and detainee rights, particularly the right of habeas corpus. The witness list in these hearings included high-ranking members of the executive—Alberto Gonzales, the attorney general, and Stephen Bradbury, the assistant attorney general, most notably. Peppered amid the witness list were Hamdan's lawyers, retired military lawyers, human rights representatives, legal scholars, and judges with experience on war crime courts and international crime tribunals. The court's ruling in *Hamdan*, by tasking Congress to work with the executive to craft military commissions legislation consistent with the Geneva Conventions, had cracked open the official discourse that dominated earlier hearings on detention and interrogation.

The Military Commissions Act—the legislation that resulted from all this discourse about Guantánamo, detainee rights, and military commissions—was widely viewed as an affront to American justice and international human rights law for its denial of habeas, its allowance of evidence gathered by coercion and torture, and its protection of those who used and authorized torture from criminal prosecution. And so, on the one hand, the court's decision in *Hamdan* led to legislation that legitimized torture by institutionalizing the evidence collected with it and undercutting efforts to hold those that engaged in it or authorized it accountable. On the other hand, the decision did contribute to the emergence of a discourse of acknowledgment. It emboldened critics, who interpreted the decision as a powerful rebuke to the Bush administration and a repudiation of its entire approach to detainee rights. Robert Byrd, during a Senate Armed Services Committee hearing on military commissions, offered this:

> The Supreme Court forcefully, with both arms, beat back this administration's transparently, shameless and ill-conceived attempt to wrest unto itself power that is properly delegated to the legislative branch, the U.S. Congress, this Congress, and this committee. The Court held that the President had no—and I repeat, no legal authority to establish the type of military commissions he created to try detainees at Guantanamo Bay. The Court found that . . . the procedures of the military commissions violated each of the four Geneva Conventions. The Supreme Court dramatically and forcefully put its foot down, and every American is all the better for it.[103]

Patrick Leahy, in a Senate Judiciary hearing on the commissions, described proposals to strip detainees of habeas corpus as "un-American"; he then noted that the Bush administration received

> a rude awakening this year in the *Hamdan* case. The court affirmed what we had—told them all along. When the terrorists brought down the Twin Towers on 9/11, they did not bring down the rule of law on which our system of government is founded. They did not supplant our form of government with one in which an unaccountable Executive can imprison people without trial for years.[104]

While Congress's passage of the Military Commissions Act limited the policy impact of the *Hamdan* decision, its impact on discourse was lasting. The decision forced opened congressional discourse to witnesses outside the executive. It also affirmed the rule of law—as embodied in long-standing military law and the Geneva Conventions—as the standard against which U.S. detention practices ought be measured. Both of these developments were vital to and, in fact, amplified by the efforts of Democrats, after the 2006 midterm election, to draw attention to the consequences of U.S. torture.

THE 2006 MIDTERM ELECTIONS AND THE EMERGENCE OF A DISCOURSE OF ACKNOWLEDGMENT

The 2006 midterm elections won the Democratic Party control over both the House of Representatives and the Senate. The party wielded this newly gained political power to arrange broad, aggressive, and investigatory hearings—with titles such as "Torture and the Cruel, Inhuman and Degrading Treatment of Detainees"—on the treatment of detainees in U.S. custody.

That this use of political power was largely unilateral is made clear in three brief sentences that appear in a December 2006 *Washington Post* article on the Democrats midterm victory and the influence of their committee staff directors. Of the Senate Armed Services Committee's new staff director, Richard D. DeBobes, the *Post* wrote: "The committee is known for its bipartisanship and, DeBobes said, 'there's no reason for that not to continue.' Still, that atmosphere may become strained. DeBobes, 68, is putting together a new three-person investigative team to challenge the administration on detainee treatment."[105]

In fact, following the 2006 midterm elections, two committees—the House Subcommittee on the Constitution, Civil Rights, and Civil Liberties and the Senate Armed Services Committee—opened series of hearings to review the administration's interrogation policies. The House Subcommittee on the Constitution focused on the Department of Justice's role in the development of interrogation rules and, over the course of their five hearings, received testimony from several former and current members of the Bush administration. The Senate Armed Services Committee focused on the Department of Defense's role in authorization of Survival, Evasion, Resistance, and Escape (SERE) techniques for use by military interrogators. The "resistance" component of SERE attempts to inoculate members of the U.S. Armed Forces to the interrogation practices and torture techniques historically used by the country's enemies; indeed, the impetus for the program was the U.S. experience of the Korean War, during which American POWs falsely confessed to war crimes after torture. Under President Bush, U.S. detention and interrogation policies, particularly those of the CIA, derived from "reverse engineering" employing the "defensive" SERE training techniques for use during interrogations.[106]

Both committees received testimony from the Bush administration's legal and policy architects of interrogation. John Ashcroft, John Yoo,

David Addington, and Douglas Feith appeared as witnesses at the Subcommittee on the Constitution's hearings. Ashcroft served as Attorney General for Bush until February 2005, overseeing the Justice Department during the period in which its lawyers, particularly Yoo, produced key legal memoranda on the application of domestic and international laws against torture in the war on terror. The memos defined torture so that it only encompassed the most extreme acts, such as those that cause organ failure or even death, and provided legal justifications for the use of painful interrogation techniques, including waterboarding and stress positions.[107] Addington served as Vice President Dick Cheney's legal counsel and chief of staff. In that capacity, according to reports, Addington was one of the most dogged and effective advocates of executive power within the administration; he was also major driving force behind the administration's decision to withhold Geneva protections from war on terror detainees.[108] Feith served in the Department of Defense as undersecretary of defense for policy and also advocated against granting detainees captured in Afghanistan prisoner of war protection under the Geneva Conventions.[109] The subcommittee compelled both Addington and Feith to appear before them by subpoena.

The Senate Armed Services Committee received testimony from William "Jim" Haynes. Haynes served as general counsel of the Department of Defense for nearly the duration of the Bush administration, May 2001 until February 2008. In that capacity, he advised Secretary of Defense Donald Rumsfeld to authorize interrogators at Guantánamo to use painful interrogation practices, including stress positions.[110] The Senate Armed Services Committee's investigation also revealed that, under Haynes, the Department of Defense's Office of the General Counsel was one of the informational hubs for interrogation policy; the office initiated a number of conversations with the Joint Personnel Recovery Agency (JPRA), the agency responsible for SERE training. The committee's hearings involved several former members of JPRA who had communicated with the Department of Defense and who coordinated trainings for military and intelligence agency interrogators.

The House Subcommittee on the Constitution and the Senate Armed Services Committee both received testimony from former members of the Bush administration and retired military officials who had advocated against the use of "enhanced interrogation" techniques. Lawrence Wilkerson, the chief of staff to former secretary of state Colin Powell, appeared

before the House subcommittee on June 18, 2008. In the months after the
September 11 terrorist attacks, the administration debated, internally, the
application of the Geneva Conventions in the war on terror. Under Powell, the Department of State advocated, in vain, for the application of the
Geneva Conventions to detainees in U.S. custody. Wilkerson would, following the 2004 elections and Powell's resignation, speak publicly and
critically about the role of the Bush administration and, in particular,
Vice President Cheney in the authorization of abusive interrogation practices.[111] The Senate Armed Services Committee also received testimony
from Alberto Mora, the former general counsel of the Navy. In late 2002
and early 2003, Mora raised concerns with Haynes about the interrogation
tactics authorized by Secretary of Defense Donald Rumsfeld. On January
15, 2003, Mora drafted, delivered, and threatened to sign a memo expressing his concerns that the interrogation techniques Rumsfeld authorized
"were violative of domestic and international legal norms, and that they
constituted, at a minimum, cruel and unusual treatment, and, at worst, torture."[112] Haynes, in response, promised Mora that Rumsfeld would rescind
his authorization, which the secretary did that day.

Congressional Democrats also transformed the tenor of committee
hearings. While the *Hamdan* decision had led congressional Republicans
to involve some external experts on international law and detainee rights,
the committees, under Democratic leadership, included numerous witnesses who did not share the executive's or military's positions on these
issues. In these years, we witness the transformation of Guantánamo from
a facility "honor bound to defend freedom" to the global stain that it is
widely considered today.

This is apparent in one of the first congressional hearings held on U.S.
detention practices after the election. On March 29, 2007, the House Committee on Armed Services held a hearing on the military commissions act.
The committee's chair, Democrat Ike Skelton, opened the hearing by wel-
coming the witnesses: William Taft IV, the great-grandson of the twenty-
seventh president (who was also a chief justice of the Supreme Court)
and, from his position within the State Department, an early internal dis-
senter on the Bush administration's interrogation policies; Patrick Philbin,
an early enabler of the administration's policies from within the Justice
Department; Neal Katyal, the lawyer who argued Hamdan's case before the
Supreme Court; and Elisa Massimino of Human Rights First.

With the witness list stacked against the administration's detention and interrogation policies, Skelton articulated an ambitious agenda for his committee: "Now, although the Military Commissions Act and Guantanamo are nominally the subjects of today's hearing, our discussion is about much more. The hearing tackles fundamental questions about who we are as a nation and how we treat those who are charged with threatening our security."[113]

Later in his statement, Skelton turned to Guantánamo, noting:

> I have no doubt that Guantanamo has become a lightning rod for criticism of American detainee policy and has undermined both our moral authority and our ability to rally necessary support for policies abroad. Secretary Gates, Secretary Rice, Senator McCain and former Secretary Powell, among many others, reportedly all have pointed to the hole that Guantanamo continues to burn in the international reputation of our country. The morale of our troops overseas and their level of security rely upon how they are perceived in other countries.[114]

Here, the rhetoric is both searing and strategic. Skelton mobilizes a litany of high-profile Republicans who have ("reportedly") described Guantánamo, in one way or another, as burning a hole in the global reputation of the United States. This hole, Skelton claims, threatens U.S. moral positioning, its international alliances, and the very safety of its troops. Later in the hearing, Taft, Katyal, and Massimino aligned their positions with Skelton's, describing the facility at Guantánamo as "legal black hole" (Katyal's words)[115] and "a law-free zone" (Massimino's)[116] that damaged the country's international reputation.

This was the beginning of a full-scale attack on Guantánamo that persisted through 2007 and 2008. During these years, we hear frequent calls for Guantánamo's closing and claims that the facility is an international stain on the country's reputation. Congressional Democrats also reheard the argument that interrogation policies designed for Guantánamo directly led to Abu Ghraib. This is exemplified by the work of the Senate Armed Services Committee in its broad investigation, *Inquiry into the Treatment of Detainees in US Custody*, of military detention and interrogation practices. Under the leadership of Levin, the committee built its report on public hearings and considerable behind-the-scenes work, including the review of documents and interviews. The resulting, bipartisan report debunked the Bush administration's explanation for Abu Ghraib, linking the scandal of that facility, in the same discursive breath, to Guantánamo (here, abbreviated as GTMO):

> The abuse of detainees at Abu Ghraib in late 2003 was not simply the result of a few soldiers acting on their own. Interrogation techniques such as stripping detainees of their clothes, placing them in stress positions, and using military working dogs to intimidate them appeared in Iraq only after they had been approved for use in Afghanistan and at GTMO.[117]

While the committee did not release the executive summary of its report until December 2008 and the full report until April 2009, Levin previewed its findings, including the link between Guantánamo and Abu Ghraib, in a lengthy and detailed opening statement on June 17, 2008. The committee's prominent (and most moderate) Republican members responded by recognizing the importance of the rule of law and human rights, while softening the committee's conclusions. John Warner, the ranking Republican and the committee's former chair, responded to Levin by saying:

> We have to look at this situation in the context of the aftermath of September 11, when this country was struggling to come to a full recognition about our vulnerability to attacks such as we experienced on that fateful day. I think men and women in uniform, as well as in the civilian community, did everything we could to try and preserve and protect our great Nation, a nation that is founded under the rule of law; and there should be no deviation from that.[118]

Warner subsequently ceded his time to Lindsey Graham, who gave a lengthy opening statement in which he attempted to cut a tenuous, rhetorical path between critique of the administration's interrogation policies and recognition that "the administration who played a major role in developing interrogation policy were motivated by anything other than a desire to protect our Nation."[119] Walking this path, Graham described the legal theories and advice that the administration used to justify "harsh interrogation techniques" as "bizarre," "irresponsible," and "short-sighted."[120] Graham also offered a qualified affirmation of Levin's claims about the connection between Abu Ghraib and Guantánamo, noting that "interrogation techniques which were supposed to be limited to GTMO may have migrated to Iraq and Afghanistan."[121] "It's hard to fathom," Graham continued, "that our Nation and the world would have to hear the United States discuss documents like the Torture Memo."[122] While highlighting that Abu Ghraib was "clearly . . . people acting on their own inappropriately in a very perverse fashion regarding detainees," Graham still rejected the "few bad apples" account for one that acknowledged "system failure" there. More broadly, Graham criticized the use of harsh interrogation techniques for marginalizing the United States and for exposing Americans to prosecution. He also recognized Congress's accomplishment when it passed the "McCain Amendment" for "putting us back on the road to upholding the best traditions of our Nation and restoring our standing in the world."[123] Despite these critiques, Graham located, near the close of his statement, the controversy surrounding interrogation in the political past. In so doing, he suggested that interrogation policy no longer required the committee's consideration and that the committee's effort was redundant. Graham summarized his thinking in this way:

> But, the overriding question is, have we learned from our mistakes? Are we all moving forward on a solid basis? The answer, in my opinion, is yes. The fact that the legal and policy decisions made from 2002 to 2005 were based on inadequate legal analysis, used to justify harsh treatment of detainees, is not new news to me. I don't think it is new news to anyone on the committee or anyone who has followed or reviewed any of the 15 different DOD investigations that had been launched in the last 5 years or the numerous hearings held in the House and Senate. This committee alone has had 17 separate briefings and hearings on detainee abuses. . . . So, respectfully, Mr. Chairman, we're not breaking new ground here. The abuses, the inconsistencies, the pattern of poor judgment in these matters are well-documented. The fact is that we have come a long way in the past 5 years. Secretary Rumsfeld is gone. Wolfowitz, Cambone, and Feith are all gone. John Yoo and Jim Haynes are gone.[124]

Despite Graham's reservations, the symbolic damage is done. The "torture word" is in play, part of even Republicans' discourse. And Guantánamo, the administration's symbolic leverage point in 2004, is caught up in narratives of lawlessness, executive overreach, and, with Abu Ghraib, international scandal.

CONCLUSION

First, Abu Ghraib, then Guantánamo. By 2005, the map of U.S. torture troubled claims that Abu Ghraib was an isolated incident, unique in its excesses and caused, primarily, by problems local to the facility. And the main reason for that trouble was that Americans—some who engaged in that torture, some who felt troubled by it—had created official, in the case of al-Qahtani's interrogation log, and quasi-official, in the case of the Abu Ghraib photographs and the FBI e-mails, records of what occurred in the two facilities. The documents that these Americans produced are not complete records of what occurred at Guantánamo and Abu Ghraib. Nor are they objective, uninfluenced by the particular vantages of those who created them. But what they all offer are *local* vantages; encountering them, one has the impression of peering into these facilities, as impossible as that is for most of us. And taking that vantage, one has the impression of watching, almost in real time, as U.S. soldiers humiliate, torment, and torture defenseless detainees in their custody.

In the months leading up to the 2008 election, a third site of detainee abuse and torture would come under congressional scrutiny. This site, though, was considerably more obscure. The CIA had run, out of classified "black sites" throughout Europe and Asia, an "enhanced interrogation" program for "high-value" detainees. The documentary record, too, was obscure. The controversy surrounding the CIA's program heightened not after the leak or release of agents' accounts of what they had witnessed at the black sites or of a photograph taken there. It heightened, instead, after the agency announced it had destroyed the very sort of evidence—video recordings of actual interrogations—that had brought down Abu Ghraib. This development and the congressional response to it is the subject of the next chapter.

CHAPTER 6

The Toxicity of Torture

*WATERBOARDING AND THE DEBATE ABOUT
"ENHANCED INTERROGATION"*

WATERBOARDING ENTERED THE AMERICAN LEXICON on May 13, 2004, amid the scandal of Abu Ghraib, when the *New York Times* described the practice—"a prisoner is strapped down, forcibly pushed under water and made to believe he might drown"—and its authorization by the Department of Justice.[1] Even as the Abu Ghraib scandal raged and despite the notoriety that would eventually attach itself to waterboarding, the practice did not register with members of Congress in 2004. There are no references to the practice in the published transcripts of Congress's hearings in 2004. And, while waterboarding appeared in the published transcripts of only thirteen hearings between 2005 and 2006, it appeared in the published transcripts of twelve hearings in 2007 and thirty-two hearings in 2008.[2] It was not until 2007, following the Democrats' victory in the 2006 midterm election, that waterboarding became a significant political issue, subject to sustained debate about its legality, effectiveness, and consequences for the nation.

This chapter considers the congressional debate about waterboarding and the CIA's "enhanced interrogation" program more generally. This debate differed from the earlier ones about Abu Ghraib and Guantánamo in an important way. Those previous debates were spurred by the release of official or quasi-official documents related to detainee abuse and torture at the two facilities; the debate about waterboarding, on the other hand, oriented to a gap in the record. This gap was the product of the CIA's decision to destroy videotapes of its interrogations, including those documenting the agency's use of waterboarding. Because of this gap, those who supported and those who opposed waterboarding had considerable freedom to describe the practice in ways consistent with their own claims. Supporters, on the one hand, described waterboarding as briefly used, restrained, and effective; they also distinguished CIA waterboarding from historical forms of water torture. Opponents, on the other hand, described the practice as dangerous, ineffective, and comparable to forms of water torture that nondemocracies had historically used. Empowered by the midterm election and attuned to a change in U.S. public opinion about terrorism, opponents also employed a rule-of-law frame to portray waterboarding as a threat to the country's international reputation and national security. This chapter follows these developments in congressional discourse, focusing on the impact of the CIA's destruction of its tapes and changes in the political context on the terms of Congress's debate about torture.

THE IRREALITY OF WATERBOARDING

In early December 2007, the CIA's director, Michael Hayden, disclosed that the agency had destroyed videotapes documenting its interrogations of Abu Zubaydah, an alleged associate of Osama bin Laden, and another high-value member of al-Qaeda. Media reporting revealed that Abu Zubaydah had been one of the detainees on whom the CIA used waterboarding.[2] Within days, the House and Senate intelligence committees, as well as the Department of Justice and the CIA's inspector general, announced investigations into the destruction of the tapes.[3]

As I discussed in chapters 2 and 3, the release of the Abu Ghraib photographs secured an underlying reality of detainee abuse among members of Congress. This was due to the fact that photographic and visually recorded representations of reality are typically viewed as "windows" onto an underlying reality. The destruction of the CIA's videotapes, then, had implications for public debate about the agency's "enhanced" techniques. This was apparent in the House Judiciary Committee's December 20, 2007, hearing, on the destruction of the tapes. John Conyers, the Democrat's committee chair, opened the hearing by describing the committee's agenda as firmly linked to the CIA's destruction of its videotapes: "The purpose of this hearing of course derives from the recent revelation of the destruction of the CIA videotapes, which involve hundreds of hours of audio and visual and we are concerned about the decision to destroy them."[4] Later in the hearing, Conyers invited Representative Robert Scott, a Democrat from Virginia and chair of the Judiciary's Subcommittee on Crime, to give an opening statement. In his, Scott referenced both the political controversy about the definition of torture and argued that the videotapes, had they been preserved, might have settled debate over whether the CIA's interrogations constituted torture: "We have heard we can't tell whether or not a particular technique is torture until we have some more specifics. If we had it on tape, people could look at the tape and ascertain whether or not that was torture, but the tape, the evidence has been destroyed."[5]

Two of the committee's witnesses made similar statements. Stephen Saltzburg, professor of law at the George Washington University Law School, suggested that public understandings of waterboarding may not correspond to the reality of the practice and referred to the videotapes as "indisputable evidence" that might have shown "that the actual implementation of waterboarding was quite a bit different than people assumed it would be."[6] Elisa Massimino, the Washington Director of Human Rights First, went further, deducing from the very destruction of the tapes "that at least some in the Administration understood what we know: that the acts depicted on those tapes were unlawful and would shock the conscience of any decent American who saw them."[7]

I do not share Saltzburg's or Massimino's confidence that the CIA videotapes, had they been viewed by the American populace, would have forced consensus on the nature of CIA interrogation generally and waterboarding specifically. The "actual implantation" of waterboarding that the videotapes showed, like what the Abu Ghraib photographs revealed, would have required interpretation and narration; U.S. politicians, no doubt, would have competed to assign meaning to what the tapes showed. Still, the political and cultural response to the release of the Abu Ghraib photographs suggests that the video recordings would have made a difference in public understandings of waterboarding. The only question is how. Part of the Abu Ghraib photograph's affective power is their portrayal of U.S. violence that appears socially organized and symbolically meaningful. Americans contorted the body of the enemy into the body of Christ on the crucifix or, at other times, into a heterosexist image of homosexuality. The photographed violence, moreover, was collectively organized; it involved groups of Americans who shared in the frenzy of violence. The photographs did not support—or, rather, could not easily be made to support—the argument that U.S. interrogators involved the controlled and clinical infliction of pain on detainees.

The CIA's destruction of their videotaped interrogations made obvious the gap between language, what U.S. politicians said about waterboarding, and reality, what actually occurred at the agency's black sites. While I am hesitant to assign meaning to this missing evidence, I would suggest that the destruction of the videotapes mattered in two ways. First, and most simply, the destruction of the videotapes permitted the CIA and proponents of "enhanced interrogation" to fill the representational lacuna with their own, preferred accounts. As I show below, the CIA and proponents of "enhanced interrogations" did just this, constructing narratives of waterboarding that fitted it to the prevailing image, which I described in chapter 1, of what legitimate state violence, in a democracy, should look like. This meant, of course, that critics of the practice also sought to fill the representational lacuna with their own, preferred accounts; they challenged the narratives of waterboarding's supporters, drew on the accounts of those who had undergone the practice as part of navy training, and associated the practice with illiberal regimes that had used water torture. The destruction of the videotapes neither silenced debate about the recent past nor did it "turn the past into a non-event."[8] Instead, the destruction of the tapes brought further scrutiny to waterboarding, as the American polity wanted "to see the 'nothing' that is so obviously present" behind the missing videos.[9] But the destruction of the tapes did provide sufficient negative space in the documentary record for proponents and critics to both construct credible but incompatible images of the practice.

Second, and more speculatively, it is likely that the CIA's videotaped interrogations would have, like the Abu Ghraib photographs before them, shown cruelty that appeared noninstrumental, poorly regulated, ferocious, if not sadistic. It is possible, in other words, that the videotapes would have revealed waterboarding to be a form of violence inconsistent with contemporary, democratic constructions of cruelty. Jose Rodriguez, the CIA officer who oversaw the destruction of the tapes, seemed to recognize this, writing that the decision to destroy the tapes was about "just getting rid of some ugly visuals."[10]

In the conclusion of this chapter, I consider these issues further. First, however, I trace the interpretive contours of supporters' and critics' portrayals of waterboarding and "enhanced interrogation" more generally.

In so doing, I consider the interpretive resources and rhetorical tactics employed by participants in House and Senate hearings in 2007 and 2008 to produce these portrayals. Proponents of waterboarding attempted to portray the practice as clinical, instrumental, modern; critics endeavored to portray waterboarding as a atavistic form of cruelty inconsistent with modern American sensibilities.

LEGITIMATING WATERBOARDING

In public debates about the CIA's "enhanced interrogation" program, much has been made about its effectiveness. This issue is central to public debate about torture, since "apologists often assume that torture works, and all that is left is the moral justification. If torture does not work, then their apology is irrelevant."[11] That waterboarding is an effective way of collecting intelligence is necessary for its defense. Waterboarding's effectiveness is, however, only part of a broader discursive construction of the practice as a legitimate use of force. To legitimize waterboarding, congressional proponents offered narratives of its use. These narratives took a particular form. They began with an initial offense: a detainee is known to have engaged in terrorism against the United States and is suspected of having knowledge of impending attacks. The detainee is then captured and traditional interrogation practices, which do not involve the application of pain, are used, but these fail to compel the detainee to provide intelligence. "Enhanced interrogation" is then used, and this results in the collection of "actionable" intelligence—information that has some practical application to the protection of U.S. interests and security. These narratives portray the use of waterboarding and "enhanced interrogation" as necessary and goal oriented. Pain, moreover, is inflicted only so long as it moves the narrative forward; it ceases once it achieves its goal. The stages of these narratives, which parallel those Dorothy Smith identified in an analysis of discourse surrounding the use of force by police, can be represented as follows:

Offense → Capture → Traditional Interrogation → "Enhanced Interrogation" → Actionable Intelligence[12]

In November 2007, a month before Hayden revealed that the CIA had destroyed tapes of its interrogations, the Subcommittee on the

Constitution, Civil Rights, and Civil Liberties of the House Judiciary Committee held a hearing entitled, "Torture and the Cruel, Inhuman, and Degrading Treatment of Detainees: The Effectiveness and Consequences of 'Enhanced' Interrogations." In his opening statement, Trent Franks, the ranking Republican on the subcommittee, called the CIA's use of waterboarding "legal" and "controlled." He then described the agency's interrogation of Khalid Sheikh Mohammed, the alleged mastermind of the September 11 terrorist attacks:

> Khalid Sheikh Mohammed, the driving force behind the 9/11 attacks, stayed quiet for months after his capture. The interrogators eventually used . . . waterboarding on him for just 90 seconds, at which point he began to reveal information that helped authorities arrest at least six major terrorists, including some who were in the process of plotting the bringing down of the Brooklyn Bridge, bombing a hotel, blowing up U.S. gas stations, poisoning American water reservoirs, detonating a radioactive dirty bomb, incinerating residential high-rise buildings by igniting apartments filled with natural gas, and carrying out large-scale anthrax attacks.[13]

Franks's depiction is typical of proponents' portrayal of waterboarding as professionally administered, briefly used, and effective. At the House Judiciary Committee's December 20 hearing on the CIA's videotapes, Lamar Smith, the committee's ranking Republican, described Mohammed's interrogation in nearly identical language: "According to reports, Khalid Sheikh Mohammed, the mastermind behind the 9/11 attacks that killed 3,000 people, stayed quiet for months until he was waterboarded for just 90 seconds."[14] Smith offered a second narrative, that of the interrogation of Abu Zubaydah, an alleged associate of Osama bin Laden:[15]

> But while we can't watch the videotapes, ABC News conducted a very telling interview with one of the former CIA officials, John Kiriakou, who was involved in one of the videotaped interrogations of terrorist Abu Zubaydah. When the terrorist Zubaydah, a logistics chief of al-Qaeda, was captured, he and two other men were caught in the act of building a bomb. A soldering gun that was used to make the bomb was still hot on the table along with building plans for a school. Zubaydah refused to offer any actual intelligence until he was waterboarded for between 30 and 35 seconds. According

to Mr. Kiriakou, from that day on he answered every question. The threat
information that he provided disrupted a number of attacks, perhaps dozens
of attacks.[16]

Smith's account of Abu Zubaydah's interrogation is notable for several
reasons. Though he cited a different instance of waterboarding than did
Franks, both offered narratives with nearly identical structures. In fact, they
are also consistent with those that President Bush offered when he acknowledged the CIA's interrogation program in a September 2006 speech on terrorism.[17] The consistency of the empirical claims and narrative structure of
these statements suggests that they may have been strategically scripted and
coordinated. It also suggests the perceived, interpretive value of this image
of waterboarding among those who advocate the practice.

Smith's account is also notable for making explicit the representational
lacuna that the videotapes might have filled. He counters, though, by filling the gap in the documentary record. In his statement, Smith cited the
account of John Kiriakou. In a December 10 interview with ABC News,
Kiriakou, a former CIA officer, acknowledged the CIA's use of waterboarding on Abu Zubaydah. Although he had not directly witnessed Zubaydah's
waterboarding, Kiriakou was Smith's source for the claim that the CIA
waterboarded Zubaydah for between thirty and thirty-five seconds. In his
interview with ABC, Kiriakou further described Zubaydah's response to
waterboarding in dramatic terms:

> A short time afterwards, in the next day or so, [Zubaydah] told his interro-
> gator that Allah had visited him in his cell during the night and told him to
> cooperate because his cooperation would make it easier on the other broth-
> ers who had been captured. And from that day on, he answered every ques-
> tion just like I'm sitting here speaking to you.[18]

Advocates of waterboarding incorporated other CIA accounts of the
practice into their own arguments. On February 5, 2008, at a Senate hearing on intelligence, Hayden publicly admitted the use of waterboarding on
three detainees.

> Let me make it very clear and to state so officially in front of this Committee
> that waterboarding has been used on only three detainees. It was used on

Khalid Shaykh Mohammed. It was used on Abu Zubaydah. And it was used on Nashiri. . . . We used it against these three high-value detainees because of the circumstances of the time. Very critical to those circumstances was the belief that additional catastrophic attacks against the homeland were imminent.[19]

Hayden later testified to reporters that two of those detainees—Zubaydah and Mohammed—provided about 25 percent of the CIA's information on al-Qaeda.[20]

Supporters subsequently incorporated Hayden's account into their defenses to stress the effectiveness of the practice and the restraint that characterized its use. A statement from Franks, made at a May 6, 2008, Subcommittee on the Constitution hearing, exemplifies this:

> The results of a total of 3 minutes of severe interrogations of three of the worst of the worst terrorists were of immeasurable benefit to the American people. CIA Director Hayden said that Mohammed and Zabeda provided roughly 25 percent of the information that the CIA had on al-Qaida from all human sources. Now we just need to kind of back up and thought [sic] about that. A full 25 percent of the human intelligence we have received on al-Qaida from just 3 minutes worth of a rarely used interrogation tactic.[21]

This portrayal of waterboarding buttressed the claim that the CIA's use of waterboarding involved "precise procedures" that prevented the practice from rising to the level of torture. The legal status of waterboarding would come, in defenses of it, to depend on these. Stephen Bradbury introduced this claim during a House Judiciary committee hearing on February 14, 2008. As Principal Deputy Assistant Attorney General for the Office of Legal Counsel, Bradbury produced two memos, in May 2005, that advised the CIA that "enhanced interrogation" practices, including waterboarding, did not violate domestic and international laws against torture. At the time of the hearings, the memos were classified, but their existence was public knowledge. Democrat Robert Scott pressed Bradbury on the legal status of waterboarding.

SCOTT: Is there any international precedence outside of this Administration that suggests that waterboarding is not torture? Anybody else in the world ever consider waterboarding not torture except this Administration?

BRADBURY: I am not aware of precedents that address the precise procedures used by the CIA. I'm simply not aware of precedents on point. And that's often what makes, frankly what makes our job difficult.[22]

To its advocates, waterboarding appears a rarely used, briefly administered, and effective practice. The incorporation of "precise procedures," furthermore, prevents the practice from satisfying the legal definition of torture and distinguishes it from historical precedents. Its use, moreover, flows toward a legitimate goal—the collection of information to prevent future terrorist attacks. Portrayed in this way, the practice is purified of the qualities that render torture toxic to democracies, containing no hint of cruelty or the illiberal desire to dominate another. It is merely another technique, a single, necessary, and controlled escalation of force that serves a legitimate function: the collection of intelligence needed to secure the nation and its populace.

CHALLENGING THE LEGITIMACY OF WATERBOARDING

The CIA closely guarded firsthand evidence of waterboarding, going so far as to destroy videotapes of its use. The accounts of those who directly observed or participated in the interrogations were publicly unavailable in 2007 and 2008. In place of such accounts, Kiriakou offered a second-hand account; Hayden offered the Central Intelligence Agency's sanctioned account. Proponents of waterboarding drew on these to legitimize waterboarding's use. But such accounts were of little use to opponents of waterboarding. Because of this, those who criticized waterboarding rarely directly attacked supporters' claims about how the CIA had employed the practice and, when they did, did so by citing unnamed sources of privileged information.

For instance, at the House Judiciary Committee's fifth and final hearing on the Department of Justice's role in the authorization of interrogation policies, Walter Dellinger, head of the Office of Legal Counsel under President Bill Clinton, alluded to "information" that suggested that the waterboarding of Khalid Sheikh Mohammed had not produced good intelligence. Dellinger's account directly challenged proponents' claims that waterboarding was necessary and effective by highlighting the effectiveness of traditional, rapport-based techniques.

I find interesting . . . the constant reference to Khalid Sheikh Mohammad and the premise that the information that has been generated from him was, as a proximate cause, a result of waterboarding, because my information contradicts that. It's when the rapport effort was undertaken that information came from Khalid Sheikh Mohammad, and that he was resistant during the course of the efforts to secure information from him as a result of waterboarding.[23]

Daniel Levin, who had served in the National Security Council and Department of Justice under Presidents George H. W. Bush and George W. Bush, appeared before the House Subcommittee on the Constitution on June 18, 2008. At the hearing, Levin challenged, albeit obliquely, the claim that waterboarding had been used for three minutes. Noting that he was "very limited in what" he could say, Levin told the committee that if they had "been informed that there was a total of 3 minutes of waterboarding, I would suggest the Subcommittee should go back and get that clarified because that, I don't believe, is an accurate statement."[24]

That neither Dellinger nor Levin could speak publicly at length and with specificity about the CIA's use of waterboarding is suggestive of the evidentiary impoverishment of critics. At the time of these hearings, the public record of the CIA's interrogation program and waterboarding was thin. The primary accounts—such as those of Kiriakou and Hayden—were produced by officials invested in maintaining the legitimacy of the CIA's program. Lacking official accounts of the CIA's use of waterboarding, congressional critics and their like-minded witnesses typically looked elsewhere for interpretive resources to construct their claims. Critics rarely directed their arguments at the CIA's specific use of practice on Abu Zubaydah or Khalid Sheikh Mohammed. Rather, they argued that waterboarding was, generally, an ineffective way of collecting intelligence and would cause severe pain equivalent to that of torture. In so doing, critics sought to cast doubt on the instrumentality of waterboarding. They also attempted to broaden the terms of the debate, recontextualizing the CIA's interrogation program within the global consequences of its use. While proponents' narrative of waterboarding tended to end with the collection of actionable intelligence and the prevention of terrorist attacks, opponents argued that the use of waterboarding harmed the reputation of the country and made it less secure. Finally, critics challenged the propriety of waterboarding by associating it with the historical use of torture by illiberal regimes.

Challenging the Instrumentality of Waterboarding

Proponents of waterboarding argued that the CIA used the practice rarely, briefly, and in a controlled manner. Critics, in contrast, portrayed waterboarding as a practice that caused significant physical pain and that could not likely be restrained.

On November 8, 2007, Malcolm Nance, a national security expert, former member of the U.S. military, and a former SERE instructor for the Navy, appeared before the House Subcommittee on the Constitution. As a SERE instructor, Nance had undergone waterboarding. In his opening statement, Nance described that experience:

> Most media representations or recreations of the waterboarding are inaccurate, amateurish, and dangerous improvisations which do not capture the true intensity of the act. Contrary to popular opinion, it is not a simulation of drowning. It is drowning. In my case, the technique was so fast and professional that I didn't know what was happening until the water entered my nose and throat. It then pushes down into the trachea and starts to process a respiratory degradation. It is an overwhelming experience that induces horror, triggers a frantic survival instinct. As the event unfolded, I was fully conscious of what was happening: I was being tortured.[25]

Later in the hearing, Democrat Artur Davis posed a series of questions to Nance about the possible outcomes of waterboarding. Davis asked Nance, in sequence, whether waterboarding, if "done in the wrong way," could "kill somebody," "cause someone to have a seizure," and "cause brain damage." Nance answered in the affirmative to each question, adding that that waterboarding could "easily" kill someone and could, "yes, of course," cause brain damage. Davis concluded the line of questioning by arguing that the context of American interrogations made it more likely that waterboarding could be misused:

> If waterboarding happens in the adrenaline-pumped setting of a real interrogation, if waterboarding happened in the context of an environment where

there really was an effort to extract information, as opposed to a simulated practice technique, it strikes me that there is a significant, quantifiable risk that it could cause a loss of human life. [26]

Lacking an interpretively useful firsthand account of the CIA's "enhanced interrogation" program, Davis drew attention to possible outcomes of waterboarding and pointed to differences within the context of SERE and the context of an actual interrogation of an enemy.

Amrit Singh, an ACLU lawyer who also appeared before the subcommittee, employed a different tactic to challenge the way that proponents depicted the CIA's interrogation program. Although Singh's statement did not specifically address waterboarding, her statement is notable for two reasons. First, it directly challenged proponents' portrayal of "enhanced interrogation" as clinically used. Second, it does so by filling in the documentary record of the CIA interrogation with the FBI's account of what military interrogators did to detainees at Guantánamo:

> Clinical descriptions of enhanced interrogation methods conceal the severity of the mental and physical damage caused by these methods. For example, in one Government document, an FBI agent describes the devastating consequences of interrogations in which military personnel employed "environmental manipulation" techniques. Environmental manipulation refers to exposure to extreme temperatures. And the FBI agent observes, "On a couple of occasions, I entered interview rooms to find a detainee chained hand and foot in a fetal position to the floor, with no chair, food or water. Most times they had urinated and defecated on themselves and had been left there for 18 to 24 hours or more. On one occasion, the air conditioning had been turned so far down and the temperature was so cold in the room that the barefooted detainee was shaking with cold. On another occasion, the air conditioning had been turned off, making the temperature in the unventilated room probably well over 100 degrees. The detainee was almost unconscious on the floor, with a pile of hair lying next to him. He had apparently literally been pulling his own hair out throughout the night."[27]

Singh's statement draws on the FBI allegations—inscribed in e-mails— about detainee abuse at Guantánamo. These allegations, which were the subject of chapter 5, are distinguished by the fact that they are generated by (critical) official sources. They are also distinguished by their sources' proximity to the primary experience of abuse. Given this proximity, the accounts retrieve the "distinctive local historical character" of detention and interrogation practices that the official vocabulary for those practices typically substitutes.[28] The FBI's accounts are, as Singh points out, especially difficult to square with the clinical image of "enhanced interrogation" that advocates promote.

By construing waterboarding as a practice that has severe, if not lethal, physical consequences, critics challenged proponents' image of it as controlled, measured, and professionally administered. This challenge aimed at proponents' suggestion that the pain of waterboarding could be effectively managed so that the minimum amount of violence would be employed in pursuit of information. Such statements also employ evocative language (Nance's "horror" and "frantic survival instinct") and images (the unconscious body and its pile of hair) that are suggestive of the boundary-breaching qualities characteristic of "enhanced interrogation."

Critics also attacked waterboarding's effectiveness. They did so by drawing attention to the historical origins of waterboarding and commonsensical understandings of how those who suffered it would respond. To do so, they cited the source of the CIA's "enhanced interrogation" program: the U.S. Armed Forces' SERE program. If the fact that "enhanced interrogations" derived from knowledge associated with SERE was once a revelation, as when Jane Mayer initially reported on it for the *New Yorker*, it was, by 2007 and 2008, undisputed.[29] The meaning of this fact, of course, remained open to debate. Proponents of waterboarding ironized congressional concern for CIA interrogation by asking whether the U.S. Navy's use of waterboarding in SERE indicated that the United States tortured its own troops. Critics, however, pointed to both the purpose of SERE and its origin in a "communist interrogation model" concerned with propaganda, not actionable intelligence, to question the use value of waterboarding.

Simply put, critics argued that, because SERE was designed to train soldiers to resist practices used by the nation's enemies to generate false confessions, practices deriving from the training are inefficient and inappropriate means of producing truth. Malcolm Nance, the former SERE instructor, told the House Judiciary Committee that the SERE community was designed over 50 years ago to show that, as a torture instrument, waterboarding is a terrifying, painful and humiliating tool that leaves no physical scars and which can be repeatedly used as an intimidation tool. Waterboarding has the ability to make the subject answer any question with a truth, a half-truth, or outright lie in order to stop the procedure.[30]

Steven Kleinman, a former interrogator and a director of intelligence for the agency responsible for SERE, made a similar point in his opening statement to the Senate Armed Services Committee on September 25, 2008:

> First, many of the methods used in SERE training are based on what was once known as a communist interrogation model; a system designed to physically and psychologically debilitate a person, a detainee, as a means of gaining compliance. Second, the model's primary objective was to compel a prisoner to generate propaganda, not provide intelligence.[31]

The fact that the administration's interrogation policies originated in SERE provided other interpretive resources. In his opening statement to the Senate Armed Services Committee's June 17, 2007 hearing, Levin, the chair of the committee, pointed out that SERE instructors are not necessarily trained in interrogation. Driving home this point, Levin referred to the instructors as "those who play the part of interrogators in the SERE school drama"; they are not, Levin continued, "real interrogators, nor are they qualified to be."[32]

In addition to drawing on SERE's history and purpose as an argumentative resource, critics cited specific, historical instances in which enemy interrogators used similar practices to extract false confessions from Americans. When he appeared before the House Judiciary's Subcommittee on the Constitution in 2007, Kleinman described such techniques as producing "compliance":

> Compliance is forcing somebody [to] do something that they would not normally want to do and, in some cases, it means against their own interests—the North Koreans, the North Vietnamese, for instance, having a POW admit to dropping chemical weapons on civilian populations, which we knew were not true, but through torture was forced to do that.[33]

Artur Davis, during the Subcommittee on the Constitution's February 14, 2008, hearing on the Office of Legal Counsel, referred to a different historical instance of torture to challenge proponents' claims that the practice produces accurate information. Davis posed a lengthy series of questions to Stephen Bradbury about the effectiveness of waterboarding. The exchange started as an exercise in commonsensical beliefs about pain. Davis began with waterboarding, first asking Bradbury whether it would lead someone to feel "distressed" and, then, "extremely frightened." Bradbury answered affirmatively to both. Davis then asked Bradbury whether such feelings would lead a person to tell "a lie." After Bradbury answered, "I suppose so," Davis rhetorically pivoted, mobilizing John McCain's well-known experience of torture to dramatize the process by which the practice produces false confessions. During the exchange, Bradbury attempted to disrupt Davis's implicit argument by noting that McCain had "bones broken," the sort of physical injuries that proponents, including Bradbury, suggest are not caused by "enhanced interrogation" practices.[34]

Taken as a whole, the statements reviewed in this section construe waterboarding and "enhanced interrogation" as a set of practices that cannot be precisely or clinically deployed and do not lead, in an instrumental fashion, to the production of truth from recalcitrant detainees. In these portrayals, "enhanced interrogation" also butts up against profane elements of liberal democratic life. Liberalism, Luban writes, "incorporates a vision of engaged, active human beings possessing an inherent dignity."[35] In critics' portrayals, "enhanced interrogation" produces the opposite: a terrorized, intimidated, humiliated, and compliant human, who is physically stripped bare—literally, as the detainee tears out his hair.

Beyond Intelligence: Recontextualizing Waterboarding

In 2007 and 2008, critics of waterboarding lacked grounds to sustain a direct challenge to advocates' claims about the waterboarding of Abu Zubaydah and Khalid Sheikh Mohammed. Instead, they leveled a broader challenge to the wisdom of employing "enhanced" techniques, particularly waterboarding. Critics insinuated that waterboarding could not be employed clinically and that it would not likely produce actionable intelligence. These critiques largely engaged with waterboarding in the same terms as proponents; the wisdom of the CIA's interrogation program could be evaluated based on a narrow understanding of its instrumentality and effectiveness. Opponents of the CIA's interrogation program, though, went further, recontextualizing it within a global context. In this context, the program's instrumentality would not merely be measured by its effectiveness at producing actionable intelligence but also by an array of global consequences.

Critics of the CIA's detention and interrogation program attempted to weaken the argument for its use value by broadening the terms of debate and enumerating the domestic and global consequences of the practice and "enhanced interrogation" more generally. Those arguing against the practice cited a range of consequences that tend to cluster into two overarching themes: waterboarding and other aggressive interrogation practices had harmed the country's global standing and had negative implications for the country's security. Within each of the themes are various subarguments. Those who argued that the program harmed the nation's global standing noted that U.S. use of torture weakened the country's position to influence other nations on matters of human rights; they also made more general statements about the practice's inconsistency with democratic values, such as the rule of law. Those who argued that such practices harmed security tended to cite the fact that the use of such practices legitimized them and put U.S. soldiers at increased risk of torture, weakened global alliances, and provided America's enemies with propaganda to use for recruitment purposes.

Critics of "enhanced interrogation" also worked to recontextualize the CIA's program within a rule of law (as opposed to national security) frame. Specifically, critics fused the pursuit of national security to the maintenance of the rule of law, arguing that the latter is a source of global strength for the nation, sustaining the global reputation of the United States and international alliances and distinguishing the nation from its enemies. In this discourse, democratic principles reinforced, rather than opposed or had to be "balanced" with, national security; to pursue the former was to pursue the latter. Plotted on this interpretive grid, human rights violations appeared as threats to national security because they were inconsistent with the fundamental values that the United States shares with its allies. As Alberto Mora, an early, internal critic of "enhanced interrogations," told the Senate Armed Services Committee on June 17, 2008:

> Because the international legal system, the legal system of many countries, and the international human rights system are all largely designed to protect

human dignity, the decision of the United States to adopt cruelty has had a devastating foreign policy consequence. The cruel treatment of detainees is a criminal act for most, and perhaps all, of our traditional allies. As these nations came to recognize the true dimensions of our policy, political fissures between us and them began to emerge, because none of them would follow our lead into the swamp of legalized abuse.[36]

The fusion of national security to human rights and the rule of law also permitted critics of the program to produce an alternative narrative of the September 11 terrorist attacks. Although proponents of the administration's detention program cited September 11 more frequently than did critics, the meaning that the attacks had in political discourse of detainee abuse in 2003 had fragmented. Critics of the administration packaged waterboarding, aggressive interrogations, and torture among other controversial policy decisions that the Bush administration made after the attacks and argued that those decisions had instigated something like a fall from secular grace—characterized by the erosion of domestic bipartisanship and international support—in the years after September 11, 2001. A statement by Senator Patrick Leahy, the chair of the Senate Judiciary Committee, exemplifies this claim. Leahy opened the Judiciary Committee's July 16, 2008, hearing, "How the Administration's Failed Detainee Policies Have Hurt the Fight Against Terrorism," with the following statement,

> In the wake of the tragic attacks on September 11th and toward the end of President Bush's first year in office, this country had an opportunity to show that we could fight terrorism, secure our Nation, and bring the perpetrators of those heinous acts to justice, and do it in a way that was consistent with our history and our most deeply valued principles. You will recall we had virtually the whole world on our side at that time. A number of us reached out to the White House, both Republicans and Democrats alike, in an effort to craft a thoughtful, effective bipartisan way forward. The White House chose another path. They diverted our forces away from al Qaeda and capturing Osama bin Laden instead to go to war and occupation in Iraq—a country that had nothing to do with 9/11, and, of course, allowing Osama bin Laden to stay loose. And they chose to enhance the power of the President and to turn the Office of Legal Counsel at the Department of Justice into an apologist for White House orders—from the warrantless wiretapping of

Americans to torture. Many of us feel, as I do, that that made our country less safe, not safer.[37]

Critics further altered the meaning of the terrorist attacks by offering their own personal accounts of September 11, 2001. Nance, for instance, told the House Subcommittee on the Constitution on November 8, 2007, that "on the morning of September 11, at the green field next to the burning Pentagon, I was a witness to one of the greatest displays of heroism in our history. American men and women, both military and civilian, repeatedly and selflessly risked their lives to save those around them." He then reflected: "but does the ultimate goal of protecting America require us to adopt policies that shift our mindset from righteous self-defense to covert cruelty? Does protecting America at all costs mean sacrificing the Constitution, our laws, and the Bill of Rights in order to save it? I do not believe that."[38]

These statements suggest that the meaning of the September 11, 2001, terrorist attacks had changed dramatically since 2003. That year, when the Senate Judiciary Committee considered the inspector general's investigation of Metropolitan Detention Center (MDC), all participants in the hearing, including those most critical of the administration, recognized the terrorist attacks of September 11, 2001 as the singular point of reference for discussing the allegations of abuse at MDC. There was relative consensus, too, about the meaning of the attacks, as hearing participants acknowledged the FBI's effectiveness at preventing follow-up attacks and highlighted that threat as reason to give the executive leeway in its pursuit of national security. Now, in the final years of the Bush administration, that consensus had fractured, and the attacks could now be spoken of as a missed moment, when the country might have affirmed its belief in the rule of law in the face of a threat, but chose another path. This change in discourse corresponds to broader changes in the political and cultural context. By 2008, American fear of terrorism was waning and, in fact, the economy, rather than terror, appeared to be the primary concern of the populace.[39]

Supporters of the CIA's interrogation program described it as having two, intertwined outcomes: the collection of actionable intelligence and the prevention of terror. Critics, however, sought to discursively reposition the program within a broader set of consequences that included the global standing of the United States and the international alliances on which the nation's security depends. Within this context, the consequentialist terms of the debate about interrogation and torture hold, but the political calculus of waterboarding changes. The consequences of the practice—the outcomes by which its instrumentality should be measured—appear far more complex, and far less favorable, than proponents allowed.

Waterboarding as the Method of the Enemy

So far, I have largely presented political discourse of waterboarding, interrogation, and torture that frames the practices in consequentialist terms—in terms that evaluate the CIA's interrogation program by its practical and political consequences. Critics, however, also mobilized collective representations of illiberal cruelty from the "modern memory" of torture to construe waterboarding as a counterdemocratic practice that is, regardless of whether it works, incompatible with democracy.[40]

Critics of waterboarding frequently associated waterboarding with an array of nondemocratic regimes that used various forms of water torture in the past. Nance, for instance, began his account of waterboarding to the House Subcommittee on the Constitution by describing the motivation for using waterboarding on American service members.

> Within the four SERE schools and the Joint Personnel Recovery community, the waterboard was rightly used as a demonstration tool that revealed to our students the techniques of brutal authoritarian enemies. SERE trained tens of thousands of service members of its historical use by the Nazis, the Japanese, the North Koreans, Iraq, the Soviet Union, the Khmer Rouge, and the North Vietnamese. SERE emphasized that the enemies of democracy and rule of law often ignored human rights, defied the Geneva Conventions, and have subjected our men and women to grievous physical and psychological harm.[41]

As discussed earlier, SERE training has its institutional origins in the experience of U.S. service members detained and tortured during the Korean War. This fact bolstered critics' argument that the "enhanced interrogation" practices derived from SERE are properly viewed as a counterdemocratic practice. Addressing the Subcommittee on the Constitution in November 2007, Steven Kleinman pointed out that coercive interrogation practices had "been used [in the SERE context] as a result of our exposure to the communist interrogation model that unfolded after World War II and essentially scared the intelligence community."[42] Carl Levin also highlighted this fact in his opening statements to the Senate Armed Services Committee's September 25 hearing on SERE.

Critics also cited historical precedent, within the United States, of prosecuting waterboarding and other SERE techniques as war crimes. At the House Judiciary's December 20, 2007, hearing on the CIA videotapes, Massimino pointed out that the United States prosecuted the use of stress positions as a war crime. Marjorie Cohn, a professor of law at Thomas Jefferson School of Law and, at the time, the president of the National Lawyers Guild, made a similar claim about waterboarding to the House Subcommittee on May 6, 2008: "The United States pushed for and got prosecutions of Japanese leaders after World War II for waterboarding. It is called the water torture, the water cure."[43]

Finally, critics of the CIA's interrogation program drew on the historical memory of the Spanish Inquisition to heighten the symbolic stakes of the debate about interrogation. In 2007, Democrat Jerrold Nadler referred to the use of "methods of interrogation so appalling they sound like—and in some cases are—techniques pioneered by the Spanish Inquisition."[44] Nadler offered a more specific comment on waterboarding in 2008: "That is why what is now euphemistically called 'waterboarding' has for centuries been more bluntly known as the water torture, from the Inquisition to the U.S. prosecution in the last century of both enemy captors and Americans alike for practicing waterboarding."[45] John Hutson, a former Navy judge advocate general, offered an evocative critique of waterboarding when he appeared at the Senate Judiciary Committee's confirmation hearing for Michael Mukasey, who President Bush had nominated to replace Alberto Gonzales as attorney general. Earlier in the hearing, Mukasey had refused to offer a clear judgment of the legal status of waterboarding, noting only, "If it amounts to torture, it is not constitutional."[46] Hutson, in response, denied this ambivalent rendering of waterboarding. Instead, he clustered the practice with other, notorious forms of classical torture—the "rack and thumbscrews"—and referred to waterboarding as "the most iconic example of torture in history. It was devised, I believe, in the Spanish Inquisition. It has been repudiated for centuries." Hutson continued, alluding back to Mukasey's testimony, "It's a little disconcerting to hear now that we're not quite sure where water-boarding fits in the scheme of things."[47]

The association of waterboarding and SERE with illiberal regimes and, in fact, the pre-Enlightenment Inquisition is consistent with two phenomena documented in human rights research and research of torture. Human rights organizations frequently use "shaming" to influence state behavior. They do so by mobilizing the symbolic association of violations, including torture, to denounce norm-violating states as "pariahs which do not belong to the community of civilized nations."[48] This sort of shaming also appears at play in the U.S. debate about torture, and critics attempted to cluster waterboarding with a litany of illiberal symbols of repression. Similarly, research on torture suggests that, within Western collective memories, the practice arrives on the cultural scene with a web of counterdemocratic associations and is, typically, purified of its democratic history.[49] We find, for instance, few references to the U.S. use of water torture in the Philippines at the turn of the twentieth century or in Vietnam in critical accounts of the practice.[50] In their portrayals of waterboarding, critics of the practice strategically deployed these associations to code waterboarding as unworthy of a democracy.

There are, though, pockets of recognition of democratic histories of torture by both advocates of "enhanced interrogation" and critics. The most notable, extended, and complex recognition comes from the testimony of Democratic John Conyers during the November 2007 House Subcommittee on the Constitution hearing. Conyers's testimony and his line of questioning is, within the sample of hearings that I analyzed, unique and is worth reprinting at length.

CONYERS: Naomi Klein in *The Nation* has raised the question that the admission that the embrace of torture by U.S. officials long predates the Bush administration and has, in fact, been integral to U.S. foreign policy since the Vietnam War. Do you have any opinion on that, Ms. Singh?

SINGH: I am not in a position to comment on the basis of the documentary record that the ACLU has obtained . . .

CONYERS: . . . I have got a bit of literature here that shows [water torture] goes back thousands and thousands of years, but nobody talks about what was being done with it, for example, just since World War II, in all the military excursions and expeditions we have been on. What do you think, Colonel and Mr. Nance? . . .

KLEINMAN: The heart of the problem we have with interrogation, is our lack of progress . . . It is one of the most important, most difficult activities that an operations officer can undertake, [and] to leave it to people with limited life experience, to leave it to contractors, to dumb it down, so to speak—is going to be wholly ineffective.

CONYERS: Mr. Nance, did you want to comment before the Chairman closes this down?

NANCE: Yes. I think that, as a whole, I believe that until recently we have seen an only what I would call uncontrolled field expedient interrogations, which may have been done in Latin America and other environments.

NADLER: Meaning that someone local decided to do something that wasn't approved or ordered from higher up?

NANCE: Yes, sir. . . . However, we can't say that it wasn't done, as we saw in the *Washington Post* article, which showed that field expedient interrogation being carried out in Vietnam. . . . Those things will happen on the battlefield. However, what we are seeing now is a systematic process.[51]

Here is an instance in which the interpretive contours of the modern memory of torture are momentarily breached. But the meaning of that breach is ambiguous. First, the most provocative claim in it is Conyers's first one that torture has "been integral to U.S. foreign policy since the Vietnam War." Conyers, however, does not own the claim. He attributes it to Klein and poses it as a question, displaying his neutrality to it.[52] Conyers then asks the Singh, an ACLU staff attorney and coeditor of *Administration of Torture: A Documentary Record from Washington to Abu Ghraib and Beyond*, for her opinion of the claim. Singh, citing the limitations of the documentary record of torture, declines to offer an opinion. In response, Conyers attempts to restate the issue; in so doing, he zooms out from "U.S. foreign policy since the Vietnam War" to the history of water torture over "thousands and thousands of years," before returning to U.S. torture since World War II and asking the other two witnesses to offer an opinion.

In response, Kleinman offers a general statement on the need to make progress on interrogation. Nance, in turn, opaquely acknowledges U.S. torture as "uncontrolled field expedient interrogations." Later in the exchange, Nance specifically references a *Washington Post* article documenting water torture in Vietnam; the reference is likely to either a January 21, 1968, cover image depicting that torture or an October 5, 2006, article about the image from 1968.[53] But Nance, in an exchange with another Democrat, Jerrold Nadler, isolates these historical instances of torture from U.S. policy. In Nadler's words, they were the result of "someone local [who] decided to do something that wasn't approved or ordered from higher up." They are "things that will happen on the battlefield." A very similar claim was made by General Ricardo Sanchez, military investigators, and Senate Republicans, as I discussed in chapter 3, to downplay allegations of widespread detainee abuse in Iraq after the release of the Abu Ghraib photographs. Denial is not only a tool for those advocating painful interrogation techniques. Here, Nadler and Nance employ the claim that historical instances of water torture should be treated as the outcome of forces "that supposedly have nothing to do with the government and are beyond its control" to construe the CIA's use of waterboarding and the Bush administration's approval of the practice as an unprecedented historical deviation. What we witness in this portion of dialogue is a momentary, ambivalent challenge to the strong distinction between democracies and torture and, subsequently, a shoring up of that distinction by distinguishing the historical instances of U.S. torture from the contemporary use of waterboarding, posing the former as isolated incidents of minor historical importance.

Proponents of waterboarding also fend off the associations that critics make between contemporary waterboarding and illiberal torture. Specifically, proponents disassociated waterboarding from critics' historical references by using "advantageous comparisons" that drew attention to the laudable qualities of waterboarding and the most reprehensible qualities of historical forms of water torture.[54] Proponents distinguished between waterboarding and types of water torture that involve pumping, which involves "forcibly filling the stomach and intestines with water."[55] During pumping, "the organs stretch and convulse, causing 'some of the most intense pain that visceral tissues can experience.'"[56] Supporters also referred to the "precise procedures" that the CIA used to advance the claim that waterboarding is a professionally administered practice that does not constitute torture.

This juxtaposition between waterboarding and pumping was made apparent during a February 14, 2008, House Judiciary Committee's February hearing. During the hearing, Franks questioned Bradbury about the comparisons critics drew between waterboarding and the historical use of water torture:

I've heard a lot of reports in the press that waterboarding was developed in the Spanish Inquisition and that the United States repeatedly prosecuted it. Is that true? Do you believe that these past historical practices bear any resemblance to the waterboarding as done by the CIA?[57]

In his lengthy response, Bradbury distinguished between CIA waterboarding and historical instances of water torture. In so doing, he described, in excruciating detail, the effect of pumping on its victims:

> To my knowledge, they bear no resemblance to what the CIA did in 2002 and 2003. The only thing in common is, I think, the use of water. The historical examples that have been referenced in public debate have all involved a course of conduct that everyone would agree constituted egregious cases of torture. And with respect to the particular use of water in those cases, as I've indicated, in most of those cases they involved the forced consumption of large amounts of water, to such extent that—beyond the capacity in many cases of the victim's stomach, so that the stomach would be distended. And then in many cases weight or pressure, including in the case of the Japanese, people standing on or jumping on the stomach of the victim, blood would come out of the mouth. And in the case of the Spanish Inquisition, there truly would be agony and, in many cases, death.[58]

Bradbury then criticized the use of "these historical examples" as inaccurate portrayals of "the careful procedures that the CIA was authorized to use with strict time limits, safeguards, restrictions, and not involving the same kind of water torture that was involved in most of those cases."[59]

Bradbury's testimony to the House Judiciary Committee are the only occasions, within the sample of hearings that I analyzed, in which the comparisons between waterboarding and historical instances of water torture were directly attacked. More generally, the presentation of waterboarding as briefly and rarely used, carefully administered, and effective implicitly called into question these comparisons. The historical comparisons, however, continued to resonate in the debate about waterboarding after the inauguration of Barack Obama. For instance, in February 2010, two prominent political bloggers, liberal Matthew Yglesias and former Bush administration speechwriter Marc Thiessen, debated the merits of comparisons between waterboarding and Inquisition torture in a series of caustic, if not occasionally juvenile, posts to their respective blogs.[60] Yglesias, in his posts, drew out the similarities between waterboarding and the use of water torture during the Inquisition, as well as by People's Liberation Army and Khmer Rouge interrogators. In response, Thiessen, like Bradbury, highlighted the practical distinctions between CIA waterboarding, Inquisition water torture, and pumping more generally. Thiessen used these distinctions to distinguish between legitimate interrogation practices and the torture of "despotic regimes":

> The CIA never "forced water" down the throats of terrorists. This is a technique called "pumping" that was employed by Imperial Japan and other despotic regimes. They would force water into their victims until their internal organs expanded painfully . . . and the victims passed out from the pain. The torturers would then jump on the victims' stomachs to make them vomit— reviving them so they could then start the process over again. The CIA never did anything even remotely like this. A few seconds of water being poured over the mouths of terrorists, never entering their stomach or lungs, does not compare to these tortures.[61]

Bradbury's and Thiessen's defenses of waterboarding leave intact the cultural logic of critics, the opposition of democracy and torture, and instead challenge the validity of clustering the CIA's use of waterboarding with the tortures employed by illiberal or "despotic" regimes. Both sides, then, align themselves against *torture*; both sides imply that the practice is incompatible with U.S. values and laws. Here, for instance, is how Trent Franks prefaces his justification of the waterboarding of Khalid Sheikh Mohammed during the Judiciary Committee's November 8, 2007, hearing:

> On the American side of the ledger, let me be very clear, Mr. Chairman: Torture is illegal. Torture is banned by various provisions of law, including the Uniform Code of Military Justice . . . and the 2005 Senate amendment prohibiting the cruel, inhuman or degrading treatment of anyone in U.S. custody.[62]

The point of disagreement between the two sides of this debate is cast not at torture but whether waterboarding and other "enhanced interrogation" techniques should be classified as such. Given the gap, in 2007 and 2008, in

public knowledge surrounding the practice, both sides possessed the interpretive space to promote portrayals of the practice that best fit their arguments. The videotaped use of the practice does not air. There is no firsthand
account of the practice against which both sides of the debate feel compelled to check their arguments. And so waterboarding is simultaneously
restrained and excessive, effective and a waste, befitting the United States
and a practice found in the interrogation rooms of despots.

CONCLUSION

Michael Hayden's admission that the CIA destroyed video recordings of its
interrogation brought the gap in the documentary record of waterboarding to the foreground of debate. Drawing on diverse and often incompatible resources—the statements of CIA officials, the firsthand experiences of
those who experienced waterboarding in a training context, and the historical lineage of SERE practices—proponents and opponents of the practice
competed to fill this gap with their preferred accounts. Their claims, moreover, oriented to broader, cultural understandings of democratic states' use
of force. Supporters of waterboarding portrayed the practice as clinically
and professionally administered; portrayed in this way, the interrogator
administers pain only after traditional interrogation techniques have failed,
in a controlled fashion, and only until the end—the extraction of intelligence—is reached. Thirty to thirty-five seconds for Abu Zubaydah; just
ninety seconds for Khalid Sheikh Mohammed. This image drains waterboarding of the excesses that torture historically has contained and that liberalism cannot tolerate—the wielding of brute, aimless power, in the form
of violence, over another.

Critics challenged this image of waterboarding by drawing attention to
the severe physical consequences of the practice and to its origin in models
of interrogation that produced false confessions, not actionable intelligence.
They also altered the political calculus associated with the practice by elabo-
rating the global harms of torture. Finally, critics mobilized symbols of illiberal cruelty from the "modern memory" of torture to deny waterboarding a
place in the democratic toolkit of interrogation.[63] In their rendering, waterboarding is in tension with democratic and national values. The practice leaves
those on whom it is used physically savaged; it produces compliant humans
who lack the very qualities that liberalism values—will and autonomy.

It is significant that proponents' image of "enhanced interrogation" as professionally administered and restrained does not simply structure public defenses of it. It also appears to have neutralized prohibitions on torture for the lawyers, policy makers, and interrogators who reviewed, authorized, and used it.[64] Indeed, it is this image of "enhanced interrogation" that Department of Justice lawyers and administration officials engaged with in the myriad documents that described and authorized the practice. As a model of interrogation, this image presumes a science of violence—the possibility of controlling and incrementally increasing pain; it is "a cold, statistically-detached," bureaucratic form of violence "that appears . . . to float free of the bodies" on which it is deployed.[65]

This, for instance, is how the CIA described "dietary manipulation" to Steven Bradbury, who, as the head of the Office of Legal Counsel, reviewed and reapproved the CIA's interrogation program in 2005:

> The CIA generally follows as a guideline a calorie requirement of 900 kcal/ day + 10 kcal/kg/day. This quantity is multiplied by 1.2 for a sedentary activity level or 1.4 for a moderate activity level. Regardless of this formulate, the recommended minimum calorie intake is 1500 kcal/day, and in no event is the detainee allowed to receive less than 1000 kcal/day. Calories are provided using commercial liquid diets (such as Ensure Plus), which also supply other essential nutrients and make for nutritionally complete meals.[66]

Of waterboarding, the CIA proposed:

> In this technique, the detainee is lying on a gurney that is inclined at an angle of 10 to 15 degrees to the horizontal, with the detainee on his back and his head toward the lower end of the gurney. A cloth is placed over the detainee's face, and cold water is poured on the cloth from a height of approximately 6 to 18 inches. . . . A single "application" of water may not last for more than 40 seconds, with the duration of an "application" measured from the moment when water—of whatever quantity—is first poured onto the cloth until the moment when the cloth is removed from the subject's face.[67]

The CIA's proposal also discusses the use of "saline solution instead of plain water to reduce the possibility of hyponatremia . . . if the detainee drinks the water." And, as Khalid Sheikh Mohammed alleged to the International

Committee of the Red Cross, the CIA may have attached blood-oxygen monitors to those who they waterboarded.[68]

These descriptions of "enhanced interrogation" imply a science of pain and violence that neither empirical research nor the CIA's experience, as best we now understand it, supports.[69] Indeed, the reality of torture haunts proponents' image of "enhanced interrogation," always threatening to pierce its interpretive borders. I find support for this claim in a flood of documents, released in April 2009 that, opaquely and through lines of redacted material, described the "actual implementation" of "enhanced interrogation" in terms very different from those of proponents. That month, the Obama administration released a series of Department of Justice memoranda on the CIA's interrogation program; the administration also released previously unpublished portions of the CIA inspector general's investigation of the agency's detention and interrogation program. The documents suggested that the CIA had used waterboarding "with far greater frequency than initially indicated . . . and also . . . in a different manner."[70] Media reports based on the inspector general's report noted that waterboarding had been used 266 times on Abu Zubaydah and Khalid Sheikh Mohammed.[71] While the precise meaning of this figure was contested,[72] it appears that the "precise procedures" that the practices allegedly involved might not have been precisely followed.

Later that month, Mark Danner, writing in the *New York Review of Books*, released an International Committee of the Red Cross (ICRC) report on the treatment of fourteen "high-value" detainees who had been transferred from the CIA's black sites to Guantánamo in 2006. Among the detainees were Abu Zubaydah, Khalid Sheikh Mohammed, and Al Nashiri, the three detainees that the CIA has admitted waterboarding. Zubaydah's account of the practice suggests that the CIA's official version of his interrogation overlooked elements of its implementation that did not well-fit proponents' image of the practice.

> I was then . . . put on what looked like a hospital bed, and strapped down very tightly with belts. A black cloth was then placed over my face and the interrogators used a mineral water bottle to pour water on the cloth so that I could not breathe. After a few minutes the cloth was removed and the bed was rotated into an upright position. The pressure of the straps on my wounds was very painful.[73] I vomited.[74] The bed was then again lowered to

horizontal position and the same torture carried out again with the black cloth over my face and water poured on from a bottle. On this occasion my head was in a more backward, downwards position and the water was poured on for a longer time. I struggled against the straps, trying to breathe, but it was hopeless. I thought I was going to die. I lost control of my urine. Since then I still lose control of my urine when under stress.[75]

This, perhaps, is what the CIA's videotapes documented: "inconvenient, involuntary memories"[76]—the excesses of violence, the leaky, suffering body—that democracies, when they turn to torture, repress, as they must.

CHAPTER 7

From "Enhanced Interrogation" to Drones

U.S. COUNTERTERRORISM AND THE LEGACY OF TORTURE

BETWEEN 2003 AND 2008, A discourse that acknowledged torture emerged in U.S. politics. In this discourse, the "torture word"—previously kept at arm's length—was applied to U.S. detention and interrogation practices, including the use of stress positions, forced nudity, "gender coercion," sleep deprivation, and waterboarding. Those who articulated this discourse construed these practices and the facilities at which the practices were used (Abu Ghraib, Guantánamo, the "black sites") as symbols of the excesses of the Bush administration. They also produced a frame for torture in which respect for the rule of law and the protection of human rights strengthened U.S. security. In this frame, torture weakened the country by eroding the country's global image and its alliances with nations who valued the laws of war.

The 2008 U.S. presidential election appeared to signal the success of the discourse of acknowledgment. Both major party candidates took antitorture positions, accepting that torture harmed U.S. interests. The Democrat's candidate, Barack Obama, won the 2008 election and, two days after his inauguration, signed executive orders that ordered the closure of the detention facility at Guantánamo Bay, limited U.S. interrogators to the practices listed in the Army's Field Manual for interrogation, and closed all CIA detention facilities. In so doing, President Obama institutionalized the discourse of acknowledgment, transforming it into policy.

Critics of "enhanced interrogation," however, neither have achieved their full policy aims nor have they settled debate about the nature and effectiveness of painful interrogation practices. The Obama administration failed to close Guantánamo during its first term, stymied by Republican resistance in Congress and its own unwillingness to meaningfully challenge that resistance.[1] Guantánamo had all but disappeared from public consciousness until the spring and summer of 2013, when a widespread hunger strike by detainees and the military's decision to force-feed dozens of those detainees, drew sustained media attention. During a May 23, 2013, national security speech, Obama addressed these issues directly, lamenting that Congress had restricted his ability to transfer of detainees out of Guantánamo and asking of the force-feeding of detainees at the facility, "Is this who we are? Is that something our Founders foresaw? Is that the America we want to leave our children?"

Since July 2013, the hunger strike at the facility has apparently died down. In late December 2013, the military recognized fifteen detainees as hunger strikers—all of whom were being force-fed—before imposing a blackout on the figures; this was down from 106 in late June and early July.[2] The administration has stepped up efforts to transfer detainees out of the facility, reducing the population of the facility from 166 to 148 by November 2014.[3] Despite this progress, there are frequent reminders of Guantánamo's troubled human rights and political legacies. On January 11, 2014, protestors marked the twelfth anniversary of Guantánamo's operation at the gates of the White House.[4] Some donned that ubiquitous symbol of the facility's excesses, the orange jumpsuit. Later that month, Obama referred to the need to close Guantánamo in his State of the Union address. The remarks were his first reference to Guantánamo in a State of the Union address, and they came just over five years after Obama signed an executive order to close the facility.[5]

On torture, the legacy of the discourse of acknowledgment is equally troubled. In the months after Obama's victory, Democrats in Congress, most notably Senator Patrick Leahy, advocated an independent investigation or "truth commission" to investigate Bush-era abuses of power, including torture.[6] President Obama, however, refused to support such efforts, observing that he "was more interested in looking forward" than he was "in looking backward."[7] The Department of Justice, for its part, opened an investigation into the CIA's program, focusing on the death of two detainees in CIA custody. The investigation closed in August 2012, however, with no charges.[8] Instead of pursuing meaningful investigations, the administration released a set of documents—four Bush-era Department of Justice memos describing and authorizing the CIA's interrogation program and previously redacted portions of the CIA inspector general's report on the program—in April 2009.[9] Later that spring, the president reversed himself on the release of photographs showing detainee abuse, refusing, in May, to release them after earlier suggesting that he would. Reports indicated that the photographs came from Abu Ghraib and a number of military detention facilities and included both "personal snapshots" taken by soldiers and military criminal investigators' photos, including autopsy photographs of detainees who died in custody.[10] In late October 2014, a federal judge ordered the Obama administration to justify its continued classification of the approximately 2,100 photographs depicting U.S. detention and interrogation operations. The order requires the administration to offer, by December 12, 2014, an explanation for the classification of each individual photograph. Alex Abdo, an ACLU staff attorney involved in the Freedom of Information Act suit, highlighted the potential evidentiary value of the photographs, telling *Newsweek*,

> These photographs come from at least seven different detention facilities throughout Afghanistan and Iraq. . . . We think this would once and for all end the myth that the abuse that took place at Abu Ghraib was an aberration . . . It was essentially official policy. It was widespread at different facilities under different commanders.[11]

At the time of writing, a 6,000-page Senate Intelligence Committee report on the CIA's program also remains classified; however, the report's executive summary was released on December 9, 2014. This exhaustive document chronicles the CIA's "repeated misleading of the White House, Congress and the public about the value of brutal and lawless methods that yielded little valuable intelligence."[12] The report also finds that the CIA used techniques that were not legally approved by the Department of Justice and "failed to keep an accurate account of the number of individuals it held" and on whom it used "enhanced interrogation" techniques.[13] Supporters of "enhanced interrogation" reject the report, describing it as a methodologically flawed, partisan document. Specifically, they emphasize that the committee did not speak to any CIA interrogators or former directors.

Without a meaningful investigation of the previous administration's interrogation policies and with so much of the documentary record still classified, the discursive divide that I described in the previous chapter has become a lasting feature of the debate about "enhanced interrogation." And, if the Obama administration hoped to foreclose debate about interrogation by declaring itself forward-looking rather than backward-looking, it erred. Once out of office, members of the Bush administration—most notably former vice president Dick Cheney, former speechwriter Marc Thiessen, and former CIA director Michael Hayden—continue to justify the CIA's "enhanced interrogation" program and publicly criticize the limits that the Obama administration set on CIA interrogations. Caught between the known and unknown, the recognized and redacted, the U.S. debate about torture idles, characterized by assertions without proof and allusions to privileged knowledge.

The precariousness of the discourse of acknowledgment may be observed, even, in how Obama speaks of torture. As a candidate, Obama referred to torture as a "key issue." "Torture has metamorphosed," Mark Danner wrote a month after the 2008 presidential election, "from an execrable war crime to a 'key issue.' From something forbidden by international treaty and condemned by domestic law to . . . something to be debated."[14] As president, Obama fitted tortured into a similar discourse, often saying that he had "prohibited torture." We should notice, Danner wrote, "that torture violates international and domestic law and that the notion that our new president has the power to prohibit it follows insidiously from the pretense that his predecessor had the power to order it."[15] Danner's analysis appears prescient. During a November 13, 2012, Republican debate, the party's candidates were asked their "stance" on torture. While no candidate supported torture, Herman Cain and Michele Bachman both distinguished waterboarding from torture and expressed their support of the controversial practice.[16] Just over two weeks later, Newt Gingrich took a similar position.[17] Mitt Romney, the Republican's choice to run against Obama, also put his support behind "enhanced interrogation."[18] Long gone were the politics of 2008, when both the Democratic and Republican candidates called waterboarding torture, lamented the harms of torture, and argued against its use.

On their face, these trends in U.S. political culture seem to challenge the claims that I presented at the start of this book. In chapter 1, I suggested that torture arrives on the contemporary political scene with a bundle of historical associations that renders the practice toxic.[19] That torture is practiced covertly, that interrogators prefer techniques that are difficult to document, and that state officials deny torture suggest that governments, particularly those that seek domestic and international legitimacy, are loath to be observed torturing or, even, advocating torture. Within U.S. political discourse, the precariousness of antitorture politics appears, on its face, to undermine this claim. One might argue, with Danner, that U.S. political culture has normalized or legitimated torture—that torture is no longer, as Malise Ruthven once called it, the "threshold of outrage" of contemporary societies, but, merely, one of many "key issues."[20]

Versions of the normalization hypothesis also appeared in scholarly work in the past decade.[21] The argument involves a subtle, but consequential move. It requires viewing each discursive justification of "enhanced interrogation" as, in fact, a discursive justification of torture. It involves, in other words, siding with the Bush administration's critics in Congress and allowing that "enhanced interrogation" is actually torture. Politically, such a move is necessary to resist the discursive conditions that make torture viable.[22] It is also, from a human rights and legal perspective, a valid naming of these practices and is consistent with historical precedent.[23] By conflating "enhanced interrogation" and torture, we fail to observe the force that international laws and human rights norms continue to exert in U.S. politics.

Within U.S. political discourse, "torture" remains coded as counterdemocratic and the "torture word" is itself still toxic. Those who support "enhanced interrogation" engage in substantial and often precarious discursive work to prevent the practices from becoming collectively recognized as "torture." Advocates of "enhanced interrogation" pay rhetorical respect to domestic and international prohibitions on torture. They also construe their favored practices, including waterboarding, as instrumentally and clinically practiced, as "enhanced interrogation" rather than "torture." They further distinguished between those practices and historical instances of torture by drawing attention to the legal reviews and safeguards involved in the use of "enhanced interrogation." We may and often should read these efforts with great skepticism, as the strategic and possibly cynical effort of public officials to protect their preferred policies and the legacies of those who created those policies. At the same time, a more optimistic interpretation is available: the liberal repugnance to torture and the international prohibition on torture remained active and operative forces even as U.S. political elites, CIA agents, contractors, and soldiers turned to the practice. These forces—sustained by the commitments of those who oppose torture—exert pressure on those who advocate "enhanced interrogation," leading them to distinguish these techniques from torture and assert, repetitively, that the United States does not condone torture. By acknowledging this seeming contradiction—that even as the country embraced torture, it recognized the sanctity of the international prohibition on torture—those concerned with human rights may confront proponents of "enhanced interrogation" on a shared moral terrain.

KNOWLEDGE AND CULTURE IN POLITICAL DISCOURSE

Members of Congress oriented their statements about detention and interrogation to a documentary record produced by military interrogators, military police, FBI agents, and official investigators. Inscribed in photographs, investigations, interrogation logs, and e-mails, these accounts provided the rudimentary facts that U.S. politicians used when debating the practice. U.S. politicians find it difficult to ignore or outright deny firsthand accounts of detainee abuse and torture produced by the country's own interrogators and soldiers. These observers cannot be accused of lying about abuse and torture, as "terrorists" are.[24] They cannot be accused of misunderstanding the stakes of interrogation or of ideological bias, as human rights organizations are.[25] Political officials must still interpret the meaning of interrogators' and soldiers' accounts of torture; one thinks, for instance, of how military investigators downplayed FBI concerns over torture at Guantánamo by pointing out that the FBI has a different standard for evaluating interrogation practices than does the military. Even so, such accounts seem to be, as brute matters of fact, unavoidable and undeniable in a way that media and human rights claims are not. They also intersect with the cultural coding of torture as counterdemocratic in two ways.

First, because these accounts portray U.S. interrogations as disorderly, unprofessional, and excessive, they weaken the credibility of the claim that "enhanced interrogation" practices were employed with care, restraint, and professionalism. Many viewers of the Abu Ghraib photographs saw ferocious if not sadistic violence—violence pursued as an end in itself, rather than for instrumental reasons.[26] Other documents, though less well-known, had a similar impact. Mohammed al-Qahtani's interrogation log betrayed the professionalism of Guantánamo's "honor bound" interrogators. In it, interrogators logged their own creative combinations of pain and humiliation, engaging in puppet shows and employing forms of "gender coercion," even as they attacked al-Qahtani's body through deprivation of sleep, application of stress, and exposure to extreme conditions. The FBI's descriptions of Guantánamo, meanwhile, portrayed the excesses of the facility and the vulnerability of those in the country's custody—the isolated detainee, shackled, shivering in the fetal position amid his own bodily fluids and matter. These accounts of U.S. detention and interrogation practices took different representational forms. The Abu Ghraib photographs are, of course, visual in nature, while both the military's interrogation log and the FBI e-mails provide written accounts. Despite this core difference, the documents share important qualities. All capture the excesses of violence and allude, in their own evocative ways, to detainees' suffering. All provided something like a first-person vantage on the events they represented. Encountering these documents, one feels as if one is looking directly into these distant detention centers. This is a well-recognized quality of photographs; it is a quality less frequently recognized of written accounts.[27] The debate about Guantánamo, though, turned precisely on documents that offer similar, but not identical, vantages on U.S. torture as their predecessors, the photographs from Abu Ghraib, had on the torture that occurred in Iraq.

The second way that the documentary record of U.S. torture and culture intersect is more speculative. The strength of the cultural coding of torture may not simply shape political discourse but may also produce mechanisms for the practice's exposure from within the bureaucracies that torture. Within the organizations tasked with detaining and interrogating the U.S.'s detainees, there were soldiers, interrogators, and military lawyers who never accepted the administration's, the military's, and the CIA's rationalizations of "enhanced interrogation." Even as "the avowedly democratic state reaches deep into its reserve of pure power, breaking loose from the usual restraints on its capacity to eliminate resistance through the infliction of physical pain," some of the state's agents never follow its lead.[28] Detention and interrogation occurs in organizational settings in which state agents compete for status and prestige.[29] They also occur across several agencies; interrogators for one agency may not share the organizational values of another. FBI interrogators, who have different organizational goals and a different chain of command than do military and CIA interrogators, documented and reported the abuses that occurred at Guantánamo and have spoken publically against CIA practices, including waterboarding.[30] At Abu Ghraib, some participants in the photographed violence, particularly Sabrina Harman, photographed what they witnessed to document events about which they felt deeply conflicted.[31] And military lawyers like Alberto Mora perceived Guantánamo for what it was in the early years of its use—a toxic swamp of legalized abuse—and so registered his criticisms, wisely in written form, with the Department of Defense's lawyers. By their actions, those who felt ambivalent about or outright opposed to the abuse and torture of detainees created a shadow documentary record that proved the undoing of the administration's policies.

Even the legal and political practice of authorizing and enacting "enhanced interrogation" may have produced mechanisms for torture's exposure. To distinguish "enhanced interrogation" from torture, advocates construe "enhanced" techniques as restrained and carefully deployed, consistent with American notions of the rule of law. To sustain this portrayal, they reference the legal reviews that interrogation policies underwent and the safeguards, including the drafting of interrogation plans and the keeping of logs, incorporated into interrogation. Although these reviews, plans, and logs may not, as Rejali shows, accurately map the actual implementation of torture,[32] they produce textual traces of its use that can alter public discourse. Public responses to the April 2009 release of legal reviews of the CIA's interrogation program provide support for this claim. The documents provided grounds to challenge advocates' image of "enhanced interrogation" as careful, restrained, and lawful, as they suggested that the CIA used its "enhanced" techniques very differently than how the agency described the techniques to the Department of Justice lawyers who reviewed and approved them.

The official, documentary record of U.S. torture on which Congress relied is far from exhaustive. Abu Ghraib and Guantánamo are well covered in it, but few other detention facilities are. Human rights reporting on the subject have convincingly shown that torture was widespread during the Bush administration, occurring in U.S. detention facilities across Afghanistan and Iraq.[33] Still, the patchwork reality that U.S. politicians encountered was vivid enough to bend the debate toward acknowledgment.

THE CONTEXT OF ACKNOWLEDGMENT

I do not think that Congress would have meaningfully grappled with U.S. interrogation policy if not for the developments in the public record of torture that this book has explored. These developments, however, were not sufficient. U.S. officials encountered detainee abuse and torture within a political environment, a "context of feeling and attitude," that provided the interpretive frames in which U.S. violence became meaningful.[34] These frames were made up of political values, such as national security, the rule of law, and human rights, whose relative significance varied depending on the political context.

Chapter 2 demonstrated that the war in Iraq provided a human rights frame for understanding Abu Ghraib, since U.S. politicians recognized the need to sustain domestic support and "Iraqi hearts and minds" for the invasion. Allegations of abuse and torture in the war on terror required far more work to elevate into a pressing political problem. The September 11, 2001 terrorist attacks and the threat of terror established national security as the pinnacle of political values. Within a frame defined by these events and this value, detainee abuse and torture, at least initially, appeared a regrettable, but relatively insignificant footnote. Concern for the "balance" between national security and civil liberties was, moreover, insufficient to elevate instances of abuse into pressing political problems. Abused detainees were, typically, noncitizens; their treatment was largely irrelevant to political calculations about liberties and security. This is how politicians framed the treatment of detainees held at Metropolitan Detention Center in New York. As chapter 5 demonstrates, this is how, too, military officials and Congressional Republicans attempted to reframe the FBI's allegations of abuse at Guantánamo.

Eventually, though, respect for the rule of law and human rights became fused with national security; in this configuration, national security could only be secured by conforming to domestic and international standards of detention and interrogation. This fusion made an interpretive frame available in which the abuse and torture of detainees, even within the war on terror, weakened the nation by undermining the global image and alliances of the United States. This change occurred gradually. As I documented in chapter 5, it was a product of an event largely outside the control of members of Congress, the Supreme Court's rulings against the Bush administration in *Hamdan v. Rumsfeld*. Following the court's decision in this case, congressional hearings on detention and interrogation, even under the Republican Congress, included a diversity of positions on law and human rights and recognized the legal tug of international law and military justice.

The 2006 midterm election subsequently won Democrats control over both Houses of Congress. This provided, as chapters 5 and 6 demonstrate, Democrats with access to the political resources—notably, the control of committee agendas—necessary to stage hearings that amplified human rights perspectives. Hearings included representatives of human rights organizations and former members of the administration or the armed forces critical of the administration's policies. These hearings also assumed, in their titles and agendas, a critical stance toward the Bush administration's detention and interrogation policies.

I am hesitant to draw strong conclusions from these observations, as this study has not compared congressional responses to allegations of executive wrongdoing across cases. On one hand, these observations could suggest that Democrats are more willing to apply human rights norms to U.S. violence than are Republicans. At the same time, they could merely suggest the strategic value of ignoring or fending off allegations of torture and human rights violations when they are levied against one's own party and dwelling on them when they are levied against one's political opponents.[35] The relative indifference of congressional Democrats to the Obama administration's drone program, discussed below, would seem to support this latter position.

The fusion of human rights and the rule of law to national security was a significant, but precarious, discursive achievement. During the early years of the Obama administration, critics of Obama's detention and interrogation policies mobilized the threat of terrorism and piggybacked on attempted or actual terrorist attacks, such as Umar Farouk Abdulmutallab's attempt to blow up a plane over the United States on Christmas Day 2010, in an effort to loosen the relation between the rule of law and national security.[36] The maintenance of a political context averse to torture requires diligence. Human rights and civil liberties must be discursively reinforced and political stages must be kept open to those who articulate human rights claims. It also appears to require some amount of good fortune—the absence or prevention of terrorist attacks that proponents of "enhanced interrogation" might mobilize to weaken the fusion of human rights, the rule of law, and national security.

FROM TORTURE TO DRONES

Under Obama, "enhanced interrogation" gave way to unmanned aerial vehicles, popularly known as drone. According to Bureau of Investigative Journalism data available in January 2014, there have been nearly four hundred CIA drone strikes in the first five years of the Obama administration. The majority, about 330, were in Pakistan; however, the CIA has also launched strikes in Yemen and Somali. The bureau estimates that the strikes have killed more than 2,400 people, including at least 273 civilians.[37] By comparison, there are 136 known detainees associated with the CIA's "enhanced interrogation" and extraordinary rendition programs, although the programs may have involved an additional, unknown number of detainees.[38]

Superficially, the "enhanced interrogation" and drone programs have little in common. The intended purpose of inflicting pain on detainees by "enhanced interrogation" was to extract information to prevent future terrorist attacks. The detainees were meant to remain alive. Drones, in contrast, are used, alongside more traditional forms of human intelligence, to collect the information necessary to prevent a future terrorist attack and, subsequently, eliminate the threat of that attack by killing the terrorists or militants involved in planning and executing it.

"Enhanced interrogation," moreover, is highly personal. Interrogators and soldiers encounter detainees face to face. Those who implement the "enhanced" techniques must, at one point or another, physically meet—touch the very body of—those on whom the techniques are used. Unmanned aerial vehicles contain, in their name, their innovation: they are unmanned. The "pilot" of a drone controls the machine remotely and surveys the battlefield surrounding the drone through a monitor. In media accounts, drone pilots have described how this remoteness brings, counterintuitively, excruciating proximity to violence. From the safety of their remote rooms, drone pilots survey their potential targets for extended periods of time, getting to know their targets in ways that traditional pilots do not. The drone's gaze—and, so, the pilots gaze—does not flinch even from the carnage of a missile strike.[39] Even so, it is indisputable that drone pilots do not encounter their potential targets face to face in the traditional sense. Nor is the sensory experience of the drone pilot as immediate or vivid as it is for torturers, who feel, hear, and smell the suffering they cause.

Most important, while there is an absolute prohibition on torture in domestic and international law, drones exist in a grayer area. They are treated by their proponents as both ordinary and extraordinary. As the former, the use of drones strikes to kill alleged enemies is continuous with more traditional forms of airstrikes and, so, seemingly lawful and legitimate. As the latter, drones are, for being unmanned, wholly discontinuous with traditional forms of military action and, so, certain restrictions on military action do not apply to drones. This was made apparent when the Obama administration argued that U.S. use of drones in Libya did not require congressional authorization under the War Powers Resolution because "U.S. operations do not involve sustained fighting or active exchanges of fire with hostile forces, nor do they involve the presence of U.S. ground troops, U.S. casualties or a serious threat thereof, or any significant chance of escalation into a conflict characterized by those factors."[40]

There are real, meaningful differences between "enhanced interrogation" and drones. But there are certain points of contact between the two programs and, especially, how they are understood and discussed that are worthy of discussion. I focus on two here. The first explores the ways that drones resolve the problem of detaining terrorists. The second explores the rhetorical tactics that Bush and Obama share when legitimating the CIA's two counterterror programs.

The Problem of Detention and the Solution of Death

Having prohibited the CIA from operating detention facilities and having promised to close Guantánamo, the Obama administration faced a problem: what to do with "high-value" detainees captured outside the United States. Such detainees could not be brought to Guantánamo. Doing so would only reverse the effort to close the facility. Interrogating foreigners at federal prisons was also fraught, as Republicans in Congress have consistently resisted the administration's efforts to transfer existing detainees to federal facilities or hold new ones domestically.

In the face of these challenges, the United States has captured very few alleged terrorists or militants outside of Afghanistan and Iraq. Two especially high-profile ones—Somali Ahmed Abdulkadir Warsame, captured in 2011, and Libyan Abu Anas al-Libi, captured in 2013—were both held and interrogated on Navy ships. Warsame was held for two months on a ship before being transferred to federal custody in New York.[41] Indicted in federal court, Warsame pleaded guilty to nine charges, including to providing material support to al-Qaeda.[42] Al-Libi was held in similar conditions for over a week before being transferred to federal custody in New York.[43] The transfer was met with criticism from Senate Republicans, including from moderates Lindsey Graham and Kelly Ayotte, who argued that al-Libi should be held in Guantánamo and tried before a military commission.[44] In October 2013, he pleaded not guilty to charges related to terrorism.

The June 2014 capture of Ahmed Abu Khattala, the alleged ringleader of the attack on the U.S. embassy in Benghazi, led to a similar outcome and debate. Reports suggested that Abu Khattala was, after capture, held for interrogation on a navy ship. Though Republicans, including McCain and Graham, argued that Abu Khattala should be held in Guantánamo, he was transferred to federal custody and indicted in federal court in Washington, D.C.[45] In the face of these difficulties, the Obama administration has relied on drones to watch and, at times, kill alleged terrorists and militants. Critics have wondered whether the administration's preference for drones comes from its inability to adequately resolve the detention problem. The administration, for its part, has denied these accusations.[46] While this is a difficult—perhaps impossible—allegation to definitively prove, it is indisputable that, over Obama's two terms, it has been politically expedient to kill, rather than capture, alleged terrorists.

The Equivalent Defenses of "Enhanced Interrogation" and Drones

There is another way that the Bush and the Obama administrations' counterterror policies are intertwined. As discussed in the previous chapter, advocates of "enhanced interrogation" describe the program as having undergone rigorous, internal review before being implemented in a restrained way. They also emphasize national security, the immanence of terrorist attacks, and the effectiveness of the program at thwarting those attacks.

Obama's case for drones is strikingly similar. In his May 2013 national security speech, Obama called the use of drones effective and, under the laws of war, legal. He then offered an elaborate defense of the program. Invoking arguments similar to those who advocate "enhanced interrogation," Obama

highlighted the amount of consideration that has gone into the drone program and the restraint with which it is used:

> Over the last four years, my administration has worked vigorously to estab-
> lish a framework that governs our use of force against terrorists—insisting
> upon clear guidelines, oversight and accountability that is now codified in
> Presidential Policy Guidance that I signed yesterday. . . . Beyond the Afghan
> theater, we only target al Qaeda and its associated forces. And even then,
> the use of drones is heavily constrained. America does not take strikes when
> we have the ability to capture individual terrorists; our preference is always
> to detain, interrogate, and prosecute. . . . America does not take strikes to
> punish individuals; we act against terrorists who pose a continuing and im-
> minent threat to the American people . . . And before any strike is taken,
> there must be near-certainty that no civilians will be killed or injured—the
> highest standard we can set.[47]

Discursively, Obama associates drones with an array of qualities of
democratic governance—oversight, accountability, and restraint. Critics
of the drone program, like those of "enhanced interrogation," challenge
these claims by associating drones with counterdemocratic qualities.
They draw attention to the lack of transparency surrounding the program
and the impossibility of verifying Obama's claims because of that lack of
transparency. They also draw attention to the excesses of the program,
namely, the civilian casualties caused by drone strikes. These critiques
have gained traction in the media and, to a lesser extent, in Congress,
but the drone program appears to be on surer footing than the use of
"enhanced interrogation." There has been no sustained expression of public concern in Congress—no series of hearings to rival the Senate Armed
Services Committee's seven on Abu Ghraib in 2004 or the committee's
investigation of interrogation policy after the 2006 election.[48] There has
also been no leak of classified information about the program to rival the
release of the Abu Ghraib photographs or, even, the interrogation log
of al-Qahtani.
The Obama administration's effort to sustain the legitimacy of the CIA
drone program benefits from two things. The first is that Congress has
offered minimal resistance to drones. Democrats, who aggressively pursued

investigations of detention and interrogation policies in the run-up to 2008 elections, have not been nearly as committed to their oversight of the Obama administration's drone program. There are, of course, notable exceptions. Former senator Mark Udall, of Colorado, and Senator Ron Wyden, of Oregon, have publically advocated for increased transparency on the matter, and Representative Alan Grayson, of Florida, helped organize a briefing with victims of drone strikes in Pakistan. Republicans, however, prefer to criticize the president on the grounds that he is weak on national security.[49] Among them, Rand Paul, a Kentucky Senator with libertarian leanings, has been the most vocal and consistent critic of drones, raising concerns over the lack of due process afforded U.S. citizens targeted by drone strikes. Paul's efforts, such as filibustering Obama's nomination of John Brennan to run the CIA, have drawn the ire of leading Republicans, including McCain and Graham, who accused Paul of "distorting," in McCain's opinion, the threat that terrorism poses.[50]

The CIA's drone program also benefits from the technological sophistication and the distancing effect of unmanned aerial vehicles. These qualities are easier to imaginatively fit to the contours of legitimate violence; indeed, they seem the very outcomes of modern and rational thinking. Drones have their excesses—the civilian casualties that are often the crux of critics' case against them—but they do away with the excesses of interpersonal violence, such as the gloating perpetrators confronting their victims (as in the Abu Ghraib photographs). And because they distance those who perpetrate the violence from the act itself, drones make it less likely that a critical documentary record—produced by Americans who witnessed the violence firsthand—will emerge. To be sure, the very nature of drones can be turned back against the machines and references to "killer robots" and to the *Terminator* films occasionally appear in writing on drones. But these images do not yet resonate the way that references to Nazi torture, communist methods, and the Spanish Inquisition do.

Though the political party advocating the violence has changed, the contours of the debate about drones are strikingly similar to those of the debate about interrogation. We have, on one side, advocates of these two forms of violence pointing to legal reviews, oversight, restraint, and efficiency; on the other, critics drawing attention to the excesses of the programs, the human carnage in the wake of each.

CONCLUSION

The easy transition from the Bush administration to the Obama administration—from torturing alleged terrorists to killing them with missile strikes fired by unmanned drones—testifies to the narrowness of congressional resistance and, especially, Democratic resistance to torture. This resistance was specific to torture, a form of violence that shocks the conscience of most contemporary observer, and not to the country's use of global violence more generally. It did not take aim at the discourses that make violence against "the enemy" thinkable, possible, and likely. In fact, "the enemy"—the sufferer of U.S. torture who was often no enemy at all—was largely excluded from the debate.

The reality of torture, as we typically encounter it in congressional hearings, is represented from the standpoint of perpetrators and observers. The accounts that constitute this reality do not always replicate the legitimating logic of "enhanced interrogation." The FBI's accounts of suffering at Guantánamo portray, in evocative terms, the vulnerability of suffering humans.[51] And yet, these representations are all object and no subject; they are torture's exteriority, what Americans who witnessed the act made of it. In them, detainees lack a personal and social identity. They are

> individuals, caught up in a particular historical moment. Each has his or her own specific story. But we do not know their stories; we know nothing about them as individuals and . . . almost nothing about the circumstances that brought them here. We can only recognize . . . a common condition of being human. . . . In this vacuum of information, [they] become icons of cruelty, of injustice, of man's inhumanity to man.[52]

The documentary record of U.S. torture is replete with such icons. Abu Ghraib's "Hooded Man" and "Leashed Man" may be the best known, but Guantánamo's naked detainee in a fetal position equally testifies to generic human cruelty. These icons altered the U.S. debate about torture; they revealed a sort of stark cruelty that only fringe actors on the American political scene—namely conservative talk-show hosts such as Rush Limbaugh—were willing to justify. In confronting these icons, however, we do not encounter U.S. torture in the terms of those who survived it.

Torture's place in survivors' worlds—or where torture has placed survivors in the world—remains out of sight.

Congress's discourse of acknowledgment further avoids grappling with the implications of torture for those who suffer it by emphasizing the harms of the practice on the United States. In this discourse, the harms of torture rebound off the body of detainees and onto the body politic of the country: the nation is weaker for having tortured, our international alliances break down, our global image erodes, we are diminished as a people. Torture, too, puts our troops at increased risk; it provides terrorists with propaganda and loses us the battle for the hearts and minds of the "Muslim world."[53]

I doubt neither the evidentiary value of official or quasi-official accounts of torture nor the rhetorical power of nationalistic framings. When the state's very own soldiers and interrogators document torture and when those allegations are inscribed in official documents it becomes difficult for political leaders to ignore or outright deny those allegations. A nationalistic framing permits officials to criticize torture by drawing on well-established discursive frames, such as that of "supporting the troops," and widely shared beliefs about American exceptionalism. It also allows critics to distinguish an antitorture position from a "pro-terrorist" position. McCain put this distinction best when he addressed Congress in 2005: "Let me close by noting that I hold no brief for the prisoners. . . . The enemy we fight has no respect for human life or human rights. They don't deserve our sympathy. But this isn't about who they are; this is about who we are. These are the values that distinguish us from our enemies."[54]

One can acknowledge that the U.S. tortured detainees in its custody without ever allowing those who survived that torture to address the perpetrators, policy makers, and populace implicated in the act. One can also acknowledge torture while suppressing awareness that violence tethers those who practice it to those who suffer it. One simply keeps survivors' claims unheard, closing political and legal stages to their claims and, especially, their demands for recognition, restitution, and justice. This, for the most part, is the sort of acknowledgment of torture that congressional Democrats offered—a recognition of the act but a denial of the victim.[55] And so another task, that of opening discourse to the survivors of American torture, remains. The challenge is not only to try to apprehend torture survivors' experiences from their perspectives. It is also to encounter and reckon with the social fate of violence and suffering: the ways that torture resides both in the bodies and psyches of survivors, as well as in the relations amid survivors, their families, and their communities. And it is to recognize that torture has irrevocably tangled the U.S. in the fates of uncounted Iraqis, Afghanis, and others.

I think often of the 2008 Physicians for Human Rights report, *Broken Laws, Broken Lives: Medical Evidence of Torture by U.S. Personnel and Its Impact*. The report pursues the reality of American torture by using the tools of medicine and psychology to secure the credibility of eleven former detainees to whom the organization spoke. Those skeptical of the country's alleged enemies—alleged insurgents, alleged terrorists, but often nothing of the sort—to speak honestly of their treatment are met with a neutral, medical discourse that seeks "independent determinations of the veracity and credibility" of testimony.[56] Each profile of the eleven former detainees includes an assessment of the extent to which physical and psychological evidence supports a detainee's testimony. "In each case," the report tells us, "the clinicians, all of whom have extensive experience evaluating both torture survivors and/or individuals involved in litigation, considered the individual evaluated to be credible. There was no evidence of deliberate exaggeration in any case."[57] In this way, *Broken Laws, Broken Lives* secures a position in public discourse for former detainees of the United States to address an often-skeptical American audience.

But *Broken Laws, Broken Lives* is not simply a medical report documenting and evaluating physical evidence of torture. It elicits narratives of torture and the continuing effect of it in the lives of the eleven detainees. These narratives often appear as fragments and are restated or summarized by the report's authors. Though brief, sparse, and retold, they remain affecting. In them, U.S. torture appears as more than an encounter between Americans and their victims; it is as torture always is: a force that displaces survivors from the world.

Adeel, who was captured in Pakistan in 2002 and held in Guantánamo until 2006,

> reported having nightmares of Guantanamo that force him to wake up in the middle of the night, and not being able to go back to sleep because he ponders his misery. He reported starting to panic when somebody walks behind him and that he often feels people are looking at him, which makes him think that he is not normal.[58]

Amir, an Iraqi man in his late twenties,

> described feeling helpless and having a "dark" sense of the future. Moreover, he articulated a sense of wounded pride and stolen honor. He explained that the dissemination of photographs from Abu Ghraib on the Internet has exposed his humiliation to the world. He is plagued with an acute sense of scrutiny wherever he goes.[59]

Adeel's and Amir's very selves have been fractured by U.S. torture. Adeel "suffers from blackouts and he has lost some of his memory capacity. He cannot remember the Koran very well, and he has no desire to read like he did before."[60] Amir "reported having trouble being naked in front of his wife. He described being scared by his wife's sudden, even slight movements in sleep. Flashbacks of his torture, especially the sexual aspects, would often intrude during sex with his wife."[61]

Some of the detainees have left their homes. Kamal, an Iraqi man in his forties, became "very concerned that his wife and children were afraid of him. He began living with his sibling and only visited his family once each week because he believed his visits made them uncomfortable."[62] Hafez, an Iraqi man in his fifties, avoided his home because it "reminds me of what happened."[63] Yasser, an Iraqi man in his forties, did so for similar reasons. His experiences in U.S. custody "have made him feel very 'uncomfortable' in his home region"; he left Iraq "to avoid the frequent reminders of his imprisonment."[64] Of the eleven detainees to whom Physicians for Human Rights spoke, "all but one," the reader learns, "feel utterly hopeless and isolated, and lack the ability to sleep well, work, or engage in normal social relationships with their families."[65]

Here, after all, is American torture. It stalks the human world still, indifferent to the politics of imagining otherwise.

Constructionism and the Reality of Torture

THE QUESTIONS AT THE HEART of this book express a fundamental concern for meaning making. How does torture become meaningful to the country that uses it? How does it become, merely, *visible* when it is practiced in secret and when powerful actors strive to keep it invisible?

My interest in these questions is both politically and intellectually motivated. I have been, for much of my life, a distant spectator to U.S. violence in Iraq. I recall, though only dimly now, a Saturday morning special, aired on ABC and hosted by Peter Jennings, explaining Operation Desert Storm in children's terms. I remember especially my relief when Jennings explained that Saddam Hussein could not bomb the United States.[1] Years later, Operation Desert Fox occurred during the winter of my senior year of high school. Operation Iraqi Freedom occurred during my senior year of college. President Bush, standing beneath a Mission Accomplished banner, infamously declared victory and an end to major combat operations on my twenty-second birthday. Seven years later, as I worked to finish an early draft of this book, President Obama made a similar declaration. It is a sign of profound distance to be able to mark the passing of one's easy life by the invasions of another's land. But that is the nature of spectatorship. And it has left me wondering—and this book is an outcome of that wondering—what this sort of spectatorship means, what sort of political and ethical stances it makes available, and how recognition of the suffering that violence causes can occur.

Intellectually, I find myself curious about how people produce—sometimes cooperatively, sometimes competitively—a sense of the reality of things. This is a general interest—one not really tethered to though not distinct from my concern for spectatorship—and I am rarely intellectually happier than when discussing how this shared sense of reality is made or, as the case sometimes is, fails to come off.

My political and intellectual concerns meet at torture. The pain of torture, Elaine Scarry famously argued, finds no refuge in language.[2] Darius Rejali has qualified this claim, saying that we tend to be able to speak well enough of pain that has some reference in the physical body—a scar, a wound grounds us. But when such a mark is absent, as is often the case when contemporary forms of clean torture are used, we are left unsure of ourselves.[3] So how do we respond? What words do we use to describe this sort of violence? How do we overcome uncertainty about the very reality of torture?

To address these questions, I have examined how small but influential groups of people construct torture as a political problem. To serve the narrative of this book, I have kept, in the text's body, discussion of general concerns related to the processes and materials of reality construction to a minimum. These topics are implied throughout the text, but I address them explicitly here in this appendix. I will address a few, interrelated issues related to the "reality" of social constructionism, which I define below. The first is the (alleged) trouble that reality gives constructionists. The second is how I have dealt with "reality" in this book. The third concerns the politics of this study, addressing how and why I have taken a particular side in the debate about U.S. torture.

SOCIAL CONSTRUCTIONISM'S REALITY PROBLEM

A constructionist study of discourse takes, as its primary concerns, how discourse is constructed, of what discourse is constructed, and what that constructed discourse does.[4] This book has concerned itself with these very issues, showing the process by which and the resources with which members of Congress produced accounts of detainee abuse and torture. I have also considered what these accounts have done and how they have contained or spread the toxicity of torture through the U.S. political structure.

There is, though, something that has consistently troubled this study. Constructionists, many who believe in the principles of this theory hold, are to remain indifferent to the very reality of the topics that they examine.

Constructionists working in the social problems tradition refer to this as bracketing the reality of problems, putting it aside, at least temporarily, for the sake of impartially studying the constructive work of the claims of those with whom one agrees with and those with whom one disagrees.[5] By bracketing reality, constructionists may build an adequate theory of how claims making occurs, a theory that can explain why claims are successful or not, no matter their basis in reality. Bracketing, for this study, would involve remaining analytically indifferent to whether Abu Ghraib *really* was an isolated incident and whether waterboarding is *really* torture to concern myself solely with the arguments about these very topics.

Although it has a contentious legacy, social constructionism is well-enough established in the social sciences that its tenets inform research that does not, explicitly, take a constructionist approach. We see this with studies of torture. Most of those studies that I have cited in this book have something to say about how contemporary societies assign meaning to the practice even though the primary concern of nearly all these studies has little or nothing to do with meaning making and reality construction. In *Torture: A Definitive History of the Practice,* Edward Peters writes about the emergence of moralized and sentimentalized vocabularies of torture in the eighteenth and nineteenth centuries, even though his primary concern is for the historical fit between torture, law, and the state.[6] In the final three chapters of *Torture and Democracy,* Darius Rejali addresses contemporary meanings of torture—what apologists say, why knowledge does not accumulate, and how many of us misrecognize contemporary torture by viewing it through a misleading "modern memory" of the practice's history. The reader encounters these final seventy or so pages of discussion only after having worked through nearly five hundred pages of meticulous description of how torture is used and why it is used in that way.

Despite the broad and often taken-for-granted contribution of constructionism to the social sciences, there are limits to what nonconstructionists will allow constructionists to say. When constructionists speak about topics that many sociologists oppose—inequality, oppression, or violence—as *constructs*, they learn that nonconstructionists are unwilling to go this far. I observed this firsthand at a panel on constructionism at the Society for the Study of Social Problems' 2013 meeting in New York City. During the panel, Kathleen J. Ferraro, a sociologist who has studied domestic violence, pantomimed a punch to illustrate her acceptance of constructionism up until the point where violence happens. The implication was clear: violence has an underlying reality, a brute reality, about which constructionism has nothing to say. Where the constructionist seeks an understanding of how suffering becomes meaningful, the nonconstructionist hears only a denial of that suffering.

In fact, violence is one of the realities on which constructionists frequently stumble.[7] When we encounter accounts of violence, we are liable to give up our commitment to bracketing the validity of particular claims. Constructionists are no more exempt from the large-scale cultural trends discussed in this book—especially the cultural abhorrence to interpersonal forms of violence—than are nonconstructionists. There is no contradiction between being a constructionist and "being somebody, a member of a particular culture, having commitments, beliefs, and a common-sense notion of reality."[8] Many of us constructionists, if asked to consider our responses to accounts of atrocity, would likely reveal humanist and liberal sensibilities, perhaps only wrapped up in an antiessentialist discourse. And many of us, when we observe allegations of interpersonal violence, are repulsed, outraged, moved, so much so that we wish to speak clearly and straightforwardly about that suffering with no worries about ontological gerrymandering[9] or being accused of vulgar constructionism.[10]

The stakes are heightened when violence is committed by the state and when victims of that violence are culturally devalued or abhorred enemies, as the case typically is with torture. Constructionists—no less than nonconstructionists—are acutely aware of the power of language to erase the claims of marginalized people and to authorize, even in the face of credible evidence, official denial. So we may doubt ourselves. Perhaps I should only say that I doubt myself. As a constructionist, one must ask oneself whether treating a detainee's claim that torture occurred with the same studied indifference as the state's claim that torture did not occur sustains the sort of collective uncertainty about torture that favors the state. Stanley Cohen, whose work on both moral panics and denial is highly influential with constructionists, gives up on constructionism, at least versions that approach relativism, for this very reason.[11]

In this book, I have clumsily treaded around constructionism's apparent reality problem. Surely, readers will notice that I believe that U.S. interrogators did torture detainees in their custody. I have occasionally juxtaposed the documentary record against claims that I do not believe hold up to a good faith interpretation of that record. Admitting this is to recognize that any attempt that I made to bracket the reality of torture while studying the array of congressional claims did not express a genuine indifference to that reality. Despite this violation of one of the rules of constructionism, I have attempted to avoid falling back into an objectivist stance, from which the reality of torture appears to be simply so—unconstructed, *really* real, *straightforwardly* real, in need of no human intervention to become meaningful.

THE REALITY OF TORTURE

What, then, do I take to be the reality of torture? And on what grounds, as a constructionist, do I support certain claims and not others?

In this study, I have treated the underlying reality of torture as a resource for claims making; participants in Congress's hearings mobilize certain statements, descriptions, and accounts of U.S. detention and interrogation practices to support their claims. This approach is consistent with the constructionist analytic approach developed by James A. Holstein and Jaber F. Gubrium, which treats the context of claims making as the set of circulating institutional, cultural, and social resources on which claims makers draw.[12] The descriptions of reality on which Congress draws frequently take the form of what Dorothy Smith refers to as textual realities, objectified accounts of everyday or lived realities that are inscribed in documents.[13] (The CIA's destroyed videotapes are a notable exception, as they are a sort of absent textual reality. It is the agency's act of destroying them to which claims makers assign meaning.)

Textual realities are important for several reasons. Texts give social action a permanence and mobility that they otherwise lack. Bruno Latour aptly captures this quality of texts in his writing on what he calls "immutable mobiles."[14] As "immutable," textually inscribed accounts or information hold steady despite transmission; they are the opposite of that childhood game of telephone, in which a statement transforms during transmission for being moved by simple, face-to-face communication. As "mobile," texts allow accounts of things that occurred in one place to be scrutinized in another. Human action is extended—spatially and temporally—through the production of texts. Much of modern, social organization relies on this capacity of texts—both material and digital texts—for their structure.

Texts bring the reality "out there"—events and problems—to sites of claims making. Claims makers may "read through," as Smith puts it, texts to the underlying reality of these events or problems and, then, speak credibly about that reality.[15] To be clear, I am not arguing that all texts or any text fully or objectively represents the events and problems inscribed in it. Rather, claims makers have the impression and give off the impression of being in direct contact with reality when grounding their claims in textual realities. This impression requires, though, that other claims makers and audiences accept that (1) a textual reality adequately reflects its underlying reality and (2) the claims maker adequately describes the textual reality. While Smith argues that texts may be "a constant point of reference against which any particular interpretation can be checked," this is an emergent quality.[16] It depends on claims makers and audiences accepting that such a text may be an adequate check on claims. We see evidence of this, in this study, in military characterizations of the ICRC report about detainee abuse in Iraq (chapter 3) and the FBI e-mails about Guantánamo (chapter 5). In both cases, military officials challenged these texts' account of the underlying reality to which they referred. When Senator Mark Dayton refused to accept General Keith Alexander's argument that the ICRC's report on Iraq and the Abu Ghraib photographs documented a single event (also chapter 3), we saw how audiences may resist claims makers' attempts to speak on behalf of a text.

The sociology of social problems has long recognized that descriptions of reality are resources for claims making. I have found the most helpful work on this to be Joel Best's study of rhetoric in claims making, in which Best identifies ground statements—the "basic facts which serve as the foundation for the discussion which follows"—as one component of claims making.[17] Best recognized that grounds statements—those basic facts—are themselves socially constructed, even as they are incorporated into subsequent constructive work. He also identified statistics as one form of a ground statement. John M. Johnson identified a second form that I have discussed in this book—horror stories, "emotionally provocative stories about violence" (against children, in Johnson's case).[18] By recognizing that claims makers' ground statements are often, though not always, textually inscribed, social problems researchers can recognize a few important things about the claims-making process.

First, the texts that provide ground statements for claims makers have their own histories, typically organizational ones. Like the claims of which their accounts are part, textual realities are themselves constructed. We can better unpack claims if we follow texts backward to their point of construction and forward to the various sites where they are mobilized. Doing this, we can show how the construction process saturates social problems; it is human activity all the way down to the very basic descriptions of problems that give them their social reality.

Second, textual realities take diverse forms. Some of them provide literary descriptions of reality; others offer quantified representations. Still others are visual in nature. Some aggregate, turning discrete events into more generalized categories ("abuse at the point of capture," is a good example of this; see chapter 3). Others dwell on the discrete and local. Traditional photographs do this, but so too does a description of an event written from the first-person perspective (the FBI's e-mails sometimes do this). Accounts of this type are valuable for two reasons. First, their vividness and level of detail allow the account maker to give off the impression of being a direct witness to the documented act.[19] Second, when the account is of an act of interpersonal violence, its vividness and detail tends to shock the conscience of those who read or view the account—for reasons, I think, having to do with prevailing beliefs about the practice of violence (see chapter 1). Recognizing this about textual realities, we can consider the variety of ways that reality may appear at sites of claims making and the different ways that claims makers put these representational forms to use. This is especially important because the contemporary context of claims making is characterized by high levels of technological and multimedia development. By paying attention to the diversity of representational forms—audio-video materials, digital materials, photographs, traditional reports and other documents—that constitute the reality of social problems, research in the area can show how this context is influencing claims making.

TAKING SIDES ON TORTURE: COMMENTS ON BRACKETING

While I believe that the tools of constructionism should be brought to bear on the topic, I have chosen not to maintain a studied indifference to the validity of claims about torture. My reasons for this are both pragmatic and political. Pragmatically, one must position one's research amid a literature to which one's work will contribute. I have located this study of congressional claims about violence against detainees in U.S. custody amid what we might call generic work on constructionism—those studies that highlight the constructionist process with relative indifference to the subject of that constructive work—as well as research on denial and torture. The latter literatures show my hand.

To study denial does not require one to side against those who employ the rhetorical tactic. Sociologists working in the ethnomethodological tradition, such as Tim Berard, describe "defense accounts" in much the same way that scholars of denial speak of their object of study.[20] The difference is this vocabulary is important. Defense accounts are, simply, conversational and rhetorical techniques in response to an allegation. Denial may be equally neutral to the object of the denial; the dictionary definition of the word does not assume that the event being denied actually occurred. But it is often given a pejorative meaning. Those who study denial typically have in mind those occasions when a person, typically one in a position of power, denies an event that did occur or a phenomenon, such as climate change, that does exist.

More tellingly, to even draw on the vast, important, and enlightening literature on torture is to imply that it is appropriate to apply lessons from other historical cases of torture to the U.S. There are certain claims makers who, I believe, would think that the lessons of historical instances of torture do not apply to the U.S. case, simply because those claims makers believe that U.S. "enhanced interrogation" techniques are not torture and are, in fact, designed to operate differently than torture does. And so this simple, scholarly act would appear the political act of taking sides in the debate about "enhanced interrogation."

This leads me to a second difficulty sustaining indifference to the validity of claims about violence against detainees in U.S. custody. I struggle to think of a term to use to name the reference of the claims I have examined that does not, itself, intervene in the debate. To label the reference of claims as "violence against detainees in U.S. custody" avoids the torture word, but I suspect that advocates of "enhanced interrogation" would find it unsuitable, for they do not advocate violence but rather legitimate interrogation techniques. Perhaps "pain-inducing interrogation techniques" would suffice, but I am still not sure that it would suit an advocate of "enhanced interrogation" and, even, some critics of the technique. The former believe that there is minimal pain associated with the techniques, while some critics of "enhanced interrogation," most notably the historian Alfred W. McCoy, describe the practices as psychological, not physical in nature.[21] It is also important to recognize that many of the practices that Congress debates are not, precisely, interrogation techniques. They are, in ways, precursors to interrogation. The detainee is left, nearly naked in his cell in a stress position *before* being interrogated, not always during that interrogation. To top it off, the phrase is aesthetically unpleasing—wordy, imprecise, and nearly bureaucratic in its dreariness. I tend, too, to agree with Orwell's sentiment that the opinion that work "should have nothing to do with politics is itself a political attitude."[22] So even if I were to settle on an adequately benign and seemingly neutral phrase for U.S. torture, I would not be avoiding politics; I would, instead, be practicing a slightly different sort of politics than the stakeholders in the debate about torture practice.

Finally and most important, I believe that a fair assessment of the evidence, a careful consideration of historical and legal precedent, and commonsensical understandings of the meaning of certain phrases ("severe pain," most notably) supports the claim that the United States has tortured detainees. Those who deny that "enhanced interrogation" constitutes torture simply do not engage with the vast and rich documentary record produced by several human rights organizations using different methodologies. Those who deny that "enhanced interrogation" is torture do not even fully engage with official investigations of detainee abuse, those conducted by the military, Department of Defense, and the CIA's inspector general. And perhaps intentionally, perhaps not, they define torture in a way profoundly inconsistent with legal and historical precedent and commonsense. These claims, I admit, presume that you share my beliefs about what constitutes "good evidence" of a historical event, a "good faith" application of legal definitions and standards, and "commonsensical understandings" of the meaning of certain words. This is a situated position, staked out from within a web of representations of torture, analyses of the Bush administration's legal reasoning, and meanings that are constructed and also shared, but not universally so.

As I am antitorture and also opposed to the collective denial of torture, I have written this book in a way that highlights the conditions under which an antitorture politics thrives and denial is effectively opposed.

(Technically, the book could have been written to emphasize how to effectively distinguish "enhanced interrogation" from torture, in order to sustain support for the latter. But that is not my purpose in this study, so I have declined to write the book in this way.) I have not, however, abandoned the task of giving a truthful account of my data. Just as "the map makers' task is to produce [accurate!] maps that are pertinent to the enterprises and interests of their societies,"[23] I have endeavored to produce a sociological mapping of political discourse with the hope that it will be pertinent to the work of recognizing and acknowledging torture.

In the end, these are all tentative positions and ones that I do not think will satisfy those with realist leanings. I do not claim that the reality of U.S. torture is undeniable for being "merely, obviously, objectively, unconstructedly" so.[24] Indeed, this book provides no shelter to those who would claim any such thing. U.S. torture *is* deniable, *has* been denied, and *will* be denied the next time the nation's politicians debate it. But I am sympathetic to those who believe that the brute fact of U.S. torture speaks for itself. We both want official denial to appear a bit less plausible, and we both are pursuing a politics that empathetically recognizes the suffering of survivors of torture. My hope is that this book will be of some use in that pursuit.

INTRODUCTION

1. Commission on Presidential Debates, "September 26, 2008, Debate Transcript," accessed April 19, 2004, http://www.debates.org/index.php?page=2008-debate-transcript.

2. Commission on Presidential Debates, "October 8, 2004, Debate Transcript," accessed April 19, 2004, http://www.debates.org/index.php?page=october-8-2004-debate-transcript.

3. Gary C. Jacobson, "The 2008 Presidential and Congressional Elections: Anti-Bush Referendum and Prospects for the Democratic Majority," *Political Science Quarterly* 124, no. 1 (2009): 1–30.

4. PollingReport.com, "Bush: Job Ratings," accessed April 26, 2014, http://www.pollingreport.com/BushJob.htm.

5. Throughout this book, "enhanced interrogation" appears in quotes. This is for two reasons. First, the term has no precedent in the United States of which I am aware. The term was invented, as far as we know, by the CIA to describe the painful detention and interrogation practices that they employed at their secret prisons during the early years of the war on terror. The term appears in the CIA inspector general's May 2004 report on the agency's detention and interrogation procedures. *Washington Post* investigative reporter Dana Priest appears to have introduced the term to the public on June 27, 2004, in a report on the CIA's decision to stop using "enhanced" techniques. In the article, Priest attributed the term to the CIA. Second, while there is still a lot we still do not know about how the CIA employed painful detention and interrogation practices, I believe that a fair assessment

of the documentary record, historical and legal precedent, and medical research demonstrates that the CIA, in fact, tortured detainees in its custody. The use of the term "enhanced interrogation," whether in good faith or cynically, obscures this. See CIA Office of Inspector General, *Counterterrorism Detention and Interrogation Activities* (Langley, Va.: CIA, 2004), accessed October 24, 2014, http://www2.gwu.edu/~nsarchiv/torture _archive/20040507.pdf ; Dana Priest, "CIA Puts Harsh Tactics on Hold; Memo on Methods of Interrogation had Wide Review," *Washington Post*, June 27, 2004. http://www.washingtonpost.com/wp-dyn/articles/A8534 -2004Jun26.html. For a few of the relevant documents and historical, legal, and medical analysis related to the CIA's "enhanced interrogation" techniques, see also International Committee of the Red Cross, *ICRC Report on the Treatment of Fourteen "High Value Detainees" in CIA Custody* (Washington, D.C.: International Committee of the Red Cross, 2007); Physicians for Human Rights, *Leave No Marks: Enhanced Interrogation Techniques and the Risk of Criminality* (Cambridge, Mass.: Physicians for Human Rights, 2007), https://s3.amazonaws.com/PHR_Reports/leave -no-marks.pdf.

6. On May 15, 2007, Fox News moderated a debate among Republican presidential candidates in Columbia, South Carolina. During the debate, Brit Hume asked the candidates to consider whether they would authorize the use of "enhanced interrogations" in order to gain information about a terrorist attack. Only McCain rejected "enhanced interrogation." On November 28, 2007, CNN and YouTube jointly held a debate among Republican presidential candidates in St. Petersburg, Florida. During the debate, Mitt Romney refused to follow McCain's public denunciation of waterboarding as torture, arguing that he did not believe it to be "wise for us to describe precisely what techniques we will use in interrogating people" (Federal News Service, "Republican Presidential Debate in South Carolina," *New York Times*, May 15, 2007, http://www.nytimes .com/2007/05/15/us/politics/16repubs-text.html; CNN, "Part II: CNN/ YouTube Republican Presidential Debate Transcript," November 29, 2007, http://www.cnn.com/2007/POLITICS/11/28/debate.transcript.part2/).

7. Charlie Savage, "Election Will Decide Future of Interrogation Methods for Terrorism Suspects," *New York Times*, September 27, 2012, http://www .nytimes.com/2012/09/28/us/politics/election-will-decide-future-of -interrogation-methods-for-terrorism-suspects.html.

8. Darius Rejali, "Review Essays: 'American Torture Debates,'" *Human Rights Review* 9, no. 3 (2008): 393–400, doi:10.1007/s12142-007-0056-9.

9. Joel Best, *Social Problems* (New York: Norton, 2008); Bryan D. Jones and Frank R. Baumgartner, *The Politics of Attention: How Government Prioritizes Problems* (Chicago: University of Chicago Press, 2005); Malcolm Spector and John I. Kitsuse, *Constructing Social Problems* (New York: de Gruyter, 1987).

10. Jones and Baumgartner, *Politics of Attention*, 43–45.

11. Stanley Cohen, *States of Denial: Knowing About Atrocities and Suffering* (Malden, Mass.: Blackwell, 2001).

12. Anne E. Goldfeld et al., "The Physical and Psychological Sequelae of Torture: Symptomatology and Diagnosis," *JAMA* 259, no. 18 (May 13, 1988): 2725–29, doi:10.1001/jama.1988.03720180051032; C. Gorst-Unsworth and E. Goldenberg, "Psychological Sequelae of Torture and Organised Violence Suffered by Refugees from Iraq: Trauma-Related Factors Compared with Social Factors in Exile," *The British Journal of Psychiatry* 172, no. 1 (January 1, 1998): 90–94, doi:10.1192/bjp.172.1.90; Metin Basoglu, *Torture and Its Consequences: Current Treatment Approaches* (New York: Cambridge University Press, 1992).

13. Frantz Fanon, *The Wretched of the Earth* (New York: Grove Press, 1963); Martha Knisely Huggins, Mika Haritos-Fatouros, and Philip G. Zimbardo, *Violence Workers: Police Torturers and Murderers Reconstruct Brazilian Atrocities* (Berkeley: University of California Press, 2002); Joshua E. S. Phillips, *None of Us Were Like This Before: American Soldiers and Torture* (New York: Verso, 2010).

14. Ronald D. Crelinsten, "The World of Torture: A Constructed Reality," *Theoretical Criminology* 7, no. 3 (2003): 293–318, doi:10.1177/1362480603007003; Crelinsten "How to Make a Torturer," *Index on Censorship* 34, no. 1 (2005): 72–77, doi:10.1080/03064220512331339508.

15. Amnesty International, *Report on Torture* (New York: Farrar, Straus and Giroux, 1975); Darius Rejali, *Torture and Democracy* (Princeton, N.J.: Princeton University Press, 2007); Elaine Scarry, *The Body in Pain: The Making and Unmaking of the World* (New York: Oxford University Press, 1985).

16. Rejali, *Torture and Democracy*, 31.

17. Thomas P. Carr, *Hearings in the House of Representatives: A Guide for Preparation and Procedure* (Washington, D.C.: Congressional Research Service, 2006).

18. Richard C. Sachs, *Hearings in the US Senate: A Guide for Preparation and Procedure* (Washington, D.C.: Congressional Research Service, 2003).

19. Barbara Hinckley, *Stability and Change in Congress* (New York: Harper and Row, 1971), quoted in Jeffery C. Talbert, Bryan D. Jones, and Frank R. Baumgartner, "Nonlegislative Hearings and Policy Change in Congress," *American Journal of Political Science* 39, no. 2 (1995): 389–90, doi:10.2307/2111618.

20. Ibid., 389.

21. Sachs, *Hearings in the US Senate*, 11.

22. Talbert, Jones, and Baumgartner, "Nonlegislative Hearings and Policy Change in Congress," 389.

23. Sarah Babb, *Behind the Development Banks: Washington Politics, World Poverty, and the Wealth of Nations* (Chicago: University of Chicago Press, 2009).

24. G. R. Boynton, "When Senators and Publics Meet at the Environmental Protection Subcommittee," *Discourse and Society* 2, no. 2 (1991): 131–55, doi:10.1177/0957926591002002001.

25. Jones and Baumgartner, *Politics of Attention*.

26. Joel Best, *Threatened Children: Rhetoric and Concern About Child-Victims* (Chicago: University of Chicago Press, 1990); Gary Mucciaroni, *Deliberative Choices: Debating Public Policy in Congress* (Chicago: University of Chicago Press, 2006).

27. Jeffrey C. Alexander, "Cultural Pragmatics: Social Performance Between Ritual and Strategy," *Sociological Theory* 22, no. 4 (2004): 527–73, doi:10.1111/j.0735-2751.2004.00233.x; Leigh Payne, *Unsettling Accounts: Neither Truth nor Reconciliation in Confessions of State Violence* (Durham, N.C.: Duke University Press, 2008).

28. Babb, *Behind the Development Banks*, xiv.

29. C. Wright Mills, "The Structure of Power in American Society," *The British Journal of Sociology* 9, no. 1 (1958): 29–41, doi:10.2307/587620; G. William Domhoff, *The Higher Circles: The Governing Class* (New York: Vintage, 1970).

30. Richard Jackson, "Language, Policy, and the Construction of a Torture Culture in the War on Terrorism," *Review of International Studies* 33, no. 3 (2007): 353–71, doi:10.1017/S0260210507007553; Gregory Hooks and Clayton Mosher, "Outrages Against Personal Dignity: Rationalizing Abuse and Torture in the War on Terror," *Social Forces* 83, no. 4 (2005): 1627–45, doi:10.1353/sof.2005.0068; Marnia Lazreg, *Torture and the Twilight of Empire: From Algiers to Baghdad* (Princeton, N.J.: Princeton University Press, 2008).

31. Rejali, *Torture and Democracy*, 411.

32. Ibid., 412.

33. Associated Press, "Bush: 'We Do Not Torture' Terror Suspects," November 7, 2005, http://www.msnbc.msn.com/id/9956644/ns/us_news-security/t /bush-we-do-not-torture-terror-suspects/.

34. Rejali, *Torture and Democracy*, 10.

35. Domhoff, *The Higher Circles*, 113.

36. Nelson Phillips, *Discourse Analysis: Investigating Processes of Social Construction* (Thousand Oaks, Calif.: Sage, 2002), 4.

37. Ibid., 6.

38. Under the umbrella term of "discourse analysis" is a variety of approaches to the study of texts and talk. Discourse analysts differ on the extent to which they focus on contextual factors to make sense of their data, microprocesses of talk and conversation, and the degree of neutrality with which they treat the claims that they study. Discourse analysts also may differ on what they mean by "discourse." On the one hand, some simply mean texts and talk. Those working in a Foucauldian tradition, on the other hand, may also study the very materiality of institutions—e.g., the design of prisons—as part of discourse. This study is grounded in a variety of constructionist approaches to the study of knowledge production and meaning making, including actor-network theory, social problems theory, and institutional ethnography. I borrow from the analytic vocabulary of these approaches, as needed, to make sense of my data. Given the sort of "opportunistic" constructionism I practice here, my approach to the study of discourse has general features in common with those of other analysts who study the ways that texts and talk produce, organize, and stabilize intersubjective understandings of reality. For instance, my approach to the study of discourse shares several features with Jonathan Potter and Alexa Hepburn's discursive constructionism (see Jonathan Potter and Alexa Hepburn, "Discursive Constructionism," *Handbook of Constructionist Research* [2008]: 275–93). In particular, my approach treats discourse as "constructed" and "constructive" (277). As the former, discourse is "assembled from a range of different resources with different degrees of structural organization." For my purposes, the rhetorical forms of denial and the arguments that U.S. politicians accept as fact are especially potent resources. As the latter, discourse is constructive in that "these assemblages . . . put together and stabilize version of world." In this book, the stabilization and destabilization of torture as a political fact is my primary concern. Finally, my approach to the study of discourse shares discursive constructionism's concern for how

discourse is situated conversationally (although this is not a primary concern of mine), institutionally, and rhetorically. My approach differs from discursive constructionism in two ways. First, I am occasionally willing to move beyond the discourse that I examine "to the objects or events that seem to be the topic of such discourse," which is a strategy Potter and Hepburn reject (275). (I discuss this further in the appendix.) Second, I tend not to focus on the microdynamics of discourse, which is one of the primary concerns for Potter and Hepburn. Rather, I focus on broad shifts in the stabilized patterns of meaning for detainee abuse and torture in Congress, illustrating specific instances or expressions of these stabilized patterns and the use of discursive resources in them.

39. See Carl W. Roberts, ed., *Text Analysis for the Social Sciences* (New York: Routledge, 1997).

40. Colin Jerolmack, "How Pigeons Became Rats: The Cultural-Spatial Logic of Problem Animals," *Social Problems* 55, no. 1 (2008): 76, doi:10.1525 /sp.2008.55.1.72.

1. THE TORTURE WORD

1. U.S. Department of Defense, "Defense Department Operational Update Briefing," May 4, 2004, http://www.defenselink.mil/transcripts/transcript .aspx?transcriptid=2973.

2. Stanley Cohen, *States of Denial: Knowing About Atrocities and Suffering* (Malden, Mass.: Blackwell, 2001).

3. Darius Rejali, *Torture and Democracy* (Princeton, N.J.: Princeton University Press, 2007).

4. Ibid., 538.

5. John Langbein, *Torture and the Law of Proof: Europe and England in the Ancien Régime* (Chicago: University of Chicago Press, 1977), 3.

6. Edward Peters, *Torture* (New York: Blackwell, 1985), 150.

7. Cesare Beccaria, *On Crimes and Punishments*, trans. David Young (Indianapolis, Ind.: Hackett, 1986), 30.

8. Voltaire, "Torture," in *A Philosophical Dictionary*, vol. 7 of *The Works of Voltaire, a Contemporary Version*, trans. William F. Fleming (New York: E.R. DuMont, 1901), 118–19.

9. Henry C. Lea, *Superstition and Force: Essays on the Wager of Law, the Wager of Battle, the Ordeal, Torture*, 1st ed. (Philadelphia: Collins, 1866), 386.

10. William Edward Hartpole Lecky, *History of the Rise and Influence of the Spirit of Rationalism in Europe*, 4th ed. (London: Longmans, Green, and Co., 1870), 332.

11. Peters, *Torture*, 144.

12. UN General Assembly, *The Universal Declaration of Human Rights* 1948, accessed October 17, 2014, http://www.un.org/en/documents/udhr/; UN General Assembly, *Convention Against Torture and Other Cruel, Inhuman, or Degrading Treatment or Punishment*, 1984, accessed October 17, 2014, http://www.ohchr.org/EN/ProfessionalInterest/Pages/CAT.aspx.

13. Michel Foucault, *Society Must Be Defended: Lectures at the Collège De France, 1975–76* (New York: Picador, 2003); Marina A. Llorente, "Civilization Versus Barbarism," in *Collateral Language: A User's Guide to America's New War*, ed. John Collins and Ross Glover (New York: New York University Press, 2002), 39–51.

14. Quoted in Peters, *Torture*, 146, emphasis added.

15. Randall Collins, "Three Faces of Cruelty: Towards a Comparative Sociology of Violence," *Theory and Society* 1, no. 4 (1974): 431, doi:10.1007/BF00160802.

16. Henry C. Lea, *Superstition and Force: Essays on the Wager of Law, the Wager of Battle, the Ordeal, Torture*, 2nd ed. (1870; reprint, New York: Haskell House Publishers, 1971), 457.

17. Jean-Paul Sartre, *Colonialism and Neocolonialism* (New York: Routledge, 2001), 35.

18. Amnesty International, *Report on Torture* (New York: Farrar, Straus and Giroux, 1975), 7.

19. Piet van Reenen and Dan Jones, "Torture: What Can Be Done," in *A Glimpse of Hell: Reports on Torture Worldwide*, ed. Duncan Forrest (New York: New York University Press, 1996), 197–210; Amnesty International, *Amnesty International Report 2013: The State of the World's Human Rights* (London: Amnesty International, 2013).

20. Marnia Lazreg, *Torture and the Twilight of Empire: From Algiers to Baghdad* (Princeton, N.J.: Princeton University Press, 2008); Christopher J. Einolf, "The Fall and Rise of Torture: A Comparative and Historical Analysis," *Sociological Theory* 25, no. 2 (2007): 101–21, doi:10.1111/j.1467-9558.2007.00300.x.

21. Rejali, *Torture and Democracy*; Thomas Risse and Kathryn Sikkink, "The Socialization of International Human Rights Norms Into Domestic Practice: Introduction," in *The Power of Human Rights: International Norms and*

Domestic Change, ed. T. Risse-Kappen et al. (New York: Cambridge University Press, 1999), 5.

22. Ryan Goodman and Derek Jinks, "How to Influence States: Socialization and International Human Rights Law," *Duke Law Journal* 54, no. 3 (2004): 621–703, http://www.jstor.org/stable/40040439; Thomas Risse, "International Norms and Domestic Change: Arguing and Communicative Behavior in the Human Rights Area," *Politics and Society* 27, no. 4 (1999): 529–59, doi:10.1177/0032329299027004004; Eran Shor, "Conflict, Terrorism, and the Socialization of Human Rights Norms: The Spiral Model Revisited," *Social Problems* 55, no. 1 (2008): 117–38, doi:10.1525/sp.2008.55.1.117.

23. Rejali, *Torture and Democracy*.

24. As Jennifer J. Esala has pointed out to me, institutions other than the state may turn to nonmarking forms of violence when their public legitimacy is staked in the appearance of their being free from violence. Erving Goffman observed this of mental institutes: "if attendants in a mental ward are to maintain order and at the same time not hit patients, and if this combination of standards is difficult to maintain, then the unruly patient may be 'necked' with a wet towel and choked into submission in a way that leaves no visible evidence of mistreatment. Absence of mistreatment can be faked, not order" (Erving Goffman, *The Presentation of Self in Everyday Life* [Garden City, N.Y.: Doubleday, 1959], 45).

25. Talal Asad, "On Torture, or Cruel, Inhuman, and Degrading Treatment," in *Social Suffering*, ed. Arthur Kleinman, Veena Das, and Margaret Lock (Berkeley: University of California Press, 1997), 290.

26. Cohen, *States of Denial*.

27. Ibid., 104.

28. Ibid., 105; Duncan Forrest, Bernard Knight, and Morris Tidball-Binz, "The Documentation of Torture," in *A Glimpse of Hell: Reports on Torture Worldwide*, ed. D. Forrest (New York: New York University Press, 1996), 167–86.

29. Cohen, *States of Denial*, 105.

30. Cohen, *States of Denial*; Avery Gordon, *Ghostly Matters: Haunting and the Sociological Imagination* (Minneapolis: University of Minnesota Press, 2008); Rejali, *Torture and Democracy*.

31. Cohen, *States of Denial*, 105–6.

32. Mark Danner, *Stripping Bare the Body: Politics, Violence, War* (New York: Nation Books, 2009).

33. Cohen, *States of Denial*, 108.

34. Stephanie Athey, "Torture: Alibi and Archetype in U.S. News," in *Culture, Trauma, and Conflict: Cultural Studies Perspectives on War*, ed. Nico Carpentier (Newcastle, UK: Cambridge Scholars Publishing, 2007), 136.

35. Eric Bonds, "Indirect Violence and Legitimation: Torture, Surrogacy, and the U.S. War on Terror," *Societies Without Borders* 7, no. 3 (2012): 295–325, http://societieswithoutborders.files.wordpress.com/2012/10/bonds2012finalupdated.pdf.

36. Cohen, *States of Denial*; Risse, "International Norms and Domestic Change."

37. John Conroy, *Unspeakable Acts, Ordinary People: The Dynamics of Torture* (New York: Knopf, 2000); Rejali, *Torture and Democracy*.

38. David Luban, "Liberalism, Torture, and the Ticking Bomb," *Virginia Law Review* 91, no. 6 (2005): 1425–61, http://0-www.jstor.org/stable/3649415.

39. Cohen, *States of Denial*, 113–14.

40. Ibid., 113.

41. Risse and Sikkink, "The Power of Human Rights"; Shor, "Conflict, Terrorism, and the Socialization of Human Rights Norms."

42. Marvin B. Scott and Stanford M. Lyman, "Accounts," *American Sociological Review* 33, no. 1 (1968): 3, doi:10.2307/2092239; Frank Burton and Pat Carlen, *Official Discourse: On Discourse Analysis, Government Publications, Ideology, and the State* (Boston: Routledge & Kegan Paul, 1979).

43. William Benoit, *Accounts, Excuses, and Apologies: A Theory of Image Restoration Strategies* (Albany: State University of New York Press, 1995); Terri L. Orbuch, "People's Accounts Count: The Sociology of Accounts," *Annual Review of Sociology* 23 (1997): 455–78, doi:10.1146/annurev.soc.23.1.455; Leigh Payne, *Unsettling Accounts: Neither Truth nor Reconciliation in Confessions of State Violence* (Durham, N.C.: Duke University Press, 2008); Scott and Lyman, "Accounts"; Gresham M. Sykes and David Matza, "Techniques of Neutralization: A Theory of Delinquency," *American Sociological Review* 22, no. 6 (1957): 664–70, doi:10.2307/2089195.

44. Joel Best, *Threatened Children: Rhetoric and Concern About Child-Victims* (Chicago: University of Chicago Press, 1990).

45. Bruno Latour, *Reassembling the Social* (New York: Oxford University Press, 2005); Dorothy E. Smith, *Texts, Facts, and Femininity: Exploring the Relations of Ruling* (New York: Routledge, 1990); Dorothy E. Smith, *The Conceptual Practices of Power* (Boston: Northeastern University Press, 1990).

46. Michael Lynch and David Bogen, *The Spectacle of History: Speech, Text, and Memory at the Iran-Contra Hearings* (Durham, N.C.: Duke University Press, 1996), 114, emphasis original.

47. Smith, *Conceptual Practices of Power*, 75.

48. Sarah Babb, *Behind the Development Banks: Washington Politics, World Poverty, and the Wealth of Nations* (Chicago: University of Chicago Press, 2009), xiv.

49. Catherine Riessman, *Narrative Analysis* (Newbury Park, Calif.: Sage, 1993), 8–16, provides a more extensive discussion of these issues.

50. Derek Edwards, Malcolm Ashmore, and Jonathan Potter, "Death and Furniture: The Rhetoric, Politics, and Theology of Bottom Line Arguments Against Relativism," *History of the Human Sciences* 8, no. 2 (May 1995): 25–49, doi:10.1177/095269519500800202.

51. Rejali, *Torture and Democracy*.

52. Smith, *Texts, Facts, and Femininity*, 154.

53. Rejali, *Torture and Democracy*.

54. Joshua E. S. Phillips, *None of Us Were Like This Before: American Soldiers and Torture* (New York: Verso, 2010); Rejali, *Torture and Democracy*.

55. Rejali, *Torture and Democracy*.

56. Lazreg, *Torture and the Twilight of Empire*; Elaine Scarry, *The Body in Pain: The Making and Unmaking of the World* (New York: Oxford University Press, 1985).

57. Dora Apel, "Torture Culture: Lynching Photographs and the Images of Abu Ghraib," *Art Journal* 64, no. 2 (2005): 88–100, doi:10.1080/00043249.200 5.10791174; Lisa Hajjar, "Does Torture Work? A Sociolegal Assessment of the Practice in Historical and Global Perspective," *Annual Review of Law and Social Science* 5, no. 1 (2009): 311–45, doi:10.1146/annurev.lawsocsci .093008.131501; Mary Ann Tétreault, "The Sexual Politics of Abu Ghraib: Hegemony, Spectacle, and the Global War on Terror," *National Women's Studies Association Journal* 18, no. 3 (2006): 33–50, doi:10.1353/nwsa.2006.0064.

58. Darius Rejali, *Torture and Modernity: Self, Society, and State in Modern Iran* (Boulder, Colo.: Westview Press, 1994).

59. Don DeLillo, *Point Omega* (New York: Simon and Schuster, 2010), 65.

60. Luban, "Liberalism, Torture, and the Ticking Bomb," 1430.

61. Philip Smith, "Codes and Conflict: Towards a Theory of War as Ritual," *Theory and Society* 20, no. 1 (1991): 103–38, doi:10.1007/BF00160735.

62. Jinee Lokaneeta, *Transnational Torture: Law, Violence, and State Power in the United States and India* (New York: New York University Press, 2011).

63. David Garland, *Peculiar Institution: America's Death Penalty in an Age of Abolition* (Cambridge, Mass.: Harvard University Press, 2011); Philip Smith, *Punishment and Culture*.

64. Garland, *Peculiar Institution*; Smith, *Punishment and Culture*.

65. Claiming that people have a stake in making an allegation is one common way of discrediting them. Jonathan Potter, *Representing Reality: Discourse, Rhetoric, and Social Construction* (Thousand Oaks, Calif.: Sage, 1996).

66. Garland, *Peculiar Institution*; Herbert Haines, "Flawed Executions, the Anti-Death Penalty Movement, and the Politics of Capital Punishment," *Social Problems* 39, no. 2 (1992), 125-38, doi: 10.2307/3097033; Smith, *Punishment and Culture*.

67. Dan Eggen and R. Jeffrey Smith, "FBI Agents Allege Abuse of Detainees at Guantanamo Bay," *Washington Post*, December 21, 2004, http://www .washingtonpost.com/wp-dyn/articles/A14936-2004Dec20.html.

68. See Donald Rumsfeld's comparison of his use of a standing desk to forced standing in Guantánamo, in William J. Haynes, *Counter-Resistance Techniques* (Washington, D.C.: General Counsel of the Department of Defense, 2002), http://library.rumsfeld.com/doclib/sp/380/2002-11-27%20from%20 Haynes%20re%20Counter-Resistance%20Techniques.pdf; see also conservative talk-show host Joe Scarborough's comparison of the CIA's use of sleep deprivation to fraternity behavior, quoted in Media Matters Staff, "Scarborough Mocks Torture, Says of Sleep Deprivation: 'They Do That in Fraternities,'" *Media Matters for America*, August 25, 2009, http://mediamatters .org/video/2009/08/25/scarborough-mocks-torture-says-of-sleep-depriva /153844.

69. Paul Veyne, *Writing History: Essay on Epistemology*, (Middletown, Conn.: Wesleyan University Press, 1984), 20.

70. Ibid., 22.

71. William A. Gamson et al., "Media Images and the Social Construction of Reality," *Annual Review of Sociology* 18 (1992): 384, doi:10.1146/annurev. so.18.080192.002105.

72. Sarah Babb, " 'A True American System of Finance': Frame Resonance in the U.S. Labor Movement, 1866 to 1886," *American Sociological Review* 61, no. 6 (1996): 1034, http://0-www.jstor.org/stable/2096307.

73. R. S. Perinbanayagam, "The Definition of the Situation: An Analysis of the Ethnomethodological and Dramaturgical View," *The Sociological Quarterly* 15, no. 4 (1974): 521–41, doi:10.1111/j.1533-8525.1974.tb00912.x.

74. Jeffrey C. Alexander, "Cultural Pragmatics: Social Performance Between Ritual and Strategy." *Sociological Theory* 22, no. 4 (2004): 527–73. doi:10.1111 /j.0735-2751.2004.00233.x, 530.

75. Cohen, *States of Denial*, 249.

76. Ibid.

77 Payne, *Unsettling Accounts*.

2. THE HEARTBREAK OF ACKNOWLEDGMENT: FROM METROPOLITAN DETENTION CENTER TO ABU GHRAIB

1. CBS's report used the word "abuse" rather than torture or mistreatment in its title. This word quickly became the executive branch's and mainstream media's preferred label for the depicted violence. In this chapter, I follow this use of the word as a label for the depicted violence; however, it is important to recognize that this term was highly contested and my use of this term should not be understood as an endorsement of it. On the media's use of the term "abuse," see W. L. Bennett, R. G. Lawrence, and S. Livingston, "None Dare Call It Torture: Indexing and the Limits of Press Independence in the Abu Ghraib Scandal," *Journal of Communication* 56, no. 3 (2006): 467–85, doi:10.1111/j.1460-2466.2006.00296.x. On the use of the word "torture" to describe Abu Ghraib, see Amnesty International, "Pattern of Brutality and Cruelty—War Crimes at Abu Ghraib," Last modified May 7, 2004, http:// www.amnesty.org/en/library/asset/AMR51/077/2004/en/52b7f594-d5d9 -11dd-bb24-1fb85fe8fa05/amr510772004en.html; Mark Danner, *Torture and Truth: America, Abu Ghraib, and the War on Terror* (New York: New York Review Books, 2004); Edward Peters, "We Should Call Torture by Its Proper Name," *History News Network*, 2005, accessed June 2, 2014, http://hnn.us /articles/5352.html.

2. Fox News, "Bush Apologizes for Iraqi Prisoner Abuse," May 7, 2004, http:// www.foxnews.com/story/0,2933,119156,00.html.

3. George W. Bush, "Interview with Al-Ahram International," *American Presidency Project*, 2004, accessed April 19, 2004, http://www.presidency.ucsb.edu /ws/index.php?pid=63380#axzz1HAH1L2tI.

4. Other polls had public approval of President Bush's performance below 50 percent earlier in the year. Gallup's 1/29–2/1 and 3/5–3/7 polls in 2004 showed that 49 percent of the public approved of President Bush's performance; however, only after CBS's story on Abu Ghraib aired did Gallup's polls consistently have Bush's approval below 50 percent. Polling conducted by NBC News/*Wall Street Journal* was relatively consistent with this trend; while a late September 2003 poll found public approval of the president at

49 percent, this was the only pre–Abu Ghraib NBC News/*Wall Street Journal* poll that returned this result. After the release of the photos, this poll would find public approval of Bush at 50 percent just twice, in the polls conducted before and after his reinauguration in 2005. Polling conducted by Fox News/ Opinion Dynamics and Pew Research Center did not replicate these trends; both polls found public approval of the president at under 50 percent several times preceding CBS's report on Abu Ghraib. PollingReport.com, "Bush: Job Ratings (1)," accessed April 26, 2014, http://www.pollingreport.com /BushJob1.htm.

5. Michelle Brown, "The Abu Ghraib Torture and Prisoner Abuse Scandal," in *Crimes and Trials of the Century*, vol. 2, *From Pine Ridge to Abu Ghraib*, ed. S. Chermak and F. Y. Bailey (Westport, Conn.: Praeger Publishers, 2007), 305–23.

6. Jeffrey C. Alexander, "Culture and Political Crisis: 'Watergate' and Durkheimian Sociology," in *Durkheimian Sociology: Cultural Studies*, ed. Jeffrey C. Alexander (New York: Cambridge University Press, 1988), 187–224.

7. Ibid., 194–95.

8. Jason L. Mast, "The Cultural Pragmatics of Event-ness: The Clinton/Lewinsky Affair," in *Social Performance: Symbolic Action, Cultural Pragmatics, and Ritual*, ed. Jeffrey C. Alexander, Bernhard Giesen, and Jason L. Mast (New York: Cambridge University Press, 2006), 117.

9. David Petraeus as quoted in *Meet the Press*, transcript for February 21, 2010, NBCNews, February 24, 2010, http://www.nbcnews.com/id/35493976/ns /meet_the_press/t/meet-press-transcript-february/.

10. Federal Bureau of Investigation, "9/11 Investigation (PENTTBOM)," accessed on May 15, 2010, http://www.fbi.gov/pressrel/penttbom/penttbomb .htm; Federal Bureau of Investigation, "FBI Intelligence Timeline," accessed March 7, 2011, http://www.fbi.gov/about-us/intelligence/timeline.

11. Federal Bureau of Investigation, "9/11 Investigation (PENTTBOM)."

12. Office of the Inspector General, United States Department of Justice, *The September 11 Detainees: A Review of the Treatment of Aliens Held on Immigration Charges in Connection with the Investigation of the September 11 Attacks*, accessed June 6, 2014, http://www.justice.gov/oig/special/0306/full.pdf, 1.

13. According to the inspector general's review of the treatment of those held in Immigration and Naturalization Service (INS; precursor to Immigration and Customs Enforcement) custody, twenty-four of those held as a result of the PENTTBOM investigation were already in INS custody before September 11.

The remaining 738 were arrested after the September 11 terrorist attacks. Ibid., 2.

14. Deborah Sontag, "Who Is This Kafka That People Keep Mentioning?'" *New York Times*, October 21, 2001, http://www.nytimes.com/2001/10/21 /magazine/who-is-this-kafka-that-people-keep-mentioning.html; Amnesty International, "Amnesty International's Concerns Regarding Post–September 11 Detentions in the USA," 2002, accessed April 19, 2014, http://www .amnesty.org/en/library/asset/AMR51/044/2002/en/1823f2ff-d882-11dd -ad8c-f3d4445c118e/amr510442002en.html; Human Rights Watch, *Presumption of Guilt: Human Rights Abuses of Post-September 11 Detainees*, 2002, accessed April 20, 2014, http://www.hrw.org/reports/2002/us911/.

15. Office of the Inspector General, *September 11 Detainees*.

16. Ibid., 3.

17. Office of the Inspector General, United States Department of Justice, "Department of Justice Inspector General Issues Report on Treatment of Aliens Held on Immigration Charges in Connection with the Investigation of the September 11 Terrorist Attack," 2003, accessed June 12, 2014, http://www .justice.gov/oig/special/0306/press.htm.

18. Ibid.

19. Ibid.

20. Office of the Inspector General, *September 11 Detainees*, 143.

21. Ibid., 143–44.

22. Rolince has since been quoted in the media as an expert on interrogations and Nahmias, in his capacity as counsel to Michael Chertoff, former secretary of the Department of Homeland Security, attended meetings in 2005 with the FBI regarding the treatment of detainees at Guantánamo. In 2003, however, the events that would make Rolince and Nahmias relevant to public debates about torture had not yet occurred (Spencer Ackerman, "Ex-FBI Agent: Still No Evidence That Cheney's Torture Methods Work," *Washington Independent*, August 31, 2009, http://washingtonindependent.com/57273/ex-fbi-agent -still-no-evidence-that-cheneys-torture-methods-work; Mark Benjamin, "Did Chertoff Lie to Congress about Guantánamo?," *Salon.com*, August 28, 2007, http://www.salon.com/news/feature/2007/08/28/chertoff).

23. *Lessons Learned: The Inspector General's Report on the 9-11 Detainees, Before the Senate Committee on the Judiciary*. 108th Cong, 4 (2003) (statement of Patrick Leahy, United States Senator).

24. *Lessons Learned*, 16 (statement of Russ Feingold, United States Senator).

25. Nancy A. Naples, "The 'New Consensus' on the Gendered 'Social Contract': The 1987–1988 U.S. Congressional Hearings on Welfare Reform," *Signs* 22, no. 4 (1997): 945, doi:10.2307/3175224.

26. *Lessons Learned*, 19 (statement of Orrin Hatch, United States Senator).

27. Attorney General Ashcroft appeared in the Senate Judiciary's Department of Justice oversight hearing on June 8, 2004. The focus of this hearing was considerably broader than the committee's hearing on the inspector general's review, a fact symbolized by the hearing's title, *DOJ Oversight: Terrorism and Other Topics*. While the inspector general's findings were briefly discussed during this hearing, so too was the abuse at Abu Ghraib prison.

28. *Lessons Learned*, 19 (statements of Orrin Hatch and Russ Feingold, United States Senators).

29. Eric Lichtblau, "Threats and Responses: Detainees; Treatment of Detained Immigrants Is Under Investigation," *New York Times*, June 26, 2003, http://www.nytimes.com/2003/06/26/us/threats-responses-detainees-treatment-detained-immigrants-under-investigation.html.

30. Edward Walsh, "Treatment of Detainees Defended; FBI Official Says Risks Justified Policy," *Washington Post*, June 26, 2003.

31. *Review of Department of Defense Detention and Interrogation Operations, Day 1, Before the Senate Committee on Armed Services*,108th Cong. 2 (2004) (statement of John Warner, United States senator).

32. Ibid.

33. Ibid., 3 (statement of Carl Levin, U.S. senator).

34. Ibid., 5 (statement of Donald Rumsfeld, secretary of the Department of Defense).

35. *Lessons Learned*, 3 (statement by Orrin Hatch, United States senator).

36. On the role of beliefs, values, and symbols in U.S. political discourse, see Jeffrey C. Alexander and Philip Smith, "The Discourse of American Civil Society: A New Proposal for Cultural Studies," *Theory and Society* 22, no. 2 (1993): 151–207, doi:10.1007/BF00993497.

37. *Lessons Learned*, 8 (statement by Glenn A. Fine, inspector general of the Department of Justice).

38. Bruno Latour, *Science in Action* (Cambridge, Mass.: Harvard University Press, 1987); Bruno Latour and Steve Woolgar, *Laboratory Life: The Construction of Scientific Facts* (Princeton, N.J.: Princeton University Press, 1986).

39. *Lessons Learned,* 14 (statements of Glenn A. Fine, inspector general of the Department of Justice, and Saxby Chambliss, United States senator).

40. Ibid., 27 (statement by Henry Lappin, director of the Federal Bureau of Prisons, Department of Justice).

41. Cohen, *States of Denial.*

42. Roland Barthes, *Camera Lucida: Reflections on Photography* (New York: Hill and Wang, 1981), 176 (emphasis in original).

43. *Review of Department of Defense Detention and Interrogation Operations, Day 1,* 108th Cong. 17–18 (2004) (statement of Donald Rumsfeld, secretary of the Department of Defense).

44. On the evidentiary value of photographs, see Kendall L. Walton, "Transparent Pictures: On the Nature of Photographic Realism," *Critical Inquiry* 11, no. 2 (1984): 246–77, doi:10.1086/448287; John Taylor, "Iraqi Torture Photographs and Documentary Realism in the Press," *Journalism Studies* 6, no. 1 (2005): 39–49, doi:10.1080/1461670052000328195; John Taylor, *Body Horror: Photojournalism, Catastrophe, and War* (New York: New York University Press, 1998); Susan Sontag, *Regarding the Pain of Others* (New York: Picador, 2003); Susan Sontag, *On Photography* (New York: Farrar, Straus and Giroux, 1977).

45. Dora Apel, "Torture Culture: Lynching Photographs and the Images of Abu Ghraib." *Art Journal* 64, no. 2 (2005): 88–100. doi:10.1080/00043249.2005 .10791174; Susan Sontag, "Regarding the Torture of Others," *New York Times Magazine* 23 (2004): 23–29.

46. W. J. Thomas Mitchell, "The Unspeakable and the Unimaginable: Word and Image in a Time of Terror," *English Literary History* 72, no. 2 (2005): 291–308, doi:10.1353/elh.2005.0019; Steven C. Caton, "Coetzee, Agamben, and the Passion of Abu Ghraib," *American Anthropologist* 108, no. 1 (2006): 114–23, doi:10.1525/aa.2006.108.1.114; Stephen Eisenman, *The Abu Ghraib Effect* (London: Reaktion, 2007).

47. Darius Rejali, "Speak Frankly About Torture," 2004, accessed July 4, 2010, http://academic.reed.edu/poli_sci/faculty/rejali/rejali/articles/Speak _Frankly.htm.

48. Quoted in Philip Gourevitch and Errol Morris, "Exposure," *New Yorker,* March 4, 2008, http://www.newyorker.com/reporting/2008/03/24/080324fa _fact_gourevitch.

49. *Review of Department of Defense Detention and Interrogation Operations, Day 1,* 108th Cong. 5 (2004) (statement of Donald Rumsfeld, secretary of the Department of Defense).

50. Ibid., 20 (statement of John McCain, United States senator).

51. Ibid., 68 (statement of Mark Pryor, United States senator).

52. Mike Allen and Bradley Graham, "Bush Lauds Rumsfeld for Doing 'Superb Job,'" *Washington Post*, May 11, 2004, http://www.washingtonpost.com/wp -dyn/articles/A15946-2004May10.html.

53. Alexander, "Culture and Political Crisis," 8; Jeffrey C. Alexander et al., eds., *Cultural Trauma and Collective Identity* (Berkeley: University of California Press, 2004); Joel Best, ed., *Images of Issues: Typifying Contemporary Social Problems* (New York: de Gruyter, 1995); Murray Edelman, *Constructing the Political Spectacle* (Chicago: University of Chicago Press, 1988).

54. Stephen Pfohl, "The 'Discovery' of Child Abuse," *Social Problems* 24, no. 3 (1977): 310–23, doi:10.1525/sp.1977.24.3.03a00020; Sontag, *Regarding the Pain of Others*; Sontag, "Regarding the Torture of Others"; Ivan Zverzhanovski, "Watching War Crimes: The Srebrenica Video and the Serbian Attitudes to the 1995 Srebrenica Massacre," *Southeast European and Black Sea Studies* 7, no. 3 (2007): 417–30, doi:10.1080/14683850701566377; Michael Peel and Vincent Iacopino, *The Medical Documentation of Torture* (San Francisco: Greenwich Medical Media, 2002); Darius Rejali, *Torture and Democracy* (Princeton, N.J.: Princeton University Press, 2007).

55. Donna Haraway, "Situated Knowledges: The Science Question in Feminism and the Privilege of Partial Perspective," *Feminist Studies* 14, no. 3 (1988): 575–99, http://www.jstor.org/stable/3178066; Latour and Woolgar, *Laboratory Life*; Catherine Riessman, *Narrative Analysis* (Newbury Park, Calif.: Sage Publications, 1993).

56. The IG's initial report acknowledged the presence of video cameras at MDC. The Office of the Inspector General (OIG), however, was initially unable to acquire the video recordings from these cameras and the office's report noted that "videotapes that could have helped prove or disprove allegations of abuse raised by detainees were not available. The lack of videotape evidence hampered the OIG's investigation of detainee abuse complaints." At the Judiciary Committee's hearing, Senator Hatch questioned Lappin on the availability of video records of abuse, and Lappin testified that the department maintained video records for only thirty days because the department has a "policy that an inmate has 20 days to file a complaint or a grievance with the warden on treatment or any other issues." Lappin also testified that the department still had some video recordings of officers forcibly removing detainees from cells and from at least one incident in which a detainee made allegations of abuse.

According to the OIG, in July 2003, it learned of a storage room in which an MDC special investigative agent believed there to be videos of interactions between detainees and MDC staff. The IG's office requested all videos and, on August 13, 2003, received a "largely unhelpful" inventory of tapes in the storage room; the inventory included over 2,000 tapes, none of which was made before February 17, 2002. In late August 2003, staff of the OIG visited MDC, received access to the storage room, and found "a significant number of boxes . . . clearly marked in large handwriting, 'Tapes' with dates beginning on October 5, 2001, and continuing to February 2002" (Office of the Inspector General, *September 11 Detainees*, 150; *Lessons Learned*, 37 [statement by Harley G. Lappin, director of the Federal Bureau of Prisons, Department of Justice]; Office of the Inspector General, U.S. Department of Justice, *Supplemental Report on September 11 Detainees' Allegations of Abuse at the Metropolitan Detention Center in Brooklyn, New York*, 2003, 40–41, accessed June 13, 2014, http://www.justice.gov/oig/special/0312/final.pdf).

57. Ibid., 41.

58. A LexisNexis Academic search of references to "Metropolitan Detention Center" in major U.S. and world publications following the release of the inspector general's supplemental report returned five unique articles on the report, two of which came from international sources. For U.S. coverage, see Leslie Casimir, "Jailers Abused Muslims: Report," *Daily News*, December 19, 2003, http://articles.nydailynews.com/2003-12-19/news/18248878_1_inspector-general-glenn-fine-verbal-abuse-federal-correctional-officers; Dan Eggen, "Tapes Show Abuse of 9/11 Detainees; Justice Department Examines Videos Prison Officials Said Were Destroyed," *Washington Post*, December 18, 2003, http://www.washingtonpost.com/ac2/wp-dyn/A11865-2003Dec18; Dan Eggen, "Audio of Attorney-Detainee Interviews Called Illegal," *Washington Post*, December 20, 2003.

59. Coalition Provisional Authority, "Coalition Provisional Authority Briefing," 2004, accessed June 12, 2004, http://www.iraqcoalition.org/transcripts/20040320_Mar20_KimmittSenor.html.

60. This information is based on a LexisNexis Academic search of newspaper articles mentioning "Abu Ghraib" with either "abuse" or "mistreatment" limited to these time frames.

61. Sontag, *On Photography*, 17.

62. Physicians for Human Rights, *Broken Laws, Broken Lives: Medical Evidence of Torture by U.S. Personnel and Its Impact: A Report* (Cambridge, Mass.: Physicians for Human Rights, 2008).

63. *Lessons Learned*, 2 (statement by Orrin Hatch, United States Senator).

64. Lichtblau, "Threats and Responses."

65. *Lessons Learned*, 30 (statement by Michael E. Rolince, acting assistant director in Charge, Washington Field Office of the Federal Bureau of Investigation).

66. Ibid., 14 (statements by Saxby Chambliss, United States senator, and Glenn A. Fine, inspector general of the Department of Justice).

67. Ibid., 25 (statement of Charles Schumer, United States senator).

68. Ibid., 25 (statement of Orrin Hatch, United States senator).

69. Ibid., 45 (statement of Orrin Hatch, United States senator).

70. Darren W. Davis and Brian D. Silver, "Civil Liberties vs. Security: Public Opinion in the Context of the Terrorist Attacks on America," *American Journal of Political Science* 48, no. 1 (2004): 28–46, doi:10.1111/j.0092-5853.2004.00054.x; Diane P. Wood, "The Rule of Law in Times of Stress," *University of Chicago Law Review* 70, no. 1 (Winter 2003): 455–70, http://www.jstor.org/stable/1600569.

71. *Lessons Learned*, 1 (statement by Orrin Hatch, United States senator).

72. Ibid., 22 (statement by Charles Schumer, United States senator).

73. Ibid., 32 (statement by Michael E. Rolince, acting assistant director in charge, Washington Field Office of the Federal Bureau of Investigation).

74. Edward Walsh, "Treatment of Detainees Defended; FBI Official Says Risks Justified Policy," *Washington Post*, June 26, 2003.

75. *Lessons Learned*, 22–23 (statement by Charles Schumer, United States senator).

76. Ibid., 10 (statement by Orrin Hatch, United States senator).

77. Ibid., 34 (statement by David Nahmias, counsel to the assistant attorney general, Department of Justice).

78. Ibid., 19 (statement by Glenn A. Fine, inspector general of the Department of Justice).

79. Ibid., 31 (statement by Michael E. Rolince, acting assistant director in charge, Washington Field Office of the Federal Bureau of Investigation)

80. Kevin R. Johnson, "'Aliens' and the U.S. Immigration Laws: The Social and Legal Construction of Nonpersons," *University of Miami Inter-American Law Review* 28, no. 2 (1996): 263–92, http://www.jstor.org/stable/40176418.

81. Susan Musarrat Akram and Kevin R. Johnson, "Race, Civil Rights, and Immigration Law After September 11, 2001: The Targeting of Arabs and Muslims," *New York University Annual Survey of American Law* 58, no. 3 (2002):

295–356, http://heinonline.org/HOL/LandingPage?handle=hein.journals /annam58&div=25&id=&page=.

82. *Lessons Learned*, 39 (statement of Russell Feingold, United States senator).

83. In the absence of a religious label, this rhetorical construction of the "September 11 detainees" differs, significantly, from later constructions of "Islamic terrorism." See Richard Jackson, "Constructing Enemies: 'Islamic Terrorism' in Political and Academic Discourse," *Government and Opposition* 42, no. 3 (2007): 394–426, doi:10.1111/j.1477-7053.2007.00229.x.

84. Gordon C. Chang and Hugh B. Mehan, "Why We Must Attack Iraq: Bush's Reasoning Practices and Argumentation System," *Discourse Society* 19, no. 4 (2008): 453–82, doi:10.1177/0957926508089939.

85. *Iraq: Status and Prospects for Reconstruction: Resources, Before the Senate Committee on Foreign Relations*, 108th Cong., 48 (2003) (statement of Lincoln Chafee, United States senator).

86. Robert Kagan, "America's Crisis of Legitimacy," *Foreign Affairs* 83, no. 2 (2004): 65–87, http://www.jstor.org/stable/20033903: 65–87; Mark Danner, *Stripping Bare the Body: Politics, Violence, War* (New York: Nation Books, 2009).

87. Stephen Biddle, "Seeing Baghdad, Thinking Saigon," *Foreign Affairs* 85, no. 2 (April 2006): 2–14. http://www.jstor.org/stable/20031907; Matthew Davis, "Bush Battles for US Hearts and Minds," *BBC News*, December 7, 2005, http://news.bbc.co.uk/2/hi/americas/4505506.stm.

88. Thanassis Cambanis, "Iraqi Detentions Fuel Anti-US Sentiment," *Boston Globe*, March 28, 2004, http://www.boston.com/news/world/middleeast /articles/2004/03/28/iraqi_detentions_fuel_anti_us_sentiment/.

89. On the discursive legacy of Vietnam, see Patrick G. Coy, Lynne M. Woehrle, and Gregory M. Maney, "Discursive Legacies: The U.S. Peace Movement and 'Support the Troops,'" *Social Problems* 55, no. 2 (2008): 161–89, doi:10.1525 /sp.2008.55.2.161.

90. *Review of Department of Defense Detention and Interrogation Operations, Day 1*, 108th Cong. 20 (2004) (statement of John McCain, United States senator).

91. Ibid., 59 (statement of Elizabeth Dole, United States senator).

92. Ibid., 17 (statement of John Warner, United States senator).

93. Ibid., 24 (statement of Edward Kennedy, United States senator).

94. Ibid., 42 (statement of Susan Collins, United States senator).

95. Ibid., 5 (statement of Donald Rumsfeld, secretary of the Department of Defense).

96. Eric Lichtblau, "Ashcroft Defends Detentions as Immigrants Recount Toll," *New York Times*, June 5, 2003, http://www.nytimes.com/2003/06/05/national/05TERR.html.

97. Federal Document Clearing House E-Media, "Rumsfeld Testifies Before Senate Armed Services Committee," *Washington Post*, May 7, 2004, http://www.washingtonpost.com/wp-dyn/articles/A8575-2004May7.html.

98. Jim Drinkard, Dave Moniz, and John Diamond, "Rumsfeld Faces Lawmakers," *USA Today*, May 7, 2004.

99. "Mr. Rumsfeld's Defense," *New York Times*, May 8, 2004, http://www.nytimes.com/2004/05/08/opinion/mr-rumsfeld-s-defense.html.

100. "An Inadequate Response," *Washington Post*, May 8, 2004.

101. The treatment of the "September 11 detainees" was discussed during a broader hearing on civil liberties *America After 9/11: Freedom Preserved or Freedom Lost?*, which the committee held on November 18, 2003. On June 15, 2005, the inspector general again appeared before the committee during a broader hearing, entitled *Detainees*, on the Bush administration's detention and interrogation policies post-9/11.

102. *Review of Department of Defense Detention and Interrogation Operations, Day 1*, 108th Cong. 7 (2004) (statement of Donald Rumsfeld, secretary of the Department of Defense).

3. ISOLATING INCIDENTS

1. Terry M. Neal, "The Politics of Abu Ghraib," *Washington Post*, May 12, 2004, http://www.washingtonpost.com/wp-dyn/articles/A18316-2004May11.html.

2. Commission on Presidential Debates, "October 8, 2004, Debate Transcript," accessed April 19, 2014. http://www.debates.org/index.php?page=october-8-2004-debate-transcript.

3. Joseph W. Schneider, "Social Problems Theory: The Constructionist View," *Annual Review of Sociology* 11 (1985): 209–29, doi:10.1146/annurev.soc.11.1.209.

4. The cartographic scale of a map is the ratio between "the amount of distance on the map" and "a particular distance on the earth's surface"; thus, when a map "shows a relatively small area of the earth," it is a relatively "large scale map." D. R. Montello, "Scale in Geography," in *International Encyclopedia of the Social and Behavioral Sciences*, ed. N. J. Smelser and P. B. Baltes (New York: Elsevier, 2001), 13,502.

5. *Review of Department of Defense Detention and Interrogation Operations, Day 1*, 108th Cong. 32 (2004) (statement by Robert Byrd, United States senator).

6. Ibid., 36 (statement by General Richard Myers, chair of the Joint Chiefs of Staff).

7. Ibid., 32 (statement by Robert Byrd, United States senator).

8. Ibid., 24 (statement by Edward Kennedy, United States senator).

9. Melvin Pollner, *Mundane Reason: Reality in Everyday and Sociological Discourse* (New York: Cambridge University Press, 1987).

10. David S. Cloud, Carla Anne Robbins, and Greg Jaffe, "Red Cross Found Widespread Abuse of Iraqi Prisoners," *Wall Street Journal*, May 7, 2004, http://online.wsj.com/news/articles/SB108384106459803859; David S. Cloud, "Red Cross Cited Detainee Abuse Over a Year Ago," *Wall Street Journal*, May 10, 2004, http://online.wsj.com/news/articles/SB108414473392906282.

11. International Committee of the Red Cross, *Report of the International Committee of the Red Cross (ICRC) on the Treatment by the Coalition Forces of Prisoners of War and Other Protected Persons by the Geneva Conventions in Iraq During Arrest, Internment, and Interrogation*, 2004, accessed April 20, 2014, http://www.globalsecurity.org/military/library/report/2004/icrc_report _iraq_feb2004.htm.

12. Cloud, Robbins, and Jaffe, "Red Cross Found Widespread Abuse."

13. *Review of Department of Defense Detention and Interrogation Operations, Day 2*, 108th Cong. 294 (2004) (statement by Edward Kennedy, United States senator).

14. Ibid., 352 (statement by Antonio M. Taguba, deputy commanding general for support, Coalition Forces Land Component Command).

15. In 2005, Alexander became the director of the National Security Agency, a position he held through President Barack Obama's first term and much of Obama's second. In 2010, Obama selected Alexander to also serve as the commander of U.S. Cyber Command.

16. Inhofe is likely referring to an article by Rajiv Chandrasekaran and Scott Wilson that appeared on the front page of the *Washington Post* on May 11, 2004. Rajiv Chandrasekaran and Scott Wilson, "Mistreatment of Detainees Went Beyond Guards' Abuse," *Washington Post*, May 11, 2004, http://www .washingtonpost.com/wp-dyn/articles/A15492-2004May10.html.

17. *Review of Department of Defense Detention and Interrogation Operations, Day 2*, 108th Cong. 512–13 (2004) (statements of James Inhofe, United States senator, Keith Alexander, deputy chief of staff, G-2, and Ronald Burgess, deputy chief of staff, J-2).

18. Ibid., 400 (statement of John McCain, United States senator).

19. Ibid., 401 (statement by John McCain, United States senator).

20. Ibid., 401 (statement by John McCain, United States senator)

21. Ibid., 401 (statement by Keith Alexander, deputy chief of staff, G-2).

22. Ibid., 5 (statements by Mark Dayton, United States senator, and Keith Alexander, deputy chief of staff G-2).

23. Ibid., 401 (statement by John McCain, United States senator).

24. Ibid., 505 (statements by Mark Dayton, United States senator, and Keith Alexander, deputy chief of staff, G-2).

25. *Review of Department of Defense Detention and Interrogation Operations Day 3*, 108th Cong. 565 (2004) (statement of Carl Levin, United States senator).

26. Ibid., 588 (statements of Robert Byrd, United States senator, and John Abizaid, commander, United States Central Command).

27. This is a fairly common way of resolving disagreements about events. See Pollner, *Mundane Reason*.

28. *Review of Department of Defense Detention and Interrogation Operations, Day 4*, 108th Cong. 687 (2004) (statement of Paul Mikolashek, inspector general of the Army).

29. Independent Panel to Review DOD Detention Operations, Final Report of the Independent Panel to Review DOD Detention Operations (Arlington, VA:.Independent Panel to Review DOD Operations, 2004), accessed October 24, 2014, http://www.defense.gov/news/aug2004/d20040824finalreport .pdf.

30. *Review of Department of Defense Detention and Interrogation Operations, Day 5*, 108th Cong. 1309 (2004) (statement of John Warner, United States senator).

31. Ibid., 1350 (statement of James Talent, United States senator).

32. Ibid., 1315 (statement of Dr. James Schlesinger, chair, independent panel to review Department of Defense detention operations).

33. Ibid., 1317 (statement of Dr. Harold Brown, member, independent panel to review Department of Defense detention operations).

34. Ibid., 1350 (statement of James Talent, United States senator).

35. On quantification and Abu Ghraib, see also Gregory Hooks and Clayton Mosher, "Outrages Against Personal Dignity: Rationalizing Abuse and Torture in the War on Terror." *Social Forces* 83, no. 4 (2005): 1627–45. doi:10.1353/sof.2005.0068.

36. *Review of Department of Defense Detention and Interrogation Operations, Day 5*, 108th Cong. 1323 (2004) (statement of Joseph Lieberman, United States senator).

37. Joel Best, *Threatened Children: Rhetoric and Concern About Child-Victims* (Chicago: University of Chicago Press, 1990), 62.

38. Jonathan Potter, *Representing Reality: Discourse, Rhetoric, and Social Construction.* Thousand Oaks, Calif.: Sage, 1996).

39. Stanley Cohen, *States of Denial Knowing About Atrocities and Suffering* (Malden, Mass.: Blackwell, 2001).

40. Montello, "Scale in Geography," 13502.

41. Dorothy E. Smith, *The Conceptual Practices of Power* (Boston: Northeastern University Press, 1990), 55.

42. Judith Butler, *Frames of War: When Is Life Grievable?* (New York: Verso, 2009); Susan Sontag, *Regarding the Pain of Others* (New York: Picador, 2003).

43. John M. Johnson, "Horror Stories and the Construction of Child Abuse," in *Images of Issues: Typifying Contemporary Social Problems*, ed. Joel Best (Hawthorne, N.Y.: de Gruyter, 1995), 17–31.

44. Jeffrey C. Alexander, "Cultural Pragmatics: Social Performance Between Ritual and Strategy," *Sociological Theory* 22, no. 4 (2004): 527–73. doi:10.1111/j.0735-2751.2004.00233.x; Joseph R. Gusfield, "Constructing the Ownership of Social Problems: Fun and Profit in the Welfare State," *Social Problems* 36, no. 5 (1989): 431–41; Bruno Latour, *Reassembling the Social* (New York: Oxford University Press, 2005); Latour, *Science in Action* (Cambridge, Mass.: Harvard University Press, 1987); Mara Loveman, "The Modern State and the Primitive Accumulation of Symbolic Power," *American Journal of Sociology* 110, no. 6 (2005): 1651–83; James C. Scott, *Seeing Like a State* (New Haven, Conn.: Yale University Press, 1999); Smith, *The Conceptual Practices of Power*.

45. Mark Danner, *Torture and Truth: America, Abu Ghraib, and the War on Terror* (New York: New York Review Books, 2004).

4. SADISM ON THE NIGHT SHIFT: ACCOUNTING FOR ABU GHRAIB

1. *Review of Department of Defense Detention and Interrogation Operations, Day 1*, 108th Cong. 4 (2004) (statement of Carl Levin, United States senator).

2. Ibid., 41–42 (statements of Stephen Cambone, undersecretary of Defense for Intelligence, and Donald Rumsfeld, secretary of the Department of Defense).

3. *Review of Department of Defense Detention and Intelligence Operations, Day 1*, 108th Cong. 42 (2004) (statements of Jack Reed, United States senator, Stephen Cambone, undersecretary of Defense for Intelligence, and Donald Rumsfeld, secretary of the Department of Defense).

4. *Review of Department of Defense Detention and Interrogation Operations, Day 2*, 108th Cong. 294 (2004), 340 (statements of Jack Reed, United States senator, and Stephen Cambone, undersecretary of Defense for Intelligence).

5. Ibid (statement of Jack Reed, United States senator).

6. Ibid

7. Ibid., 333 (statement of Antonio Taguba, deputy commanding general for support, Coalition Forces Land Component).

8. Ibid., 392–93 (statement of Keith Alexander, deputy chief of staff, G-2).

9. *Review of Department of Defense Operations, Day 3*, 108th Cong. 608 (2004) (statements of Lindsey Graham, United States senator, and Geoffrey Miller, deputy commander for detainee operations, Multi-National Force–Iraq).

10. Ibid., 581 (statement of Geoffrey Miller, deputy commander for detainee operations, Multi-National Force–Iraq).

11. Ibid., 582 (statement of John McCain, United States senator).

12. Ibid., 585 (statements of Pat Roberts, United States senator, and Geoffrey Miller, deputy commander for detainee operations, Multi-National Force–Iraq).

13. After the hearing, additional information was added to the hearing transcript. This information stated that "there were a total of eight instances of minor abuse requiring administrative action" (ibid., 604).

14. Ibid., 604–5 (statements of Saxby Chambliss, United States senator, and Geoffrey Miller, deputy commander for detainee operations, Multi-National Force–Iraq).

15. On July 22, 2004, Senator Carl Levin asked General Paul Mikolashek, the inspector general of the Army, about how he interpreted Miller's recommendation and General Taguba's criticism. Mikolashek, as well as the other witnesses who appeared before the committee (Secretary of the Army Les Brownlee and Chief of Staff of the Army General Peter Schoomaker), did not criticize the policy. Brownlee and Schoomaker both noted that it did not allow for abusive practices. See *Review of Department of Defense Detention and Interrogation Operations, Day 4*, 108th Cong. (2004).

16. Scott Higham and Joe Stephens, "New Details of Prison Abuse Emerge; Abu Ghraib Detainees' Statements Describe Sexual Humiliation and Savage Beatings," *Washington Post*, May 21, 2004, http://www.washingtonpost.com/wp-dyn/articles/A43783-2004May20.html.

17. *Review of Department of Defense Detention and Interrogation Operations, Day 4*, 108th Cong. 1006 (2004) (statement of Jeff Sessions, United States senator).

18. Michael Lynch and David Bogen, *The Spectacle of History: Speech, Text, and Memory at the Iran-Contra Hearings* (Durham, N.C.: Duke University Press, 1996), 214.

19. *Review of Department of Defense Detention and Interrogation Operations, Day 2*, 108th Cong. 287 (2004) (statement of Carl Levin, United States senator).

20. The document displayed in figure 4.1 is available in several of the Taguba report's annexes, including Annex 28, Annex 40, and Annex 93. This particular image of it was copied from Annex 40. Because publicly available versions of the Interrogation Rules of Engagement Slide are not of sufficient quality to publish, I have re-created this document in PowerPoint. My re-creation closely resembles the original; however, readers are encouraged to consult the document, which can be found in Annex 40 of Antonio Taguba's report. "JIDC Joint Interrogation and Debriefing Center," University of Minnesota Human Rights Library, Accessed June 16, 2014, http://www1.umn.edu/humanrts /OathBetrayed/Taguba%20Annex%2040.pdf.

21. *Review of Department of Defense Detention and Interrogation Operations, Day 3*, 108th Cong. 605 (2004) (Hillary Rodham Clinton, United States senator).

22. Ibid., 587 (statement of Ricardo Sanchez, commander, Multi-National Force–Iraq).

23. The date of this memorandum—September 14, 2003—conflicts with the date given by Sanchez during the hearing, September 12. The hearing transcript offers no explanation of this discrepancy; it is possible, though, that Sanchez confused the date of the October memorandum, October 12, with the date of the September memorandum. This September memorandum was publicly released in late March 2005 and is available at http://www.aclu .org/files/FilesPDFs/september%20sanchez%20memo.pdf as of October 24, 2014.

24. R. Jeffrey Smith, "Memo Gave Intelligence Bigger Role," *Washington Post*, May 21, 2004, http://www.washingtonpost.com/wp-dyn/articles/A43708 -2004May20.html; R. Jeffrey Smith and Josh White, "General Granted Latitude at Prison," *Washington Post*, June 12, 2004, http://www.washingtonpost .com/wp-dyn/articles/A35612-2004Jun11.html.

25. *Review of Department of Defense Detention and Interrogation Operations, Day 3*, 108th Cong. 595 (2004) (statement of Jeff Sessions, United States senator).

26. Ibid. (statements of Jeff Sessions, United States senator, and Ricardo Sanchez, commander, Multi-National Force–Iraq).

27. Robert Jackall, *Moral Mazes: The World of Corporate Managers* (New York: Oxford University Press, 1989), 20; see also David Luban, "Liberalism, Torture, and the Ticking Bomb," *Virginia Law Review* 91, no. 6 (2005): 1425–61. http://0-www.jstor.org/stable/3649415.

28. *Review of Department of Defense Detention and Interrogation Operations, Day 3*, 614 (statements of Joseph Lieberman, United States senator, and Marc Warren, staff judge advocate, CJTF-7).

29. George W. Bush, "Humane Treatment of al Qaeda and Taliban Detainee," *National Security Archive,* accessed June 16, 2014, http://www2.gwu .edu/~nsarchiv/NSAEBB/NSAEBB127/02.02.07.pdf.

30. *Review of Department of Defense Detention and Interrogation Operations, Day 5*, 108th Cong., 1318 (2004) (statement of Dr. Harold Brown, member, independent panel to review Department of Defense detention operations).

31. Ibid., 1311 (statement of Carl Levin, United States senator).

32. Ibid., 1048 (statement of Carl Levin, United States senator).

33. Ibid., 1319 (statement of Dr. Harold Brown, member, independent panel to review Department of Defense detention operations).

34. Ibid., 1311 (statement of Carl Levin, United States senator).

35. Ibid., 1319 (statement of Dr. Harold Brown, member, independent panel to review Department of Defense detention operations).

36. Ibid., 1108 (statement of Paul Kern, commanding general, United States Army Material Command).

37. Ibid., 1315 (statement of Dr. James Schlesinger, chair, independent panel to review Department of Defense detention operations).

38. CNN, "Report: Abu Ghraib Was 'Animal House' at Night," August 25, 2004, http://www.cnn.com/2004/US/08/24/abughraib.report/index.html.

39. Bradley Graham and Josh White, "Top Pentagon Leaders Faulted in Prison Abuse," *Washington Post*, August 25, 2004, http://www.washingtonpost.com /wp-dyn/articles/A28862-2004Aug24.html; Dave Moniz and Donna Leinwand, "Panel: Top Officials Played Role in Prison Abuse," *USA Today*, August 24, 2004, http://usatoday30.usatoday.com/news/washington/2004 -08-24-abu-ghraib-report_x.htm; Eric Schmitt, "Abuse Panel Says Rules on

Inmates Need Overhaul," *New York Times*, August 25, 2004, http://www
.nytimes.com/2004/08/25/politics/25abuse.html.

40. "A Failed Investigation," *Washington Post*, September 10, 2004. http://www
.washingtonpost.com/wp-dyn/articles/A10281-2004Sep9.html; "No Accountability on Abu Ghraib," *New York Times*, September 10, 2004, http://www
.nytimes.com/2004/09/10/opinion/10fri1.html.

41. Neil A. Lewis and David Johnston, "New F.B.I. Files Describe Abuse of
Iraq Inmates," *New York Times*, December 21, 2004, http://www.nytimes
.com/2004/12/21/politics/21abuse.html.

42. Adam Zagorin and Timothy J. Duffy, "Inside the Interrogation of Detainee
063," *Time*, June 20, 2005. http://www.time.com/time/magazine/article
/0,9171,1071284,00.html

43. *Review of Department of Defense Detention and Interrogation Policy and Operations
in the Global War on Terrorism, Day 2, Before the Senate Armed Services Committee*,
109th Cong., 117 (2005) (statement of Jack Reed, United States senator).

5. "HONOR BOUND": THE POLITICAL LEGACY OF GUANTÁNAMO

1. *Review of Department of Defense Detention and Interrogation Operations,
Day 1*, 108th Cong. 27 (2004) (statement of Pat Roberts, United States senator).

2. Ibid., 64 (2004) (statement of Saxby Chambliss, United States senator).

3. Leo Cebdriwucz, "Portugal's Offer to Help the US Close Guantánamo,"
Time, December 12, 2008, http://www.time.com/time/world/article
/0,8599,1867163,00.html; Charlie Savage, "Closing Guantánamo Fades as a Priority," *New York Times*, June 25, 2010, http://www.nytimes.com/2010/06/26
/us/politics/26gitmo.html; Julia E. Sweig, "Give Guantanamo Back to Cuba,"
Washington Post, May 3, 2009, http://www.washingtonpost.com/wp-dyn
/content/article/2009/04/29/AR2009042903940.html.

4. Peter Finn, "Guantanamo Closure Called Obama Priority," *Washington Post*,
November 12, 2008, http://www.washingtonpost.com/wp-dyn/content
/article/2008/11/11/AR2008111102865.html; John McCain, "Speech on
Foreign Policy," *Council on Foreign Relations*, March 26 2008, accessed June 18,
2014, http://www.cfr.org/publication/15834/mccains_speech_on_foreign
_policy_march_2008.html.

5. Exec. Order. No. 13492. 74 Fed. Reg. 4897 (January 22, 2009) http://www
.gpo.gov/fdsys/pkg/FR-2009-01-27/pdf/E9-1893.pdf.

6. Savage, "Closing Guantánamo Fades as a Priority."

7. Naval Station Guantanamo Bay, Public Affairs Office, "Naval Station Guantanamo Bay, Cuba," accessed October 26, 2014, http://www.jtfgtmo .southcom.mil/xWEBSITE/fact_sheets/NavstaGTMO.pdf.

8. Avalon Project, "Treaty Between the United States of America and Cuba," Yale Law School, Lillian Goldman Law Library, accessed June 17, 2014, http:// avalon.law.yale.edu/20th_century/dip_cuba001.asp.

9. Naval Station Guantanamo Bay, Public Affairs Office, "Naval Station Guantanamo Bay, Cuba."

10. Matthew J. Gibney and Randall Hansen, "Guantanamo Bay," *Immigration and Asylum from 1900 to Present*, (Santa Barbara, CA: ABC-CLIO, 2005).

11. Mireya Navarro, "Last of Refugees from Cuba in '94 Flight Now Enter U.S.," *New York Times*, February 1, 1996, http://www.nytimes.com/1996/02/01 /world/last-of-refugees-from-cuba-in-94-flight-now-enter-us.html.

12. Joint Task Force–Guantanamo Public Affairs Office, "Guantanamo Facility Will Assist Refugees in Distress," *The Wire* 8, no. 32 (2007): 4, accessed October 26, 2014, http://www.jtfgtmo.southcom.mil/wire/wire/WirePDF /v8/Issue32v8.pdf.

13. Ibid.

14. George Monbiot, "Genocide or Peace," *Guardian*, October 2, 2001, http:// www.guardian.co.uk/world/2001/oct/02/afghanistan.comment.

15. Bruce Fein, "Abrogating Terrorism's Paradise," *Washington Times*, October 2, 2001, http://www.washingtontimes.com/news/2001/oct/2/20011002-025736-6454r/.

16. Matthew Purdy, "A Nation Challenged: The Law; Bush's New Rules to Fight Terror Transform the Legal Landscape," *New York Times*, November 25, 2001, http://www.nytimes.com/2001/11/25/us/nation-challenged-law-bush-s -new-rules-fight-terror-transform-legal-landscape.html.

17. CNN, "U.S. to Hold Detainees at Guantanamo Bay," CNN.com, December 28, 2001, http://edition.cnn   com/2001/US/12/27/ret.holding.detainees/.

18. Katharine Q. Seelye, "A Nation Challenged: The Prisoners; Troops Arrive at Base in Cuba to Build Jails," *New York Times*, January 7, 2002, http://www .nytimes.com/2002/01/07/us/a-nation-challenged-the-prisoners-troops -arrive-at-base-in-cuba-to-build-jails.html.

19. BBC News, "Afghan Captives Start Cuba Detention," January 12, 2002, http://news.bbc.co.uk/2/hi/americas/1754444.stm.

20. Ibid.

21. Amnesty International, "Afghanistan/USA: Prisoners Must Be Treated Humanely," last modified January 10, 2002, http://www.amnesty.org/en

/library/asset/AMR51/004/2002/en/5d2c70b4-fb03-11dd-9fca
-od1f97c98a21/amr510042002en.pdf.

22. Julian Borger, "Congress Delegates Scorn X-Ray Fears," *Guardian*, January
    26, 2002, http://www.guardian.co.uk/world/2002/jan/26/usa.afghanistan.

23. Ibid.

24. Ibid.

25. 148 Cong. Rec. S92–93 (daily ed. January 25, 2002) (statement of Sen.
    Nelson).

26. 148 Cong. Rec. E415 (March 20, 2002) (statement of Rep. Kucinich).

27. On July 16, 2003, Senator Jeff Bingaman argued for an amendment that he
    added to the 2004 Department of Defense Appropriations Act that would
    require the Department of Defense to produce a report about the legal status
    of the detainees at Guantánamo. Of the amendment, Bingaman said, "Oth-
    ers have questioned the treatment of these individuals. I have not questioned
    the treatment of these individuals in Guantánamo. There is nothing in the
    amendment that questions the treatment of these individuals." In November,
    Senator Dick Durbin introduced into the congressional record a speech by a
    law professor at the University of Chicago; the speech included some criti-
    cal, but relatively nonspecific, remarks about Guantánamo. Later that month,
    Bingaman reintroduced his legislation, which had failed as an amendment.
    This bill was referred to the Senate Armed Services Committee and was never
    brought to a vote. 149 Cong. Rec. S 9454 (daily ed. July 16, 2003) (statement
    of Sen. Bingaman).

28. A search of the *Congressional Record* returned eighty-three hits for the term
    "Guantánamo" in 2001 to 2003. In 2004, there were 102 hits.

29. Neil A. Lewis, "Broad Use of Harsh Tactics Is Described at Cuba Base,"
    New York Times, October 17, 2004, http://www.nytimes.com/2004/10/17
    /politics/17gitmo.html.

30. Neil A. Lewis, "Red Cross Finds Detainee Abuse in Guantánamo," *New
    York Times*, November 30, 2004, http://www.nytimes.com/2004/11/30
    /politics/30gitmo.html.

31. Redacted, "E-mail from [Redacted] to [Redacted]," ACLU.org, accessed
    April 16, 2004, http://www.aclu.org/torturefoia/released/FBI_5053_5054.pdf.

32. Eggen and Smith, "FBI Agents Allege Abuse of Detainees at Guantanamo Bay."

33. *Review of Department of Defense Detention and Interrogation Policy and
    Operations in the Global War on Terrorism, Day 1, Before the Senate Committee*

on Armed Services, 109th Cong. 9 (2005) (statement of Albert Church, director of Navy staff).

34. Ibid., 6 (statement of Carl Levin, United States senator).

35. Dorothy E. Smith, *Texts, Facts, and Femininity: Exploring the Relations of Ruling* (New York: Routledge, 1990), 154.

36. Though al-Qahtani is widely viewed as the likely would-be twentieth hijacker, Vice President Dick Cheney once insinuated that Zacarias Moussaoui was the intended twentieth hijacker. In 2006, al-Qaeda claimed that Fawaz al-Nashimi was to be the twentieth hijacker. Dan Eggen, "Was There a Twentieth Hijacker for Sept. 11?," *Washington Post*, June 22, 2006, http://www.washingtonpost.com/wp-dyn/content/article/2006/06/21/AR2006062101782.html.

37. Adam Zagorin, "'Twentieth Hijacker' Says Torture Made Him Lie," March 3, 2006, http://content.time.com/time/nation/article/0,8599,1169322,00.html.

38. Adam Zagorin and Timothy J. Duffy, "Inside the Interrogation of Detainee 063," *Time*, June 20, 2005. http://www.time.com/time/magazine/article/0,9171,1071284,00.html.

39. Ibid.

40. Ibid.

41. Ibid.

42. Ibid.

43. Ibid.

44. See also Steven H. Miles, "Medical Ethics and the Interrogation of Guantanamo 063," *The American Journal of Bioethics* 7, no. 4 (2007): 5–11, doi:10.1080/15265160701263535.

45. This is a relatively common practice. After severely beating prisoners' feet, the Greek military junta's torturers often forced their victims to run to decrease swelling and numbness. See Darius Rejali, *Torture and Democracy* (Princeton, N.J.: Princeton University Press, 2007), 343.

46. Jim VandeHei and Josh White, "Guantanamo Bay to Stay Open, Cheney Says," *Washington Post*, June 14, 2005, http://www.washingtonpost.com/wp-dyn/content/article/2005/06/13/AR2005061301513.html.

47. Marc Kaufman, "Cheney: U.S. Not Aiming To Close Guantanamo," *Washington Post*, June 13, 2005, http://www.washingtonpost.com/wp-dyn/content/article/2005/06/12/AR2005061201265.html; "Guantánamo Detainees Are 'Bad People,' Says Cheney," June 13, 2005, http://www.guardian.co.uk/world/2005/jun/13/afghanistan.guantanamo; Associated Press, "Rumsfeld

Says No Alternatives Exist for Guantánamo Prison," *New York Times*, June 15, 2005, http://www.nytimes.com/2005/06/15/politics/15gitmo.html.

48. Associated Press, "Republican Urges Closing Guantánamo Facility," *New York Times*, June 12, 2005, http://www.nytimes.com/2005/06/12/politics/12martinez.html.

49. Kaufman, "Cheney."

50. Associated Press, "Rumsfeld Says No Alternatives Exist for Guantánamo Prison."

51. *Detainees, Before the Senate Committee on the Judiciary. Detainees*, 109th Cong. 1 (2005) (statement of Arlen Specter, United States senator).

52. Ibid., 3–4 (statement of Patrick Leahy, United States senator).

53. Ibid., 23 (statement of Edward Kennedy, United States senator).

54. *Review of Department of Defense Detention and Interrogation Policy and Operations in the Global War on Terrorism, Day 2*, 109th Cong. 46 (2005) (statement of John Warner, United States senator).

55. Ibid.

56. Ibid., 77 (statement of Carl Levin, United States senator).

57. Ibid.

58. Ibid.

59. Ibid.

60. Ibid., 88–89.

61. Ibid., 90.

62. Ibid., 90–91.

63. Ibid., 91.

64. Ibid., 93.

65. Ibid., 128 (statement of Pat Roberts, United States senator).

66. Ibid., 126.

67. Ibid.

68. Ibid.

69. Ibid., 127.

70. Ibid.

71. Ibid., 126.

72. Ibid., 127.

73. *Review of Department of Defense Detention and Interrogation Policy and Operations in the Global War on Terrorism, Day 2*, 109th Cong. 106 (2005) (statements of John Warner, United States senator, and John Furlow, investigating officer).

74. Senator Kennedy raised this issue in his questions for the record. Generals Schmidt and Furlow explicitly articulated this view, responding that the different perspectives that the FBI and military had of interrogations "highlights the difference between the law enforcement mission of criminal prosecution and the need for actionable intelligence in the war on terror" (ibid., 155).

75. Melvin Pollner, *Mundane Reason: Reality in Everyday and Sociological Discourse* (New York: Cambridge University Press, 1987).

76. *Review of Department of Defense Detention and Interrogation Policy and Operations in the Global War on Terrorism, Day 2,* 109th Cong. 99 (2005) (statement of Randall Schmidt, senior investigating officer).

77. Ibid.

78. *Review of Department of Defense Detention and Interrogation Policy and Operations in the Global War on Terrorism, Day 2,* 109th Cong. 97 (2005) (statement of Randall Schmidt, senior investigating officer).

79. Ibid.

80. Ibid.

81. U.S. Department of the Army, *Field Manual 34-52 Intelligence Interrogation* (Washington, D.C.: Department of the Army, 1992), 3–18, accessed October 23, 2014, http://www.loc.gov/rr/frd/Military_Law/pdf/intel_interrrogation_sept-1992.pdf

82. Ibid.

83. *Review of Department of Defense Detention and Interrogation Policy and Operations in the Global War on Terrorism, Day 2,* 109th Cong. 97 (2005) (statement of Randall Schmidt, senior investigating officer).

84. Ibid., 98.

85. U.S. Department of the Army, *Field Manual 34-52,* 3–18.

86. Randall Schmidt and John T. Furlow, *Investigation Into FBI Allegations of Detainee Abuse at Guantanamo Bay, Cuba Detention Facility, US Department of Defense,* 20, accessed April 26, 2014, http://www.defense.gov/news/Jul2005/d20050714report.pdf.

87. *Review of Department of Defense Detention and Interrogation Policy and Operations in the Global War on Terrorism, Day 2,* 109th Cong. 104 (2005) (statement of Bantz Craddock, commander, U.S. Southern Command).

88. U.S. Department of the Army, *Field Manual 2-22.3 (FM 34-52) Human Intelligence Collector Operations* (Washington, D.C.: Department of the Army, 2006), 5–21, accessed October 23, 2014, http://www.loc.gov/rr/frd/Military_Law/pdf/human-intell-collector-operations.pdf.

89. David Luban, "Liberalism, Torture, and the Ticking Bomb," *Virginia Law Review* 91, no. 6 (2005), 1460.

90. David Garland, *Peculiar Institution: America's Death Penalty in an Age of Abolition* (Cambridge, Mass.: Harvard University Press, 2011); Philip Smith, *Punishment and Culture* (Chicago: University of Chicago Press, 2008).

91. Zagorin and Duffy, "Inside the Interrogation of Detainee 063."

92. Schmidt and Furlow, *Investigation Into FBI Allegations of Detainee Abuse*, 13–14.

93. *Review of Department of Defense Detention and Interrogation Policy and Operations in the Global War on Terrorism, Day 2*, 109th Cong. 77 (2005) (statement of Carl Levin, United States senator).

94. Ibid., 117 (statement of Jack Reed, United States senator).

95. *Review of Department of Defense Detention and Interrogation Policy and Operations in the Global War on Terrorism, Day 3, Before the Subcommittee on Personnel of the Senate Committee on Armed Services*, 109th Cong. 187 (2005) (statement of Edward Kennedy, United States senator).

96. Josh White, "Abu Ghraib Tactics Were First Used at Guantanamo," *Washington Post*, July 14, 2005, http://www.washingtonpost.com/wp-dyn/content/article/2005/07/13/AR2005071302380.html.

97. Neil A. Lewis, "Report Discredits F.B.I. Claims of Abuse at Guantánamo Bay," *New York Times*, July 14, 2005, http://www.nytimes.com/2005/07/14/politics/14gitmo.html.

98. "The Women of Gitmo," *New York Times*, July 15, 2005, http://www.nytimes.com/2005/07/15/opinion/15fri1.html.

99. The Supreme Court's decision in *Hamdan* was not its first to challenge the Bush administration's detention program. In June 2004, the court issued a pair of rulings against the administration in *Rasul v. Bush* and *Hamdi v. Rumsfeld*. Coming, as they did, amid the scandal surrounding Abu Ghraib, these rulings did not immediately alter congressional discourse surrounding U.S. detention policies in the war on terror. The Senate Judiciary Committee addressed the implications of the court's rulings several months after the decisions—in their confirmation hearing for Alberto Gonzales on January 6, 2005, and during their June 15, 2005, hearing, *Detainees. Hamdan*, however, inspired a rapid response from Congress; through the summer of 2006, the House Armed Services, Senate Armed Services, and Senate Judiciary Committees all held hearings related to the *Hamdan* decision. In part, the urgency of the congressional response to *Hamdan* can be explained by the fact that the decision required Congress to take some sort of legislative action in order for the Bush administration

to restart its stalled military commissions. But my reason for focusing on the influence of this decision does not only have to do with the policy implications of *Hamdan*. Instead, it has to do with the sheer fact that, discursively, the decision registered in Congress and quickly became a potent framing device for debates about Guantánamo, especially among Democrats, who viewed the decision as a powerful and clear rejection of the administration's approach to detention.

100. Jonathan Mahler, *The Challenge:* Hamdan v. Rumsfeld *and the Fight Over Presidential Power* (New York: Farrar, Straus and Giroux, 2008).

101. John Roberts, the Supreme Court's chief justice, abstained from the case because he had, when earlier serving as a federal court of appeals judge, "rejected Mr. Hamdan's challenge to the military commissions in a decision." See Linda Greenhouse, "Justices Hint That They'll Rule on Challenge Filed by Detainee," *New York Times*, March 29, 2006, http://www.nytimes.com/2006/03/29/politics/29scotus.html.

102. Linda Greenhouse, "Justices, 5–3, Broadly Reject Bush Plan to Try Detainees," *New York Times*, June 30, 2006, http://www.nytimes.com/2006/06/30/washington/30hamdan.html.

103. *Military Commissions in Light of the Supreme Court Decision in* Hamdan v. Rumsfeld*, Day 1, Before the Senate Committee on the Armed Services,* 109th Cong. 50 (2006) (statement of Robert Byrd, United States senator).

104. *Examining Proposals to Limit Guantanamo Detainees' Access to Habeas Corpus Review, Before the Senate Committee on the Judiciary,* 109th Cong. 4 (2006) (statement of Patrick Leahy, United States senator).

105. Al Kamen et al., "Senate Committee Staff Directors Set Session Agenda," *Washington Post*, December 26, 2006, http://www.washingtonpost.com/wp-dyn/content/article/2006/12/25/AR2006122500581.html.

106. Jane Mayer, *The Dark Side* (New York: Doubleday, 2008), 158.

107. Mark Mazzetti, "'03 U.S. Memo Approved Harsh Interrogations," *New York Times*, April 2, 2008, http://www.nytimes.com/2008/04/02/washington/02terror.html.

108. David Cole, "The Man Behind the Torture," *The New York Review of Books*, December 6, 2007, http://www.nybooks.com/articles/archives/2007/dec/06/the-man-behind-the-torture/; Jeffrey Rosen, "Conscience of a Conservative," *New York Times*, September 9, 2007, http://www.nytimes.com/2007/09/09/magazine/09rosen.html.

109. Phillip Sands, *Torture Team: Rumsfeld's Memo and the Betrayal of American Values* (New York: Palgrave, 2008).

110. William J. Haynes, *Counter-Resistance Techniques* (Washington, D.C.: General Counsel of the Department of Defense, 2002), http://library .rumsfeld.com/doclib/sp/380/2002-11-27%20from%20Haynes%20re%20 Counter-Resistance%20Techniques.pdf.

111. Carolyn Quinn, "Transcript of Wilkerson Interview," November 29, 2005, http://news.bbc.co.uk/2/hi/middle_east/4481092.stm.

112. *The Treatment of Detainees in U.S. Custody, Day 1, Before the Senate Committee on Armed Services,* 110th Cong. 8 (2008) (Alberto Mora quoted in statement of Carl Levin, United States senator).

113. *Military Commissions Act and the Continued Use of Guantanamo Bay as a Detention Facility, Before the House Committee on the Armed Services,* 110th Cong. 1 (2007) (statement of Ike Skelton, United States representative).

114. Ibid., 2.

115. Ibid., 12 (statement of Neal Kaytal, professor of law, Georgetown University).

116. Ibid., 14 (statement of Elisa Massimino, director of the Washington, D.C. Office, Human Rights First).

117. Senate Armed Services Committee, *Inquiry into the Treatment of Detainees in U.S. Custody,* United States Senate, 110th Cong. xxix, accessed June 17, 2014, http://www.armed-services.senate.gov/imo/media/doc/Detainee-Report -Final_April-22-2009.pdf.

118. *The Treatment of Detainees in U.S. Custody, Day 1,* 110th Cong. 12 (2008) (statement of John Warner, United States senator).

119. Ibid., 13 (statement of Lindsey Graham, United States senator).

120. Ibid., 12–13.

121. Ibid., 14.

122. Ibid.

123. Ibid., 15.

124. Ibid., 16.

6. THE TOXICITY OF TORTURE: WATERBOARDING AND THE DEBATE ABOUT "ENHANCED INTERROGATION"

1. James Risen, David Johnston, and Neil A. Lewis, "Harsh C.I.A. Methods Cited in Top Qaeda Interrogations," *New York Times,* May 13, 2004, http:// www.nytimes.com/2004/05/13/world/struggle-for-iraq-detainees-harsh-cia -methods-cited-top-qaeda-interrogations.html?pagewanted=all&src=pm.

2. This information is based on a search for "waterboarding" in published congressional hearing transcripts on October 27, 2014. Some references to the technique may be in the questions or answers submitted for the record of hearing participants.

3. Mark Mazzetti, "C.I.A. Destroyed 2 Tapes Showing Interrogations," *New York Times*, 2007, http://www.nytimes.com/2007/12/07/washington/07intel.html; Dan Eggen and Joby Warrick, "CIA Destroyed Videos Showing Interrogations," *Washington Post*, December 7, 2007, http://www.washingtonpost.com/wp-dyn/content/article/2007/12/06/AR2007120601828.html.

4. Mark Mazzetti and David Johnston, "Inquiry Begins Into Destruction of Tapes," *New York Times*, December 7, 2007, http://www.nytimes.com/2007/12/09/washington/09zubaydah.html; Eric Lichtblau, "Congress Looks Into Obstruction as Calls for Justice Inquiry Rise," *New York Times*, December 8, 2007, http://query.nytimes.com/gst/fullpage.html?res=9500E2DA1031F93BA35751C1A9619C8B63.

5. *Applicability of Federal Criminal Laws to the Interrogation of Detainees, Before the House Committee on the Judiciary*, 110th Cong. 1 (2007) (statement of John Conyers, United States representative).

6. Ibid., 6 (statement of Robert Scott, United States representative).

7. Ibid., 9 (statement of Stephen Saltzburg, professor of law, George Washington University).

8. Ibid., 21 (statement of Elisa Massimino, Washington director, Human Rights First).

9. Leigh Payne, *Unsettling Accounts: Neither Truth nor Reconciliation in Confessions of State Violence* (Durham, N.C.: Duke University Press, 2008), 194.

10. Ibid.

11. Adam Goldman and Matt Apuzzo, "Ex-Spy: Destroying CIA Tapes Purged 'Ugly Visuals,'" *Yahoo News*, April 24, 2012, http://news.yahoo.com/ex-spy-destroying-cia-tapes-purged-ugly-visuals-212042971.html.

12. Darius Rejali, *Torture and Democracy* (Princeton, N.J.: Princeton University Press, 2007), 447.

13. Dorothy E. Smith, *Texts, Facts, and Femininity: Exploring the Relations of Ruling* (New York: Routledge, 1990).

14. *Torture and the Cruel, Inhuman, and Degrading Treatment of Detainees: The Effectiveness and Consequences of "Enhanced" Interrogation, Before the House Subcommittee on the Constitution, Civil Rights, and Civil Liberties of the*

Committee on the Judiciary. 110th Cong. 3 (2007) (statement by Trent Franks, United States representative).

15. *Applicability of Federal Criminal Laws to the Interrogation of Detainees*, 4 (statement of Lamar Smith, United States representative).

16. In March of 2009, the *Washington Post* reported that, though President George W. Bush described Abu Zubaydah as "al-Qaeda's chief of operations" and other government officials referred to Abu Zubaydah's involvement in the September 11, 2001, terrorist attacks, Abu Zubaydah had no direct ties with al-Qaeda at the time of the attacks. Peter Finn and Joby Warrick, "Detainee's Harsh Treatment Foiled No Plots," *Washington Post*, March 29, 2009, http://www.washingtonpost.com/wp-dyn/content/article/2009/03/28/AR2009032802066.html.

17. *Applicability of Federal Criminal Laws to the Interrogation of Detainees*, 4 (statement of Lamar Smith, United States representative).

18. George W. Bush, "President Bush's Speech on Terrorism," *New York Times*, September 6, 2006, http://www.nytimes.com/2006/09/06/washington/06bush_transcript.html.

19. Richard Esposito and Brian Ross, "Coming in From the Cold: CIA Spy Calls Waterboarding Necessary but Torture," December 10, 2007, http://abcnews.go.com/Blotter/story?id=3978231&page=1.

20. *Current and Projected Threats to the National Security of the United States, Before the Senate Select Committee on Intelligence.* 110th Cong. 71–72 (2008) (statement of Michael Hayden, director, Central Intelligence Agency).

21. Richard Esposito, "CIA Chief: We Waterboarded," February 5, 2008, http://abcnews.go.com/Blotter/TheLaw/story?id=4244423&page=1.

22. *From the Department of Justice to Guantanamo Bay: Administration Lawyers and Administration Interrogation Rules (Part I), Before the House Subcommittee on the Constitution, Civil Rights, and Civil,* 110th Cong. 3 (2008) (statement of Trent Franks, United States representative).

23. *Justice Department's Office of Legal Counsel, Before the House Subcommittee on the Constitution, Civil Rights, and Civil Liberties,* 110th Cong. 28 (2008) (statements of Robert Scott, United States representative, and Steven Bradbury, principal deputy assistant attorney general, Office of the Legal Counsel, U.S. Department of Justice).

24. *From the Department of Justice to Guantanamo Bay (Part V), Before the House Committee on the Judiciary,* 110th Cong. 51 (2008) (statement of Walter

Dellinger, former assistant attorney general, Office of Legal Counsel, U.S. Department of Justice).

25. *From the Department of Justice to Guantanamo Bay (Part II), Before the House Subcommittee on the Constitution, Civil Rights, and Civil Liberties,* 110th Cong. 9 (2008) (statement of Daniel Levin, White & Case LLP).

26. *Torture and the Cruel, Inhuman, and Degrading Treatment of Detainees,* 22–23 (statement of Malcolm Nance, former Survival, Evasion, Resistance, Escape [SERE] instructor, U.S. Navy).

27. Ibid., 56 (statements of Artur Davis, United States representative, and Malcolm Nance, former SERE instructor).

28. Ibid., 37 (statement of Amrit Singh, staff attorney, American Civil Liberties Union).

29. Smith, *Texts, Facts, and Femininity,* 154.

30. Jane Mayer, "The Experiment," *New Yorker,* July 11, 2005. http://www.newyorker.com/archive/2005/07/11/050711fa_fact4.

31. *Torture and the Cruel, Inhuman, and Degrading Treatment of Detainees,* 22 (statement of Malcolm Nance, former SERE instructor).

32. *The Treatment of Detainees in U.S. Custody, Day 2,* 110th Cong. 175 (2008) (statement of Steven Kleinman, former director of intelligence, Personnel Recovery Academy, Joint Personnel Recovery Agency).

33. Ibid., 3 (statement of Carl Levin, United States senator).

34. *Torture and the Cruel, Inhuman, and Degrading Treatment of Detainees,* 53 (statement of Steven Kleinman, former director of intelligence, Personnel Recovery Academy, Joint Personnel Recovery Agency).

35. *Justice Department's Office of Legal Counsel,* 20–21 (statements of Artur Davis, United States representative, and Steven Bradbury, principal deputy assistant attorney general, Office of the Legal Counsel, U.S. Department of Justice).

36. David Luban, "Liberalism, Torture, and the Ticking Bomb," *Virginia Law Review* 91, no. 6 (2005): 1433.

37. *The Treatment of Detainees in U.S. Custody, Day 1,* 69 (statement of Alberto Mora, former general counsel, United States Navy).

38. *How the Administration's Failed Detainee Policies Have Hurt the Fight Against Terrorism: Putting the Fight Against Terrorism on Sound Legal Foundations, Before the Senate Committee on the Judiciary,* 110th Cong. 1 (2008) (statement of Patrick Leahy, United States senator).

39. *Torture and the Cruel, Inhuman, and Degrading Treatment of Detainees*, 23 (statement of Malcolm Nance, former SERE instructor).

40. Alan Silverleib, "Poll: Terrorism Fears Are Fading," *CNN.com*, July 2, 2008, http://www.cnn.com/2008/POLITICS/07/02/terrorism.poll/; Lymari Morales, "Americans Prioritize the Economy Over Terrorism," *Gallup Politics*, June 27, 2008, http://www.gallup.com/poll/108415/americans-prioritize -economy-over-terrorism.aspx.

41. Rejali, *Torture and Democracy*.

42. *Torture and the Cruel, Inhuman, and Degrading Treatment of Detainees*, 22 (statement of Malcolm Nance, former SERE instructor).

43. Ibid., 30 (statement of Steven Kleinman, former director of intelligence, Personnel Recovery Academy, Joint Personnel Recovery Agency).

44. *Department of Justice to Guantanamo Bay (Part I)*, 124 (statement of Marjorie Cohn, professor of law, Thomas Jefferson School of Law).

45. *Torture and the Cruel, Inhuman, and Degrading Treatment of Detainees*, 1 (statement of Jerrold Nalder, United States representative).

46. *Justice Department's Office of Legal Counsel*, 2 (statement of Jerrold Nalder, United States representative).

47. *Confirmation Hearing on the Nomination of Michael B. Mukasey to Be Attorney General of the United States, Day 1, Before the Senate Committee on the Judiciary*, 110th Cong. 187 (October 17, 2007) (statement of Michael Mukasey, nominee to be attorney general).

48. *Confirmation Hearing on the Nomination of Michael B. Mukasey to Be Attorney General of the United States, Day 2*, 108th Cong. 222 (2007) (statement of John Hutson, president and dean, Franklin Pierce Law Center).

49. Thomas Risse and Kathryn Sikkink, "The Socialization of International Human Rights Norms into Domestic Practice: Introduction," in *The Power of Human Rights: International Norms and Domestic Change*, ed. T. Risse-Kappen, T. Risse, S. C Ropp, and K. Sikkink (New York: Cambridge University Press, 1999), 15.

50. Edward Peters, *Torture* (New York: Blackwell, 1985); Rejali, *Torture and Democracy*.

51. Evan Wallach, "Drop by Drop: Forgetting the History of Water Torture in U.S. Courts," *Columbia Journal of Transnational Law* 45, no. 2 (2007): 468–506. http://heinonline.org/HOL/LandingPage?handle=hein.journals /cjtl45&div=17&id=&page=.

52. *Torture, and the Cruel, Inhuman, and Degrading Treatment of Detainees,* 468 (statements of John Conyers, United States representative, Amrit Singh, staff attorney, ACLU, Steven Kleinman, former director of intelligence, Personnel Recovery Academy, Joint Personnel Recovery Agency, Malcolm Nance, former SERE instructor, and Jerrold Nadler, United States representative).

53. Jonathan Potter, *Representing Reality: Discourse, Rhetoric, and Social Construction* (Thousand Oaks, Calif.: Sage, 1996).

54. Walter Pincus, "Waterboarding Historically Controversial," *Washington Post,* October 5, 2006, http://www.washingtonpost.com/wp-dyn/content/article/2006/10/04/AR2006100402005.html.

55. Stanley Cohen, *States of Denial: Knowing About Atrocities and Suffering* (Malden, Mass.: Blackwell, 2001).

56. Rejali, *Torture and Democracy,* 279.

57. Ibid.

58. *Justice Department's Office of Legal Counsel,* 18 (statement of Trent Franks, United States representative).

59. Ibid., 18 (statement of Steven Bradbury, principal deputy assistant attorney general, Office of the Legal Counsel, U.S. Department of Justice).

60. Marc Thiessen, "Yglesias Admits His Ignorance," *National Review,* February 9, 2010, http://www.nationalreview.com/corner/194573/yglesias-admits-his-ignorance/marc-thiessen; Marc Thiessen, "Yglesias and the Slow Learners at Think Progress," National Review Online, February 8, 2010, http://www.nationalreview.com/corner/194550/yglesias-and-slow-learners-think-progress/marc-thiessen; Matthew Yglesias, "If Marc Thiessen Doesn't Want to Be Compared to the Spanish Inquisition, He Should Stop Advocating Torture Techniques Used in the Spanish Inquisition," *ThinkProgress,* February 8, 2010, http://thinkprogress.org/yglesias/2010/02/08/196096/if-marc-thiessen-doesnt-want-to-be-compared-to-the-spanish-inquisition-he-should-stop-advocating-torture-techniques-used-in-the-spanish-inquisition/; Matthew Yglesias, "No One Expects the Spanish Inquisition," *ThinkProgress,* February 8, 2010, http://thinkprogress.org/yglesias/2010/02/08/196102/no-one-expects-the-spanish-inquisition/.

61. Thiessen, "Yglesias Admits His Ignorance."

62. *Torture and the Cruel, Inhuman, and Degrading Treatment of Detainees,* 2 (statement of Trent Franks, United States representative).

63. Rejali, *Torture and Democracy*.

64. On neutralizations, see Gresham M. Sykes and David Matza, "Techniques of Neutralization: A Theory of Delinquency," *American Sociological Review* 22, no. 6 (1957): 664–70. doi:10.2307/2089195.

65. Stephen Pfohl, "Twilight of the Parasites: Ultramodern Capital and the New World Order," *Social Problems* 40, no. 2 (May 1, 1993): 128, doi:10.1525/sp.1993.40.2.03x0322j.

66. In a footnote in this passage, Bradbury compares these restrictions to those that "individuals who voluntarily engage in commercial weight-loss programs" adhere. "While we do not equate," he writes, "commercial weight loss programs and this interrogation technique, the fact that these calorie levels are used in the weight-loss programs, in our view, is instructive in evaluating the medical safety of the interrogation technique." These comments recall a brief note that Secretary of Defense Donald Rumsfeld added to his December 2, 2002, authorization of harsh techniques: "I stand for 8–10 hours a day. Why is standing limited 4 hours?" In these descriptions, we see how the superficial resemblances between "enhanced interrogation" techniques and everyday deprivations obscure the practices' severity. See Steven G. Bradbury, *Re: Application of 18 U.S.C. §§ 2340–2340A to Certain Techniques That May Be Used in the Interrogation of a High Value Al Qaeda Detainee* (Washington, D.C.: Office of the Principal Deputy Assistant Attorney General, 2005), 9, http://www.fas.org/irp/agency/doj/olc/techniques.pdf; William J. Haynes, *Counter-Resistance Techniques* (Washington, D.C.: General Counsel of the Department of Defense, 2002), http://library.rumsfeld.com/doclib/sp /380/2002-11-27%20from%20Haynes%20re%20Counter-Resistance %20Techniques.pdf.

67. Bradbury, *Re: Application of 18 U.S.C. §§ 2340–2340A*, 15.

68. International Committee of the Red Cross, *ICRC Report on the Treatment of Fourteen "High Value Detainees" in CIA Custody*.

69. Rejali, *Torture and Democracy*.

70. Bradbury, *Re: Application of 18 U.S.C. §§ 2340–2340A*, 43.

71. Scott Shane, "Waterboarding Used 266 Times on 2 Suspects," *New York Times*, April 19, 2009, http://www.nytimes.com/2009/04/20/world/20detain.html.

72. Joseph Abrams, "Despite Reports, Khalid Sheikh Mohammed Was Not Waterboarded 183 Times," *Fox News*, April 28, 2009, http://www .foxnews.com/politics/2009/04/28/despite-reports-khalid-sheikh -mohammed-waterboarded-times/.

73. Zubaydah suffered significant wounds from being shot during capture.

74. Department of Justice memoranda indicate that the CIA attempted to prevent waterboarding from causing vomiting by putting detainees on a liquid diet (Bradbury, *Re: Application of 18 U.S.C. §§ 2340–2340A*).

75. International Committee of the Red Cross, *ICRC Report on the Treatment of Fourteen "High Value Detainees" in CIA Custody*, 10.

76. Rejali, *Torture and Democracy*, 550.

7. FROM "ENHANCED INTERROGATION" TO DRONES: U.S. COUNTERTERRORISM AND THE LEGACY OF TORTURE

1. Daniel Klaidman, *Kill or Capture: The War on Terror and the Soul of the Obama Presidency* (Boston: Houghton Mifflin Harcourt, 2012); Chris McGreal, "Barack Obama Abandons Guantánamo Closure Plan After Congress Veto," *Guardian*, January 20, 2011, http://www.guardian.co.uk/world/2011/jan/20/barack-obama-guantanamo-congress-veto.

2. Lazaro Gamio and Carol Rosenberg, "Tracking the Hunger Strike in Guantanamo," *Miami Herald,* accessed May 5, 2014, http://www.miamiherald.com/static/media/projects/gitmo_chart/index.html.

3. Charlie Savage, "Kuwaiti Prisoner Held for Thirteen Years Is Released from Guantánamo," *New York Times*, November 5, 2014, http://www.nytimes.com/2014/11/06/us/guantanamo-kuwait-fawzi-al-odah-released.html.

4. "Guantánamo Twelfth Anniversary Protests," accessed January 27, 2014, http://www.miamiherald.com/2014/01/11/3864497/jan-11-2014-guantanamo-12th-anniversary.html.

5. Liz Goodwin, "Obama Vows to Close Guantanamo in State of the Union," *Yahoo News*, January 28, 2014, http://news.yahoo.com/for-first-time-in-five-years-obama-vows-to-close-guantanamo-in-state-of-the-union-023956545.html.

6. Patrick Leahy, "A Truth Commission to Investigate Bush-Cheney Administration Abuses," *Huffington Post*, February 12, 2009, http://www.huffingtonpost.com/sen-patrick-leahy/a-truth-commission-to-inv_b_166461.html.

7. "A Truth Commission for the Bush Era?," *New York Times*, March 2, 2009, http://roomfordebate.blogs.nytimes.com/2009/03/02/a-truth-commission-for-the-bush-era/.

8. Scott Shane, "Holder Rules Out Prosecutions in C.I.A. Interrogations," *New York Times*, August 30, 2012, http://www.nytimes.com/2012/08/31/us/holder-rules-out-prosecutions-in-cia-interrogations.html.

9. Peter Finn, Joby Warrick, and Julie Tate, "CIA Report Calls Oversight of Early Interrogations Poor," *Washington Post*, August 25, 2009, http://www.washingtonpost.com/wp-dyn/content/article/2009/08/24/AR2009082402220.html.

10. Jeff Zeleny and Thom Shanker, "Obama Moves to Bar Release of Detainee Abuse Photos," *New York Times*, May 14, 2009, http://www.nytimes.com/2009/05/14/us/politics/14photos.html.

11. Lauren Walker, "Remember the Abu Ghraib Torture Pictures? There Are More That Obama Doesn't Want You to See," *Newsweek*, October 22, 2014, http://www.newsweek.com/remember-abu-ghraib-torture-pictures-there-are-more-obama-doesnt-want-you-see-279254.

12. "Release the Torture Reports," *New York Times*, December 19, 2013, http://www.nytimes.com/2013/12/20/opinion/release-the-torture-reports.html.

13. Ali Watkins, Jonathan S. Landay, and Marisa Taylor, "CIA's Use of Harsh Interrogation Went Beyond Legal Authority, Senate Report Says," *McClatchy*, April 11, 2014, http://www.mcclatchydc.com/2014/04/11/224085_cias-use-of-harsh-interrogation.html.

14. Mark Danner, "Frozen Scandal," *New York Review of Books*, December 4, 2008, http://www.nybooks.com/articles/archives/2008/dec/04/frozen-scandal/.

15. Mark Danner, "After September 11: Our State of Exception," *New York Review of Books*, October 13, 2011, http://www.nybooks.com/articles/archives/2011/oct/13/after-september-11-our-state-exception/.

16. CBS News, "CBS News/NJ Debate Transcript, Part 1," *CBS News*, November 13, 2011, http://www.cbsnews.com/news/cbs-news-nj-debate-transcript-part-1/8/.

17. Ben Armbruster, "Gingrich Changes His Position: 'Waterboarding Is, By Every Technical Rule, Not Torture,'" *ThinkProgress*, November 29, 2011, http://thinkprogress.org/security/2011/11/29/377907/gingrich-waterboarding-not-torture/.

18. Charlie Savage, "Election Will Decide Future of Interrogation Methods for Terrorism Suspects," *New York Times*, September 27, 2012, http://www.nytimes.com/2012/09/28/us/politics/election-will-decide-future-of-interrogation-methods-for-terrorism-suspects.html.

19. Lisa Hajjar, "Does Torture Work?" A Sociolegal Assessment of the Practice in Historical and Global Perspective," *Annual Review of Law and Social Science* 5, no. 1 (December 2009): 311–45. doi:10.1146/annurev.lawsocsci.093008.131501; Edward Peters, *Torture*; Darius Rejali, *Torture and Democracy*.

20. Malise Ruthven quoted in Peters, *Torture*, 151.

21. Richard Jackson, "Language, Policy, and the Construction of a Torture Culture in the War on Terrorism," *Review of International Studies* 33, no. 3 (2007): 353–71. doi:10.1017/S0260210507007553; Luban, "Liberalism, Torture, and the Ticking Bomb"; Tzvetan Todorov, *Torture and the War on Terror* (New York: Seagull Books, 2009).

22. Ronald D. Crelinsten, "How to Make a Torturer," *Index on Censorship* 34, no. 1 (2005): 72–77, doi:10.1080/03064220512331339508; and Crelinsten, "The World of Torture: A Constructed Reality." *Theoretical Criminology* 7, no. 3 (2003): 293–318, doi:10.1177/1362480603007003

23. Physicians for Human Rights, *Leave No Marks*.

24. Nina Philadelphoff-Puren, "Hostile Witness: Torture Testimony in the War on Terror," *Life Writing* 5, no. 2 (2008): 219–36, doi:10.1080/14484520802386568.

25. Stanley Cohen, *States of Denial: Knowing About Atrocities and Suffering* (Malden, Mass.: Blackwell, 2001).

26. Gregory Hooks and Clayton Mosher, "Outrages Against Personal Dignity: Rationalizing Abuse and Torture in the War on Terror," *Social Forces* 83, no. 4 (2005): 1627–45, doi:10.1353/sof.2005.0068

27. Jonathan Potter and Dorothy Smith both give written or literary accounts of events their due. Jonathan Potter, *Representing Reality: Discourse, Rhetoric, and Social Construction* (Thousand Oaks, Calif.: Sage, 1996); Dorothy E. Smith, *Texts, Facts, and Femininity: Exploring the Relations of Ruling* (New York: Routledge, 1990).

28. Marnia Lazreg, *Torture and the Twilight of Empire: From Algiers to Baghdad* (Princeton, N.J.: Princeton University Press, 2008), 253.

29. Rejali, *Torture and Democracy*.

30. Ali Soufan, "My Tortured Decision," *New York Times*, April 22, 2009, http://www.nytimes.com/2009/04/23/opinion/23soufan.html.

31. Philip Gourevitch and Errol Morris, *Standard Operating Procedure* (New York: Penguin Press, 2008).

32. Rejali, *Torture and Democracy*.

33. Center for Human Rights and Global Justice, Human Rights First, and Human Rights Watch, *By the Numbers: Findings of the Detainee Abuse and Accountability Project*, 2006; Human Rights Watch, *No Blood, No Foul, Human Rights Watch*, 2006, accessed April 20, 2014, http://www.hrw.org/reports/2006/07/22/no-blood-no-foul; Physicians for Human Rights,

Broken Laws, Broken Lives: Medical Evidence of Torture by US Personnel and Its Impact.

34. Susan Sontag, *On Photography* (New York: Farrar, Straus and Giroux, 1977), 17.

35. Morris S. Ogul and Bert A. Rockman, "Overseeing Oversight: New Departures and Old Problems," *Legislative Studies Quarterly* 15, no. 1 (February 1, 1990): 5–24, doi:10.2307/439999; Tara M. Sugiyama and Marisa Perry, "The NSA Domestic Surveillance Program: An Analysis of Congressional Oversight During an Era of One-Party Rule," *University of Michigan Journal of Law Reform* 40, no. 1 (2006): 149–89, http://heinonline.org/HOL /LandingPage?handle=hein.journals/umijlr40&div=10&id=&page=; Alan Rosenthal, "Legislative Behavior and Legislative Oversight," *Legislative Studies Quarterly* 6, no. 1 (1981): 115–31, doi:10.2307/439716.

36. Jacqueline Klingebiel, "Dick Cheney: Waterboarding Should Have Been Option with Underwear Bomber," *ABC News*, February 14, 2010, http:// blogs.abcnews.com/thenote/2010/02/cheney-waterboarding-should -have-been-option-with-underwear-bomber.html; Marc Thiessen, "Could a Captured Taliban Leader Have Warned Us of the Times Square Plot?," *The National Review*, May 11, 2010, http://www.nationalreview.com/corner /199225/could-captured-taliban-leader-have-warned-us-times-square-plot /marc-thiessen.

37. Bureau of Investigative Journalism, "More Than 2,400 Dead as Obama's Drone Campaign Marks Five Years," January 30, 2014, http://www .thebureauinvestigates.com/2014/01/23/more-than-2400-dead-as-obamas -drone-campaign-marks-five-years/.

38. Open Society Justice Initiative, *Globalizing Torture: CIA Secret Detention and Extraordinary Rendition*, 2013, accessed June 2, 2014. http://www .opensocietyfoundations.org/sites/default/files/globalizing-torture-20120205.pdf.

39. James Dao, "Drone Pilots Found to Get Stress Disorders Much as Those in Combat Do," *New York Times*, February 22, 2013, http://www.nytimes .com/2013/02/23/us/drone-pilots-found-to-get-stress-disorders-much-as -those-in-combat-do.html.

40. William Saletan, "Koh Is My God Pilot," *Slate*, accessed April 26, 2014, http:// www.slate.com/articles/health_and_science/human_nature/2011/06/koh _is_my_god_pilot.html.

41. Ed Pilkington, "Obama Under Fire Over Detention of Terror Suspect on US Navy Ship," *The Guardian*, July 6, 2011, http://www.theguardian.com /law/2011/jul/06/obama-detention-terror-suspect-us-navy-ship.

42. Benjamin Weiser, "Since 2011 Guilty Plea, Somali Terrorist Has Cooperated with Authorities," *New York Times*, March 25, 2013, http://www.nytimes.com/2013/03/26/nyregion/since-2011-guilty-plea-somali-terrorist-has-cooperated-with-authorities.html.

43. Evan Perez and Susan Candiotti, "Alleged Al Qaeda Operative Al Libi Taken to New York Week After Capture in Libya," October 15, 2013, http://www.cnn.com/2013/10/14/justice/al-libi/index.html.

44. Aki Peritz and Mieke Eoyang, "Even Al Qaeda Operatives Deserve Their Day in Court—and Justice," *Huffington Post*, October 16, 2013, http://www.huffingtonpost.com/aki-peritz/even-al-qaeda-operatives-_b_4109812.html.

45. Howard Koplowitz, "Ahmed Abu Khattala, Alleged Benghazi Attack Ringleader, Captured in Libya by US Forces," *International Business Times*, June 17, 2014, http://www.ibtimes.com/ahmed-abu-khattala-alleged-benghazi-attack-ringleader-captured-libya-us-forces-1603516; Ed O'Keefe, Wesley Lowery, and Sean Sullivan, "Republicans Call for Captured Benghazi Suspect to be Held at Guantanamo," *Washington Post*, June 17, 2004, http://www.washingtonpost.com/blogs/post-politics/wp/2014/06/17/mccain-graham-call-for-captured-benghazi-suspect-to-be-held-at-guantanamo/; Phil Stewart and Jeff Mason, "U.S. Captures Suspected Ringleader of 2012 Attack in Benghazi," Reuters, June 18, 2004, http://uk.reuters.com/article/2014/06/17/uk-usa-politics-benghazi-idUKKBN0ES24I20140617; Eyder Peralta, "Benghazi Suspect, Ahmed Abu Khattala, Is Indicted On Seventeen New Charges," NPR, October 14, 2004, http://www.npr.org/blogs/thetwo-way/2014/10/14/356196973/benghazi-suspect-ahmed-abu-khattala-is-indicted-on-17-new-charges.

46. Jo Becker and Scott Shane, "Secret 'Kill List' Tests Obama's Principles," *New York Times*, May 29, 2012, http://www.nytimes.com/2012/05/29/world/obamas-leadership-in-war-on-al-qaeda.html; Karen DeYoung and Joby Warrick, "Under Obama, More Targeted Killings Than Captures in Counterterrorism Efforts," *Washington Post*, February 14, 2010, http://www.washingtonpost.com/wp-dyn/content/article/2010/02/13/AR2010021303748.html; Klaidman, *Kill or Capture*.

47. "Text of President Obama's May 23 Speech on National Security (Full Transcript)," *Washington Post*, May 23, 2013, http://www.washingtonpost.com/politics/president-obamas-may-23-speech-on-national-security-as-prepared-for-delivery/2013/05/23/02c35e30-c3b8-11e2-9fe2-6ee52d0eb7c1_story.html.

48. On April 22, 2013, the Senate Judiciary's Subcommittee on the Constitution, Civil Rights, and Human Rights held a hearing on drones and the targeted killing of alleged terrorists. No Department of Justice or administration officials testified to the committee.

49. Neela Banerjee, "Republicans Criticize Obama's New Approach on Fighting Terrorism," *Los Angeles Times*, May 26, 2013, http://articles.latimes.com/2013/may/26/news/la-pn-obama-drones-terror-sunday-talk-shows-20130526.

50. Paul Harris, "Rand Paul Anti-drone Filibuster Draws Stinging Criticism from Republicans," *Guardian*, March 7, 2013, http://www.theguardian.com/world/2013/mar/07/rand-paul-drones-policy-filibuster.

51. The photographs taken at Abu Ghraib prison are more ambiguous. Many of them include gloating U.S. soldiers and dehumanized and emasculated Iraqi men. The photographs, further, were tangled in the violence that they record. Some photographs appear staged or partially staged for the camera, in so far as the Americans present in the pictures orient to the camera lens. Photographs were also used to repeat and intensify the humiliation and shame experienced by detainees. One detainee described this to Physicians for Human Rights: "You feel insulted, you feel humiliated. It became kind of a joke with the soldiers. They were showing the pictures and saying, 'Which butt is yours?'" Still, the photographs betray the professional image of interrogation that the Bush administration and its supporters in Congress employed to legitimate the administration's policies on detention and interrogation. Physicians for Human Rights, *Broken Laws, Broken Lives Medical Evidence of Torture by US Personnel and Its Impact: A Report* (Cambridge, Mass.: Physicians for Human Rights, 2008), 37

52. The American anthropologist Lindsay French originally argued this about a Museum of Modern Art in New York exhibit featuring prison photographs of detainees held by the Khmer Rouge in S-21, a prison in Cambodia's capital, Phnom Penh. See Lindsay French, "Exhibiting Terror," in *Truth Claims*, ed. Mark Philip Bradley and Patrice Petro (Camden, N.J.: Rutgers University Press, 2002), 138–40.

53. These sorts of statements, which narrowly articulate the risks and harms of U.S. violence for the country, its citizens, and its soldiers and ignore the costs of this violence for others, appear to be typical of U.S. political discourse. See Douglas V. Porpora, Alexander Nikolaev, Julia Hagemann May, and Alexander Jenkins, *Post-ethical Society: The Iraq War, Abu Ghraib, and the Moral Failure of the Secular* (Chicago: University of Chicago Press, 2013).

54. 151. Cong. Rec. S11061–S11076 (daily ed. October 5, 2005) (statement of Sen. McCain).

55. Murat Kurnaz's appearance at a hearing held by the House Committee on Foreign Affairs on May 20, 2008 is one notable exception. The U.S. detained Kurnaz, a Turkish citizen raised in Germany, in Guantánamo from late 2001 until 2006. Kurnaz testified to the committee that, while in U.S. custody in a prison in Kandahar, Afghanistan, and later Guantánamo, he was dunked under water, electrocuted, hung by his hands, deprived of food and sleep, kept in solitary confinement, subject to extreme temperatures, beaten, and subject to religious and sexual humiliation. During the hearing, Jerrold Nadler directly apologized to Kurnaz for his treatment by the United States, which Nadler described as torture—vicious, savage, and highly illegal. House Subcommittee on International Organizations, Human Rights, and Oversights of the Committee on Foreign Affairs, *City on the Hill or Prison on the Bay? The Mistakes of Guantanamo and the Decline of America's Image, Part II*, 110th Cong., 2nd. sess., May 20, 2008.

56. Physicians for Human Rights. *Broken Laws, Broken Lives: Medical Evidence of Torture by U.S. Personnel and Its Impact: A Report* (Cambridge, Mass.: Physicians for Human Rights, 2008), 16.

57. Ibid., 16.

58. Ibid., 55.

59. Ibid., 45.

60. Ibid., 55.

61. Ibid., 45.

62. Ibid., 19.

63. Ibid., 23.

64. Ibid., 31.

65. Ibid., 9.

APPENDIX: CONSTRUCTIONISM AND THE REALITY OF TORTURE

1. Scott Williams, "ABC, NBC Let Children Ask Questions About the Gulf War," *AP News Archive*, 1991, accessed May 5, 2014, http://www.apnewsarchive .com/1991/ABC-NBC-Let-Children-Ask-Questions-About-the-Gulf-War /id-ae7bc214175119859db0a76c57322571.

2. Elaine Scarry, *The Body in Pain: The Making and Unmaking of the World* (New York: Oxford University Press, 1985).

3. Darius Rejali, *Torture and Democracy* (Princeton, N.J.: Princeton University Press, 2007).

4. Jonathan Potter and Alexa Hepburn, "Discursive Constructionism," *Handbook of Constructionist Research* (2008): 275–93; James A. Holstein and Jaber F. Gubrium, "A Constructionist Analytics for Social Problems," in *Challenges and Choices: Constructionist Perspectives on Social Problems*, ed. James A. Holstein and Gale Miller (Hawthorne, N.Y.: de Gruyter, 2003), 187–208.

5. In their foundational text in the sociology of social problems, Malcolm Spector and John I. Kitsuse initially advised sociologists of social problems to treat the validity of claims or the reality of problems with indifference in order to clear out a scholarly space for the study of claims making. This pragmatic advice transformed, over the better part of two decades, into something of an epistemological quagmire. See Malcolm Spector and John I. Kitsuse, *Constructing Social Problems* (New York: de Gruyter, 1987); Joel Best, "But Seriously Folks: The Limitations of the Strict Constructionist Interpretation of Social Problems," in *Reconsidering Social Constructionism: Debates in Social Problems Theory*, ed. James A. Holstein and Gale Miller (Hawthorne, N.Y.: Aldine de Gruyter, 1993), 129–47.

6. Edward Peters, *Torture* (New York: Blackwell, 1985).

7. Derek Edwards, Malcolm Ashmore, and Jonathan Potter, "Death and Furniture: The Rhetoric, Politics, and Theology of Bottom Line Arguments Against Relativism," *History of the Human Sciences* 8, no. 2 (May 1995): 25–49, doi:10.1177/095269519500800202.

8. Ibid., 35.

9. Steve Woolgar and Dorothy Pawluch, "Ontological Gerrymandering: The Anatomy of Social Problems Explanations," *Social Problems* 32, no. 3 (1985): 214–27.

10. Best, "But Seriously Folks."

11. Stanley Cohen, *States of Denial: Knowing About Atrocities and Suffering* (Malden, Mass.: Blackwell, 2001).

12. Holstein and Gubrium, "Challenges and Choices."

13. Dorothy E. Smith, *The Conceptual Practices of Power* (Boston: Northeastern University Press, 1990).

14. Bruno Latour, *Reassembling the Social* (New York: Oxford University Press, 2005); and Latour, *Science in Action* (Cambridge, Mass.: Harvard University Press, 1987).

15. Smith, *The Conceptual Practices of Power*.

16. Dorothy E. Smith, "Texts and the Ontology of Organizations and Institutions," *Culture and Organization* 7, no. 2 (2001): 175, doi:10.1080/10245280108523557.

17. Joel Best, "Rhetoric in Claims-Making: Constructing the Missing Children Problem." *Social Problems* 34, no. 2 (1987): 104.

18. John M. Johnson, "Horror Stories and the Construction of Child Abuse," in *Images of Issues: Typifying Contemporary Social Problems*, ed. Joel Best (Hawthorne, N.Y.: de Gruyter, 1995), 17.

19. Jonathan Potter, *Representing Reality: Discourse, Rhetoric, and Social Construction* (Thousand Oaks, Calif.: Sage, 1996); Potter and Hepburn, "Discursive Constructionism."

20. Tim Berard, "Collective Action, Collective Reaction: Inspecting Bad Apples in Accounts for Organizational Deviance and Discrimination," *Interaction and Everyday Life: Phenomenological and Ethnomethodological Essays in Honor of George Psathas* (Lanham, Md.: Lexington, 2012): 261–77; Kwang-ki Kim and Tim Berard, "Typification in Society and Social Science: The Continuing Relevance of Schutz's Social Phenomenology," *Human Studies* 32, no. 3 (2009): 263–89, doi:10.1007/s10746-009-9120-6.

21. Alfred W. McCoy, "The U.S. Has a History of Using Torture," *History News Network*, December 6, 2006, accessed February 4, 2014, http://www.hnn.us/article/32497.

22. George Orwell, "Why I Write," in *A Collection of Essays* (New York: Harvest Books, 1981), 313.

23. On mapmaking as a metaphor for scientific inquiry, see Philip Kitcher, *Science, Truth, and Democracy* (New York: Oxford University Press, 2001), 59.

24. Edwards, Ashmore, and Potter, "Death and Furniture," 39.

BIBLIOGRAPHY

Abrams, Joseph. "Despite Reports, Khalid Sheikh Mohammed Was Not Waterboarded 183 Times." *Fox News*, April 28, 2009. http://www.foxnews .com/politics/2009/04/28/despite-reports-khalid-sheikh-mohammed -waterboarded-times/.

Ackerman, Spencer. "Ex-FBI Agent: Still No Evidence That Cheney's Torture Methods Work." *Washington Independent*, August 31, 2009. http://washington independent.com/57273/ex-fbi-agent-still-no-evidence-that-cheneys-torture -methods-work.

Akram, Susan Musarrat, and Kevin R. Johnson. "Race, Civil Rights, and Immigration Law After September 11, 2001: The Targeting of Arabs and Muslims." *New York University Annual Survey of American Law* 58, no. 3 (2002): 295–356. http://heinonline.org/HOL/LandingPage?handle=hein.journals /annam58&div=25&id=&page=.

Alexander, Jeffrey C. "Cultural Pragmatics: Social Performance Between Ritual and Strategy." *Sociological Theory* 22, no. 4 (2004): 527–73. doi:10.1111 /j.0735-2751.2004.00233.x.

——. "Culture and Political Crisis: 'Watergate' and Durkheimian Sociology." In *Durkheimian Sociology: Cultural Studies*, edited by Jeffrey C. Alexander, 187–224. New York: Cambridge University Press, 1988.

Alexander, Jeffrey C., Ron Eyerman, Bernhard Giesen, Neil J. Smelser, and Piotr Sztompka, eds. *Cultural Trauma and Collective Identity*. Berkeley: University of California Press, 2004.

Alexander, Jeffrey C., and Philip Smith. "The Discourse of American Civil Society: A New Proposal for Cultural Studies." *Theory and Society* 22, no. 2 (1993): 151–207. doi:10.1007/BF00993497.

Allen, Mike, and Bradley Graham. "Bush Lauds Rumsfeld for Doing 'Superb Job.'" *Washington Post*, May 11, 2004. http://www.washingtonpost.com /wp-dyn/articles/A15946-2004May10.html.

Amnesty International. "Afghanistan/USA: Prisoners Must Be Treated Humanely." Last modified January 10, 2002. http://www.amnesty.org/en/library/asset/AMR51 /004/2002/en/5d2c70b4-fb03-11dd-9fca-0d1f97c98a21/amr510042002en.pdf.

——. *Amnesty International Report 2013: The State of the World's Human Rights*. London: Amnesty International, 2013. Accessed May 5, 2014. http://files.amnesty .org/air13/AmnestyInternational_AnnualReport2013_complete_en.pdf

——. "Amnesty International's Concerns Regarding Post-September 11 Detentions in the USA." Accessed April 19, 2014. http://www.amnesty.org/en /library/asset/AMR51/044/2002/en/1823f2ff-d882-11dd-ad8c-f3d4445c118e /amr510442002en.html.

——. "Pattern of Brutality and Cruelty—War Crimes at Abu Ghraib." Last modified May 7, 2004. http://www.amnesty.org/en/library/asset/AMR51/077/2004 /en/52b7f594-d5d9-11dd-bb24-1fb85fe8fa05/amr510772004en.html.

——. *Report on Torture*. New York: Farrar, Straus and Giroux, 1975.

Apel, Dora. "Torture Culture: Lynching Photographs and the Images of Abu Ghraib." *Art Journal* 64, no. 2 (2005): 88–100. doi:10.1080/00043249.2005.10791174.

Armbruster, Ben. "Gingrich Changes His Position: 'Waterboarding Is, By Every Technical Rule, Not Torture.'" *ThinkProgress*, November 29, 2011. http://think progress.org/security/2011/11/29/377907/gingrich-waterboarding-not -torture/.

Asad, Talal. "On Torture, or Cruel, Inhuman, and Degrading Treatment." In *Social Suffering*, edited by Arthur Kleinman, Veena Das, and Margaret Lock, 285–308. Berkeley: University of California Press, 1997.

Associated Press. "Bush: 'We Do Not Torture' Terror Suspects." MSNBC.com, November 7, 2005. http://www.msnbc.msn.com/id/9956644/ns/us_news -security/t/bush-we-do-not-torture-terror-suspects/.

——. "Republican Urges Closing Guantánamo Facility." *New York Times*, June 12, 2005. http://www.nytimes.com/2005/06/12/politics/12martinez.html.

——. "Rumsfeld Says No Alternatives Exist for Guantánamo Prison." *New York Times*, June 15, 2005. http://www.nytimes.com/2005/06/15/politics/15gitmo .html.

Athey, Stephanie. "Torture: Alibi and Archetype in U.S. News." In *Culture, Trauma and Conflict: Cultural Studies Perspectives on War*, edited by Nico Carpentier, 135–60. Newcastle, UK: Cambridge Scholars Publishing, 2007.

Avalon Project, "Treaty Between the United States of America and Cuba." Yale Law School, Lillian Goldman Law Library. Accessed June 17, 2014. http:// avalon.law.yale.edu/20th_century/dip_cuba001.asp.

Babb, Sarah. *Behind the Development Banks: Washington Politics, World Poverty, and the Wealth of Nations*. Chicago: University of Chicago Press, 2009.

——. "'A True American System of Finance': Frame Resonance in the U.S. Labor Movement, 1866 to 1886." *American Sociological Review* 61, no. 6 (1996): 1033–52. http://0-www.jstor.org/stable/2096307.

Banerjee, Neela. "Republicans Criticize Obama's New Approach on Fighting Terrorism." *Los Angeles Times*, May 26, 2013. http://articles.latimes.com/2013 /may/26/news/la-pn-obama-drones-terror-sunday-talk-shows-20130526.

Barthes, Roland. *Camera Lucida: Reflections on Photography*. New York: Hill and Wang, 1981.

Basoglu, Metin. *Torture and Its Consequences: Current Treatment Approaches*. New York: Cambridge University Press, 1992.

BBC News. "Afghan Captives Start Cuba Detention." *BBC News*, January 12, 2002. http://news.bbc.co.uk/2/hi/americas/1754444.stm.

Beccaria, Cesare. *On Crimes and Punishments*. 1764. Translated by David Young. Indianapolis, Ind.: Hackett Publishing Company, 1986.

Becker, Jo, and Scott Shane. "Secret 'Kill List' Tests Obama's Principles." *New York Times*, May 29, 2012. http://www.nytimes.com/2012/05/29/world/obamas -leadership-in-war-on-al-qaeda.html.

Benjamin, Mark. "Did Chertoff Lie to Congress about Guantánamo?" *Salon.com*, August 28, 2007. http://www.salon.com/news/feature/2007/08/28/chertoff.

Bennett, W. L., R. G. Lawrence, and S. Livingston. "None Dare Call It Torture: Indexing and the Limits of Press Independence in the Abu Ghraib Scandal." *Journal of Communication* 56, no. 3 (2006): 467–85. doi:10.1111/j.1460-2466.2006.00296.x.

Benoit, William. *Accounts, Excuses, and Apologies: A Theory of Image Restoration Strategies*. Albany: State University of New York Press, 1995.

Berard, Tim. "Collective Action, Collective Reaction: Inspecting Bad Apples in Accounts for Organizational Deviance & Discrimination." *Interaction and Everyday Life: Phenomenological and Ethnomethodological Essays in Honor of George Psathas* (2012): 261–77.

Berger, John. *About Looking*. New York: Vintage, 1991.

Best, Joel. "But Seriously Folks: The Limitations of the Strict Constructionist Interpretation of Social Problems." In *Reconsidering Social Constructionism:*

Debates in Social Problems Theory, edited by James A. Holstein and Gale Miller, 129–47. Hawthorne, N.Y.: Aldine de Gruyter, 1993.

——, ed. *Images of Issues: Typifying Contemporary Social Problems*. New York: de Gruyter, 1995.

——. "Rhetoric in Claims-Making: Constructing the Missing Children Problem." *Social Problems* 34, no. 2 (1987): 101–21. doi:10.2307/800710.

——. *Social Problems*. New York: Norton, 2008.

——. *Threatened Children: Rhetoric and Concern About Child-Victims*. Chicago: University of Chicago Press, 1990.

Biddle, Stephen. "Seeing Baghdad, Thinking Saigon." *Foreign Affairs* 85, no. 2 (2006): 2–14. http://www.jstor.org/stable/20031907.

Boltanski, Luc. *Distant Suffering: Morality, Media, and Politics*. New York: Cambridge University Press, 1999.

Bonds, Eric. "Indirect Violence and Legitimation: Torture, Surrogacy, and the U.S. War on Terror." *Societies Without Borders* 7, no. 3 (2012): 295–325. Accessed May 5, 2014. http://societieswithoutborders.files.wordpress.com/2012/09/bonds2012.pdf

Borger, Julian. "Congress Delegates Scorn X-Ray Fears." *Guardian*, January 26, 2002. http://www.guardian.co.uk/world/2002/jan/26/usa.afghanistan.

Boynton, G. R. "When Senators and Publics Meet at the Environmental Protection Subcommittee." *Discourse and Society* 2, no. 2 (1991): 131–55. doi:10.1177/0957926591002002001.

Bradbury, Steven G. *Re: Application of 18 U.S.C. §§ 2340–2340A to Certain Techniques That May Be Used in the Interrogation of a High Value Al Qaeda Detainee*. Washington, D.C.: Office of the Principal Deputy Assistant Attorney General, 2005. http://www.fas.org/irp/agency/doj/olc/techniques.pdf.

Brown, Michelle. "The Abu Ghraib Torture and Prisoner Abuse Scandal." In *Crimes and Trials of the Century,* vol. 2, *From Pine Ridge to Abu Ghraib,* edited by S. Chermak and F. Y. Bailey, 305–23. Westport, Conn.: Praeger, 2007.

Bureau of Investigative Journalism. "More Than 2,400 Dead as Obama's Drone Campaign Marks Five Years," January 23, 2014. http://www.thebureauinvestigates.com/2014/01/23/more-than-2400-dead-as-obamas-drone-campaign-marks-five-years/.

Burton, Frank, and Pat Carlen. *Official Discourse: On Discourse Analysis, Government Publications, Ideology, and the State*. Boston: Routledge & Kegan Paul, 1979.

Bush, George W. "Humane Treatment of al Qaeda and Taliban Detainee." *The National Security Archive*. Accessed June 16, 2014. http://www2.gwu.edu/~nsarchiv/NSAEBB/NSAEBB127/02.02.07.pdf.

———. "Interview with Al-Ahram International." *The American Presidency Project*, May 6, 2004. Accessed April 19, 2014. http://www.presidency.ucsb.edu/ws/index.php?pid=63380#axzz1HAH1L2tI.

———. "President Bush's Speech on Terrorism." *New York Times*, September 6, 2006. http://www.nytimes.com/2006/09/06/washington/06bush_transcript.html.

Butler, Judith. *Frames of War: When Is Life Grievable?* New York: Verso, 2009.

———. *Precarious Life: The Powers of Mourning and Violence*. New York: Verso, 2004.

Cambanis, Thanassis. "Iraqi Detentions Fuel Anti-US Sentiment." *Boston Globe*, March 28, 2004. http://www.commondreams.org/headlines04/0328-04.htm.

Carr, Thomas P. *Hearings in the House of Representatives: A Guide for Preparation and Procedure*. Washington, D.C.: Congressional Research Service, 2006.

Casimir, Leslie. "Jailers Abused Muslims: Report." *Daily News*, December 19, 2003. http://www.nydailynews.com/archives/news/jailers-abused-muslims-report-article-1.525543.

Caton, Steven C. "Coetzee, Agamben, and the Passion of Abu Ghraib." *American Anthropologist* 108, no. 1 (2006): 114–23. doi:10.1525/aa.2006.108.1.114.

CBS News. "CBS News/NJ Debate Transcript, Part 1." *CBS News*, November 13, 2011. http://www.cbsnews.com/news/cbs-news-nj-debate-transcript-part-1/8/.

Cebdriwucz, Leo. "Portugal's Offer to Help the US Close Guantánamo." *Time*, December 18, 2008. http://www.time.com/time/world/article/0,8599,1867163,00.html.

Center for Human Rights and Global Justice, Human Rights First, and Human Rights Watch. *By the Numbers: Findings of the Detainee Abuse and Accountability Project*, 2006. Accessed May 5, 2014. http://www.chrgj.org/docs/By_The_Numbers.pdf.

Chandrasekaran, Rajiv, and Scott Wilson. "Mistreatment of Detainees Went Beyond Guards' Abuse." *Washington Post*, May 11, 2004. http://www.washingtonpost.com/wp-dyn/articles/A15492-2004May10.html.

Chang, Gordon C., and Hugh B. Mehan. "Why We Must Attack Iraq: Bush's Reasoning Practices and Argumentation System." *Discourse Society* 19, no. 4 (2008): 453–82. doi:10.1177/0957926508089939.

CIA Office of Inspector General. *Counterterrorism Detention and Interrogation Activities*. Langley, Va.: CIA, 2004. Accessed October 24, 2014. http://www2.gwu.edu/~nsarchiv/torture_archive/20040507.pdf.

Cloud, David S. "Red Cross Cited Detainee Abuse Over a Year Ago." *Wall Street Journal*, May 10, 2004. http://online.wsj.com/news/articles/SB108414473392906282.

Cloud, David S., Carla Anne Robbins, and Greg Jaffe. "Red Cross Found Wide-spread Abuse of Iraqi Prisoners." *Wall Street Journal*, May 7, 2004. http://online.wsj.com/news/articles/SB108384106459803859.

CNN. "Part II: CNN/YouTube Republican Presidential Debate Transcript," November 29, 2007. CNN.com, http://www.cnn.com/2007/POLITICS/11/28/debate.transcript.part2/.

——. "Report: Abu Ghraib Was 'Animal House' at Night," CNN.com, August 25, 2004. http://www.cnn.com/2004/US/08/24/abughraib.report/index.html.

——. "U.S. to Hold Detainees at Guantanamo Bay." CNN.com, December 28, 2001. http://edition.cnn.com/2001/US/12/27/ret.holding.detainees/.

Coalition Provisional Authority. "Coalition Provisional Authority Briefing." *The Coalition Provisional Authority*, 2004. http://www.iraqcoalition.org/transcripts/20040320_Mar20_KimmittSenor.html.

Coetzee, J. M. *Waiting for the Barbarians*. New York: Penguin, 1982.

Cohen, Stanley. *States of Denial: Knowing About Atrocities and Suffering*. Malden, Mass.: Blackwell, 2001.

Cole, David. "The Man Behind the Torture." *The New York Review of Books*, December 6, 2007, http://www.nybooks.com/articles/archives/2007/dec/06/the-man-behind-the-torture/.

Collins, Randall. "Three Faces of Cruelty: Towards a Comparative Sociology of Violence." *Theory and Society* 1, no. 4 (1974): 415–40. doi:10.1007/BF00160802.

Commission on Presidential Debates. "October 8, 2004, Debate Transcript." Accessed April 19, 2014. http://www.debates.org/index.php?page=october-8-2004-debate-transcript.

——. "September 26, 2008, Debate Transcript." Accessed April 19, 2014. http://www.debates.org/index.php?page=2008-debate-transcript.

Conroy, John. *Unspeakable Acts, Ordinary People: The Dynamics of Torture*. New York: Knopf, 2000.

Cowan, Alison Leigh. "A Nation Challenged: Civil Rights; Detainees' Lawyers Complain of Unfair Treatment." *New York Times*, 2001. http://www.nytimes.com/2001/10/21/us/a-nation-challenged-civil-rights-detainees-lawyers-complain-of-unfair-treatment.html?pagewanted=1.

Coy, Patrick G., Lynne M. Woehrle, and Gregory M. Maney. "Discursive Legacies: The U.S. Peace Movement and 'Support the Troops.'" *Social Problems* 55, no. 2 (2008): 161–89. doi:10.1525/sp.2008.55.2.161.

Crelinsten, Ronald D. "How to Make a Torturer." *Index on Censorship* 34, no. 1 (2005): 72–77. doi:10.1080/03064220512331339508.

——. "The World of Torture: A Constructed Reality." *Theoretical Criminology* 7, no. 3 (2003): 293–318. doi:10.1177/13624806030073003.

Danner, Mark. "After September 11: Our State of Exception." *New York Review of Books*, October 13, 2011. http://www.nybooks.com/articles/archives/2011 /oct/13/after-september-11-our-state-exception/.

——. "Frozen Scandal." *New York Review of Books*, December 4, 2008. http:// www.nybooks.com/articles/archives/2008/dec/04/frozen-scandal/.

——. *Stripping Bare the Body: Politics, Violence, War*. New York: Nation Books, 2009.

——. *Torture and Truth: America, Abu Ghraib, and the War on Terror*. New York: New York Review Books, 2004.

——. "We Are All Torturers Now." *New York Times*, January 6, 2005. http://www .nytimes.com/2005/01/06/opinion/06danner.html.

Dao, James. "Drone Pilots Found to Get Stress Disorders Much as Those in Combat Do." *New York Times*, February 22, 2013. http://www.nytimes .com/2013/02/23/us/drone-pilots-found-to-get-stress-disorders-much-as -those-in-combat-do.html.

Davis, Darren W., and Brian D. Silver. "Civil Liberties vs. Security: Public Opinion in the Context of the Terrorist Attacks on America." *American Journal of Political Science* 48, no. 1 (2004): 28–46. doi:10.1111/j.0092-5853.2004.00054.x.

Davis, Matthew. "Bush Battles for US Hearts and Minds." *BBC News*, December 7, 2005. http://news.bbc.co.uk/2/hi/americas/4505506.stm.

DeLillo, Don. *Point Omega*. New York: Simon and Schuster, 2010.

DeYoung, Karen, and Joby Warrick. "Under Obama, More Targeted Killings than Captures in Counterterrorism Efforts." *Washington Post*, February 14, 2010. http://www.washingtonpost.com/wp-dyn/content/article/2010/02/13 /AR2010021303748.html.

Domhoff, G. William. *The Higher Circles: The Governing Class*. New York: Vintage, 1970.

Drinkard, Jim, Dave Moniz, and John Diamond. "Rumsfeld Faces Lawmakers." *USA Today*, May 7, 2004.

Edelman, Murray. *Constructing the Political Spectacle*. Chicago: University of Chicago Press, 1988.

Edwards, Derek, Malcolm Ashmore, and Jonathan Potter. "Death and Furniture: The Rhetoric, Politics and Theology of Bottom Line Arguments Against Relativism." *History of the Human Sciences* 8, no. 2 (May 1995): 25–49. doi:10.1177/095269519500800202.

Eggen, Dan. "Audio of Attorney-Detainee Interviews Called Illegal." *Washington Post*, December 20, 2003.

——. "Tapes Show Abuse of 9/11 Detainees; Justice Department Examines Videos Prison Officials Said Were Destroyed." *Washington Post*, December 18, 2003.

——. "Was There a 20th Hijacker for Sept. 11?" *Washington Post*, June 22, 2006. http://www.washingtonpost.com/wp-dyn/content/article/2006/06/21/AR2006062101782.html.

Eggen, Dan, and R. Jeffrey Smith. "FBI Agents Allege Abuse of Detainees at Guantanamo Bay." *Washington Post*, December 21, 2004. http://www.washingtonpost.com/wp-dyn/articles/A14936-2004Dec20.html.

Eggen, Dan, and Joby Warrick. "CIA Destroyed Videos Showing Interrogations." *Washington Post*, December 7, 2007. http://www.washingtonpost.com/wp-dyn/content/article/2007/12/06/AR2007120601828.html.

Einolf, Christopher J. "The Fall and Rise of Torture: A Comparative and Historical Analysis." *Sociological Theory* 25, no. 2 (2007): 101–21. doi:10.1111/j.1467-9558.2007.00300.x.

Eisenman, Stephen. *The Abu Ghraib Effect*. London: Reaktion, 2007.

Esposito, Richard. "CIA Chief: We Waterboarded." *ABC News*, February 5, 2008. http://abcnews.go.com/Blotter/TheLaw/story?id=4244423&page=1.

Esposito, Richard, and Brian Ross. "Coming in from the Cold: CIA Spy Calls Waterboarding Necessary But Torture." *ABC News*, December 10, 2007. http://abcnews.go.com/Blotter/story?id=3978231&page=1.

Fanon, Frantz. *The Wretched of the Earth*. New York: Grove Press, 1963.

Federal Bureau of Investigation. "FBI Intelligence Timeline." Accessed March 7, 2011. http://www.fbi.gov/about-us/intelligence/timeline.

——. "9/11 Investigation (PENTBOMB)." Accessed May 15, 2010. http://www.fbi.gov/pressrel/penttbom/penttbomb.htm.

Federal Document Clearing House E-Media. "Rumsfeld Testifies Before Senate Armed Services Committee." *Washington Post*, May 7, 2004. http://www.washingtonpost.com/wp-dyn/articles/A8575-2004May7.html.

Federal News Service. "Republican Presidential Debate in South Carolina." *New York Times*, May 15, 2007. http://www.nytimes.com/2007/05/15/us/politics/16repubs-text.html.

Fein, Bruce. "Abrogating Terrorism's Paradise." *Washington Times*, October 2, 2001. http://www.washingtontimes.com/news/2001/oct/2/20011002-025736-6454r/.

Finn, Peter. "Guantanamo Closure Called Obama Priority." *Washington Post*, November 12, 2008, http://www.washingtonpost.com/wp-dyn/content/article/2008/11/11/AR2008111102865.html.

Finn, Peter, and Joby Warrick. "Detainee's Harsh Treatment Foiled No Plots." *Washington Post*, March 29, 2009, http://www.washingtonpost.com/wp-dyn/content/article/2009/03/28/AR2009032802066.html

Finn, Peter, Joby Warrick, and Julie Tate. "CIA Report Calls Oversight of Early Interrogations Poor." *Washington Post*, August 25, 2009. http://www.washingtonpost.com/wp-dyn/content/article/2009/08/24/AR2009082402220.html.

Forrest, Duncan, Bernard Knight, and Morris Tidball-Binz. "The Documentation of Torture." In *A Glimpse of Hell: Reports on Torture Worldwide*, edited by D. Forrest, 167–86. New York: New York University Press, 1996.

Foucault, Michel. *Society Must Be Defended: Lectures at the Collège De France, 1975–76*. New York: Picador, 2003.

Fox News. "Bush Apologizes for Iraqi Prisoner Abuse." *FoxNews*, May 7, 2004. http://www.foxnews.com/story/0,2933,119156,00.html.

French, Lindsay. "Exhibiting Terror." In *Truth Claims*, edited by Mark Philip Bradley and Patrice Petro, 131–54. Camden, N.J.: Rutgers University Press, 2002.

Gamio, Lazaro, and Carol Rosenberg. "Tracking the Hunger Strike in Guantanamo." *Miami Herald*. Accessed May 5, 2014. http://www.miamiherald.com/static/media/projects/gitmo_chart/index.html.

Gamson, William A., David Croteau, William Hoynes, and Theodore Sasson. "Media Images and the Social Construction of Reality." *Annual Review of Sociology* 18 (January 1, 1992): 373–93. doi:10.1146/annurev.so.18.080192.002105.

Garland, David. *Peculiar Institution: America's Death Penalty in an Age of Abolition*. Cambridge, Mass.: Harvard University Press, 2011.

Glaberson, William. "A Nation Challenged: The Arrests; Detainees' Accounts Are at Odds with Official Reports of an Orderly Investigation." *New York Times*, September 29, 2001. http://www.nytimes.com/2001/09/29/us/nation-challenged-arrests-detainees-accounts-are-odds-with-official-reports.html?pagewanted=1.

Goffman, Erving. *The Presentation of Self in Everyday Life*. Garden City, N.Y.: Doubleday, 1959.

Goldfeld, Anne E., Richard F. Mollica, Barbara H. Pesavento, and Stephen V. Faraone. "The Physical and Psychological Sequelae of Torture: Symptomatology and Diagnosis." *JAMA* 259, no. 18 (May 13, 1988): 2725–29. doi:10.1001 /jama.1988.03720180051032.

Goldman, Adam, and Matt Apuzzo. "Ex-Spy: Destroying CIA Tapes Purged 'Ugly Visuals.'" *Yahoo News*, April 24, 2012. http://news.yahoo.com/ex-spy -destroying-cia-tapes-purged-ugly-visuals-212042971.html.

Goodman, Ryan, and Derek Jinks. "How to Influence States: Socialization and International Human Rights Law." *Duke Law Journal* 54, no. 3 (December 2004): 621–703. http://www.jstor.org/stable/40040439.

Goodwin, Liz. "Obama Vows to Close Guantanamo in State of the Union." *Yahoo News*, January 28, 2014. http://news.yahoo.com/for-first-time-in-five-years --obama-vows-to-close-guantanamo-in-state-of-the-union-023956545.html.

Gordon, Avery. *Ghostly Matters: Haunting and the Sociological Imagination*. Minneapolis: University of Minnesota Press, 2008.

Gorst-Unsworth, C., and E. Goldenberg. "Psychological Sequelae of Torture and Organised Violence Suffered by Refugees from Iraq: Trauma-Related Factors Compared with Social Factors in Exile." *The British Journal of Psychiatry* 172, no. 1 (January 1, 1998): 90–94. doi:10.1192/bjp.172.1.90.

Gourevitch, Philip, and Errol Morris. "Exposure." *The New Yorker*, March 24, 2008. http://www.newyorker.com/reporting/2008/03/24/080324fa_fact _gourevitch.

——. *Standard Operating Procedure*. New York: Penguin Press, 2008.

Grady, Denise. "Tugging at Threads to Unspool Stories of Torture." *New York Times*, May 2, 2011. http://www.nytimes.com/2011/05/03/health/03torture .html.

Graham, Bradley, and Josh White. "Top Pentagon Leaders Faulted in Prison Abuse." *Washington Post*, August 25, 2004. http://www.washingtonpost.com /wp-dyn/articles/A28862-2004Aug24.html.

Greenhouse, Linda. "Justices, 5–3, Broadly Reject Bush Plan to Try Detainees." *New York Times*, June 30, 2006. http://www.nytimes.com/2006/06/30 /washington/30hamdan.html.

——. "Justices Hint That They'll Rule on Challenge Filed by Detainee." *New York Times*, March 29, 2006. http://www.nytimes.com/2006/03/29 /politics/29scotus.html.

Guardian. "Guantánamo Detainees Are 'Bad People,' Says Cheney," June 13, 2005. http://www.guardian.co.uk/world/2005/jun/13/afghanistan.guantanamo.

Gusfield, Joseph R. "Constructing the Ownership of Social Problems: Fun and Profit in the Welfare State." *Social Problems* 36, no. 5 (1989): 431–41. doi:10.2307/3096810.

Haines, Herbert. "Flawed Executions, the Anti-Death Penalty Movement, and the Politics of Capital Punishment." *Social Problems* 39, no. 2 (1992): 125–38, doi:10.2307/3097033.

Hajjar, Lisa. "Does Torture Work? A Sociolegal Assessment of the Practice in Historical and Global Perspective." *Annual Review of Law and Social Science* 5, no. 1 (2009): 311–45. doi:10.1146/annurev.lawsocsci.093008.131501.

Haney, Craig, Curtis Banks, and Philip Zimbardo. "Interpersonal Dynamics in a Simulated Prison." *International Journal of Criminology and Penology* 1, no. 1 (1973): 69–97. http://psycnet.apa.org/psycinfo/1974-32677-001.

Haraway, Donna. "Situated Knowledges: The Science Question in Feminism and the Privilege of Partial Perspective." *Feminist Studies* 14, no. 3 (1988): 575–99. http://www.jstor.org/stable/3178066.

Harris, Paul. "Rand Paul Anti-drone Filibuster Draws Stinging Criticism from Republicans." *Guardian*, March 7, 2013. http://www.theguardian.com/world/2013/mar/07/rand-paul-drones-policy-filibuster.

Haynes, William J. *Counter-Resistance Techniques*. Washington, D.C.: General Counsel of the Department of Defense, 2002. Accessed November 4, 2014. http://library.rumsfeld.com/doclib/sp/380/2002-11-27%20from%20Haynes%20re%20Counter-Resistance%20Techniques.pdf.

Higham, Scott, and Joe Stephens. "New Details of Prison Abuse Emerge; Abu Ghraib Detainees' Statements Describe Sexual Humiliation and Savage Beatings." *Washington Post*, May 21, 2004. http://www.washingtonpost.com/wp-dyn/articles/A43783-2004May20.html.

Holstein, James A., and Jaber F. Gubrium. "A Constructionist Analytics for Social Problems." In *Challenges and Choices: Constructionist Perspectives on Social Problems*, edited by James A. Holstein and Gale Miller, 187–208. Hawthorne, N.Y.: de Gruyter, 2003.

Hooks, Gregory, and Clayton Mosher. "Outrages Against Personal Dignity: Rationalizing Abuse and Torture in the War on Terror." *Social Forces* 83, no. 4 (2005): 1627–45. doi:10.1353/sof.2005.0068.

Huggins, Martha Knisely, Mika Haritos-Fatouros, and Philip G. Zimbardo. *Violence Workers: Police Torturers and Murderers Reconstruct Brazilian Atrocities*. Berkeley: University of California Press, 2002.

Human Rights Watch. *No Blood, No Foul.* 2006. Accessed April 20, 2014. http://
www.hrw.org/reports/2006/07/22/no-blood-no-foul.

——. "Presumption of Guilt: Human Rights Abuses of Post-September 11 Detainees." 2002. Accessed April 20, 2014. http://www.hrw.org/reports/2002/us911/.

Independent Panel to Review DoD Detention Operations. *Final Report of the
Independent Panel to Review DoD Detention Operations.* Arlington, Va.: Independent Panel to Review DoD Operations, 2004. Accessed October 24, 2014,
http://www.defense.gov/news/aug2004/d20040824finalreport.pdf.

International Committee of the Red Cross. *ICRC Report on the Treatment of Fourteen "High Value Detainees" in CIA Custody.* Washington, D.C.: International
Committee of the Red Cross, 2007. Accessed April 20, 2014. http://assets
.nybooks.com/media/doc/2010/04/22/icrc-report.pdf.

——. *Report of the International Committee of the Red Cross (ICRC) on the Treatment by the Coalition Forces of Prisoners of War and Other Protected Persons
by the Geneva Conventions in Iraq during Arrest, Internment, and Interrogation,* 2004. Accessed April 20, 2014. http://www.globalsecurity.org/military
/library/report/2004/icrc_report_iraq_feb2004.htm.

Jackall, Robert. *Moral Mazes: The World of Corporate Managers.* New York:
Oxford University Press, 1989.

Jackson, Richard. "Constructing Enemies: 'Islamic Terrorism' in Political and
Academic Discourse." *Government and Opposition* 42, no. 3 (2007): 394–426.
doi:10.1111/j.1477-7053.2007.00229.x.

——. "Language, Policy, and the Construction of a Torture Culture in the War on
Terrorism." *Review of International Studies* 33, no. 3 (2007): 353–71. doi:10.1017
/S0260210507007553.

Jacobson, Gary C. "The 2008 Presidential and Congressional Elections: Anti-
Bush Referendum and Prospects for the Democratic Majority." *Political Science
Quarterly* 124, no. 1 (2009): 1–30. doi:10.1002/j.1538-165X.2009.tb00640.x.

Jerolmack, Colin. "How Pigeons Became Rats: The Cultural-Spatial Logic
of Problem Animals." *Social Problems* 55, no. 1 (2008): 72–94. doi:10.1525
/sp.2008.55.1.72.

Johnson, John M. "Horror Stories and the Construction of Child Abuse." In
Images of Issues: Typifying Contemporary Social Problems, edited by Joel Best,
17–31. Hawthorne, N.Y.: de Gruyter, 1995.

Johnson, Kevin R. " 'Aliens' and the U.S. Immigration Laws: The Social and Legal
Construction of Nonpersons." *The University of Miami Inter-American Law
Review* 28, no. 2 (Winter 1996): 263–92. http://www.jstor.org/stable/40176418.

Joint Task Force–Guantanamo Public Affairs Office. "Guantanamo Facility will Assist Refugees in Distress." *The Wire* 8, no. 32 (2007): 4. Accessed October 26, 2014. http://www.jtfgtmo.southcom.mil/wire/wire/WirePDF/v8/Issue32v8 .pdf

Jones, Bryan D., and Frank R. Baumgartner. *The Politics of Attention: How Government Prioritizes Problems*. Chicago: University of Chicago Press, 2005.

Kagan, Robert. "America's Crisis of Legitimacy." *Foreign Affairs* 83, no. 2 (2004): 65–87. http://www.jstor.org/stable/20033903.

Kamen, Al, Lyndsey Layton, Elizabeth Williamson, and Zachary A. Goldfarb. "Senate Committee Staff Directors Set Session Agenda." *Washington Post*, December 26, 2006. http://www.washingtonpost.com/wp-dyn/content /article/2006/12/25/AR2006122500581.html.

Kaufman, Marc. "Cheney: U.S. Not Aiming to Close Guantanamo." *Washington Post*, June 13, 2005. http://www.washingtonpost.com/wp-dyn/content /article/2005/06/12/AR2005061201265.html.

Kim, Kwang-ki, and Tim Berard. "Typification in Society and Social Science: The Continuing Relevance of Schutz's Social Phenomenology." *Human Studies* 32, no. 3 (September 1, 2009): 263–289. doi:10.1007/s10746-009-9120-6.

Kitcher, Philip. *Science, Truth, and Democracy*. New York: Oxford University Press, 2001.

Klaidman, Daniel. *Kill or Capture: The War on Terror and the Soul of the Obama Presidency*. Boston: Houghton Mifflin Harcourt, 2012.

Klingebiel, Jacqueline. "Dick Cheney: Waterboarding Should Have Been Option with Underwear Bomber." *ABC News,* February 14, 2010. http://blogs .abcnews.com/thenote/2010/02/cheney-waterboarding-should-have-been -option-with-underwear-bomber.html.

Koplowitz, Howard. "Ahmed Abu Khattala, Alleged Benghazi Attack Ringleader, Captured in Libya by US Forces." *International Business Times*, June 17, 2014, http://www.ibtimes.com/ahmed-abu-khattala-alleged-benghazi-attack-ring leader-captured-libya-us-forces-1603516

Kucinich, Dennis. "A Prayer for America," February 26, 2002. Accessed April 20, 2014. http://www.commondreams.org/views02/0226-09.htm.

Langbein, John. *Torture and the Law of Proof: Europe and England in the Ancien Régime*. Chicago: University of Chicago Press, 1977.

Latour, Bruno. *Reassembling the Social*. New York: Oxford University Press, 2005.

——. *Science in Action*. Cambridge, Mass.: Harvard University Press, 1987.

Latour, Bruno, and Steve Woolgar. *Laboratory Life: The Construction of Scientific Facts.* Princeton, N.J.: Princeton University Press, 1986.

Lazreg, Marnia. *Torture and the Twilight of Empire: From Algiers to Baghdad.* Princeton, N.J.: Princeton University Press, 2008.

Lea, Henry C. *Superstition and Force: Essays on the Wager of Law, the Wager of Battle, the Ordeal, Torture,* 1st ed. Philadelphia: Collins, 1866.

——. *Superstition and Force: Essays on the Wager of Law, the Wager of Battle, the Ordeal, Torture,* 2nd ed. 1870. Reprint, New York: Haskell House Publishers, 1971.

Leahy, Patrick. "A Truth Commission to Investigate Bush-Cheney Administration Abuses." *Huffington Post,* February 12, 2009. http://www.huffingtonpost.com /sen-patrick-leahy/a-truth-commission-to-inv_b_166461.html.

Lecky, William Edward Hartpole. *History of the Rise and Influence of the Spirit of Rationalism in Europe,* 4th ed. London: Longmans, Green, and Co., 1870.

Lewis, Neil A. "Broad Use of Harsh Tactics Is Described at Cuba Base." *New York Times,* October 17, 2004. http://www.nytimes.com/2004/10/17 /politics/17gitmo.html.

——. "Red Cross Finds Detainee Abuse in Guantánamo." *New York Times,* November 30, 2004. http://www.nytimes.com/2004/11/30/politics/30gitmo .html.

——. "Report Discredits F.B.I. Claims of Abuse at Guantánamo Bay." *New York Times,* July 14, 2005. http://www.nytimes.com/2005/07/14/politics/14gitmo .html.

Lewis, Neil A., and David Johnston. "New F.B.I. Files Describe Abuse of Iraq Inmates." *New York Times,* December 21, 2004. http://www.nytimes .com/2004/12/21/politics/21abuse.html.

Lichtblau, Eric. "Ashcroft Defends Detentions as Immigrants Recount Toll." *New York Times,* June 5, 2003. http://www.nytimes.com/2003/06/05 /national/05TERR.html.

——. "Congress Looks Into Obstruction as Calls for Justice Inquiry Rise." *New York Times,* December 8, 2007. http://query.nytimes.com/gst/fullpage.html ?res=9500E2DA1031F93BA35751C1A9619C8B63.

——. "Threats and Responses: Detainees; Treatment of Detained Immigrants Is Under Investigation." *New York Times,* June 26, 2003. http://www.nytimes .com/2003/06/26/us/threats-responses-detainees-treatment-detained -immigrants-under-investigation.html.

Llorente, Marina A. "Civilization versus Barbarism." In *Collateral Language: A User's Guide to America's New War,* edited by John Collins and Ross Glover, 39–51. New York: New York University Press, 2002.

Lokaneeta, Jinee. *Transnational Torture: Law, Violence, and State Power in the United States and India*. New York: New York University Press, 2011.

Loveman, Mara. "The Modern State and the Primitive Accumulation of Symbolic Power." *American Journal of Sociology* 110, no. 6 (2005): 1651–83. http://www .jstor.org/stable/10.1086/428688.

Luban, David. "Liberalism, Torture, and the Ticking Bomb." *Virginia Law Review* 91, no. 6 (2005): 1425–61. http://0-www.jstor.org/stable/3649415.

Lynch, Michael, and David Bogen. *The Spectacle of History: Speech, Text, and Memory at the Iran-Contra Hearings*. Durham, N.C.: Duke University Press, 1996.

Madden, Mike. "Rumsfeld: Architect of Torture." *Salon.com*, April 22, 2009. http://www.salon.com/2009/04/22/madden_2/.

Mahler, Jonathan. *The Challenge:* Hamdan v. Rumsfeld *and the Fight Over Presidential Power*. 1st ed. New York: Farrar, Straus and Giroux, 2008.

Maratea, Ray. "The E-Rise and Fall of Social Problems: The Blogosphere as a Public Arena." *Social Problems* 55, no. 1 (2008): 139–60. doi:10.1525/sp.2008.55.1.139.

Mast, Jason L. "The Cultural Pragmatics of Event-ness: The Clinton/Lewinsky Affair." In *Social Performance: Symbolic Action, Cultural Pragmatics, and Ritual*, edited by Jeffrey C. Alexander, Bernhard Giesen, and Jason L. Mast, 115–45. New York: Cambridge University Press, 2006.

Mayer, Jane. *The Dark Side*. New York: Doubleday, 2008.

——. "The Experiment." *New Yorker*, July 11, 2005. http://www.newyorker.com /archive/2005/07/11/050711fa_fact4.

Mark, Mazzetti, "'03 U.S. Memo Approved Harsh Interrogations," *New York Times*, April 2, 2008, http://www.nytimes.com/2008/04/02/washington/02terror .html.

——. "C.I.A. Destroyed 2 Tapes Showing Interrogations." *New York Times*, December 7, 2007. http://www.nytimes.com/2007/12/07/washington/07intel.html.

Mazzetti, Mark, and David Johnston. "Inquiry Begins Into Destruction of Tapes." *New York Times*, December 9, 2007. http://www.nytimes.com/2007/12/09 /washington/09zubaydah.html.

McCain, John. "McCain's Speech on Foreign Policy," *Council on Foreign Relations*, March 26 2008. Accessed June 18, 2014. http://www.cfr.org/publication /15834/mccains_speech_on_foreign_policy_march_2008.html.

McCoy, Alfred W. "The U.S. Has a History of Using Torture." Accessed February 4, 2014. http://www.hnn.us/article/32497.

McGreal, Chris. "Barack Obama Abandons Guantánamo Closure Plan After Congress Veto." *Guardian*, January 20, 2011. http://www.theguardian.com /world/2011/jan/20/barack-obama-guantanamo-congress-veto.

Media Matters Staff. "Scarborough Mocks Torture, Says of Sleep Deprivation: 'They Do That in Fraternities.'" *Media Matters for America*, August 25,
2009. http://mediamatters.org/video/2009/08/25/scarborough-mocks-torture
-says-of-sleep-depriva/153844.

Meet the Press. Transcript for February 21, 2010. NBC News, February 24, 2010.
http://www.nbcnews.com/id/35493976/ns/meet_the_press/t/meet-press
-transcript-february/.

Miami Herald. "Guantánamo Twelfth Anniversary Protests." Accessed January
27, 2014. http://www.miamiherald.com/2014/01/11/3864497/jan-11-2014
-guantanamo-12th-anniversary.html.

Miles, Steven H. "Medical Ethics and the Interrogation of Guantanamo 063." *The American Journal of Bioethics* 7, no. 4 (2007): 5–11.
doi:10.1080/15265160701263535.

Mills, C. Wright. "The Structure of Power in American Society." *The British Journal of Sociology* 9, no. 1 (1958): 29–41. doi:10.2307/587620.

Mitchell, W. J. Thomas. "The Unspeakable and the Unimaginable: Word and
Image in a Time of Terror." *English Literary History* 72, no. 2 (2005): 291–308,
doi:10.1353/elh.2005.0019.

Monbiot, George. "Genocide or Peace." *Guardian*, October 2, 2001. http://www
.theguardian.com/world/2001/oct/02/afghanistan.comment.

Moniz, Dave, and Donna Leinwand. "Panel: Top Officials Played Role in Prison
Abuse." Iraq Abuse Report Holds Top Officials Responsible." *USA Today*,
August 24, 2004.

Montello, D. R. "Scale in Geography." In *International Encyclopedia of the Social
and Behavioral Sciences*, edited by N. J. Smelser and P. B. Baltes, 13501–4. New
York: Elsevier, 2001.

Morales, Lymari. "Americans Prioritize the Economy Over Terrorism." *Gallup*,
June 27, 2008. Accessed April 20, 2014. http://www.gallup.com/poll/108415
/americans-prioritize-economy-over-terrorism.aspx.

Mucciaroni, Gary. *Deliberative Choices: Debating Public Policy in Congress*.
Chicago: University of Chicago Press, 2006.

Naples, Nancy A. "The 'New Consensus' on the Gendered 'Social Contract': The
1987–1988 U.S. Congressional Hearings on Welfare Reform." *Signs* 22, no. 4
(1997): 907–45. doi:10.2307/3175224.

Naval Station Guantanamo Bay, Public Affairs Office. "Naval Station Guantanamo Bay, Cuba." Accessed October 26, 2014. http://www.jtfgtmo.southcom
.mil/xWEBSITE/fact_sheets/NavstaGTMO.pdf

Navarro, Mireya. "Last of Refugees from Cuba in '94 Flight Now Enter U.S." *New York Times*, February 1, 1996. http://www.nytimes.com/1996/02/01/world /last-of-refugees-from-cuba-in-94-flight-now-enter-us.html.

Neal, Terry M. "The Politics of Abu Ghraib." *Washington Post*, May 12, 2004. http://www.washingtonpost.com/wp-dyn/articles/A18316-2004May11.html.

New York Times. "Mr. Rumsfeld's Defense." May 8, 2004. http://www.nytimes .com/2004/05/08/opinion/mr-rumsfeld-s-defense.html.

——. "No Accountability on Abu Ghraib." September 10, 2004. http://www .nytimes.com/2004/09/10/opinion/10fri1.html?_r=0

——. "Release the Torture Reports." December 19, 2013. http://www.nytimes .com/2013/12/20/opinion/release-the-torture-reports.html.

——. "A Truth Commission for the Bush Era?" March 2, 2009. http:// roomfordebate.blogs.nytimes.com/2009/03/02/a-truth-commission-for-the -bush-era/.

——. "The Women of Gitmo." July 15, 2005. http://www.nytimes.com/2005 /07/15/opinion/15fri1.html.

Office of the Inspector General, United States Department of Justice, "Department of Justice Inspector General Issues Report on Treatment of Aliens Held on Immigration Charges in Connection with the Investigation of the September 11 Terrorist Attack." 2003. Accessed June 12, 2014. http://www .justice.gov/oig/special/0306/press.htm.

——. *The September 11 Detainees: A Review of the Treatment of Aliens Held on Immigration Charges in Connection with the Investigation of the September 11 Attacks*. Accessed June 6, 2014. http://www.justice.gov/oig/special/0306/full.pdf, 1.

——. *Supplemental Report on September 11 Detainees' Allegations of Abuse at the Metropolitan Detention Center in Brooklyn, New York*. 2003. Accessed June 13, 2014. http://www.justice.gov/oig/special/0312/final.pdf.

Ogul, Morris S., and Bert A. Rockman. "Overseeing Oversight: New Departures and Old Problems." *Legislative Studies Quarterly* 15, no. 1 (February 1, 1990): 5–24. doi:10.2307/439999.

O'Keefe, Ed, Wesley Lowery, and Sean Sullivan. "Republicans Call for Captured Benghazi Suspect to be Held at Guantanamo." *Washington Post*, June 17, 2004, http://www.washingtonpost.com/blogs/post-politics/wp/2014/06/17 /mccain-graham-call-for-captured-benghazi-suspect-to-be-held-at -guantanamo/

Open Society Justice Initiative. *Globalizing Torture: CIA Secret Detention and Extraordinary Rendition*, 2013. Accessed June 2, 2014. http://www

.opensocietyfoundations.org/sites/default/files/globalizing-torture-20120205
.pdf.

Orbuch, Terri L. "People's Accounts Count: The Sociology of Accounts." *Annual Review of Sociology* 23 (1997): 455–78. doi:10.1146/annurev.soc.23.1.455.

Orwell, George. "Why I Write." In *A Collection of Essays*, 309–16. New York: Harvest Books, 1981.

Payne, Leigh. *Unsettling Accounts: Neither Truth nor Reconciliation in Confessions of State Violence*. Durham, N.C.: Duke University Press, 2008.

Peel, Michael, and Vincent Iacopino. *The Medical Documentation of Torture*. San Francisco: Greenwich Medical Media, 2002.

Peralta, Eyder. "Benghazi Suspect, Ahmed Abu Khattala, Is Indicted On 17 New Charges." *NPR*, October 14, 2004. http://www.npr.org/blogs/thetwo-way /2014/10/14/356196973/benghazi-suspect-ahmed-abu-khattala-is-indicted -on-17-new-charges.

Perez, Evan, and Candiotti, Susan. "Alleged Al Qaeda Operative Al Libi Taken to New York Week After Capture in Libya." October 15, 2013. http://www.cnn .com/2013/10/14/justice/al-libi/index.html.

Perinbanayagam, R. S. "The Definition of the Situation: An Analysis of the Ethno-methodological and Dramaturgical View." *The Sociological Quarterly* 15, no. 4 (October 1, 1974): 521–41. doi:10.1111/j.1533-8525.1974.tb00912.x.

Peritz, Aki, and Mieke Eoyang. "Even Al Qaeda Operatives Deserve Their Day in Court—and Justice." *Huffington Post*, October 16, 2013. http://www .huffingtonpost.com/aki-peritz/even-al-qaeda-operatives-_b_4109812.html.

Peters, Edward. *Torture*. New York: Blackwell, 1985.

——. "We Should Call Torture by Its Proper Name." History News Network, 2005. Accessed June 2, 2014. http://hnn.us/articles/5352.html.

Pfohl, Stephen. "The 'Discovery' of Child Abuse." *Social Problems* 24, no. 3 (February 1977): 310–323. doi:10.1525/sp.1977.24.3.03a00020.

——. "Twilight of the Parasites: Ultramodern Capital and the New World Order." *Social Problems* 40, no. 2 (May 1, 1993): 125–51. doi:10.1525 /sp.1993.40.2.03x0322j.

Philadelphoff-Puren, Nina. "Hostile Witness: Torture Testimony in the War on Terror." *Life Writing* 5, no. 2 (October 2008): 219–36. doi:10.1080/14484520802386568.

Phillips, Joshua E. S. *None of Us Were Like This Before: American Soldiers and Torture*. New York: Verso, 2010.

Phillips, Nelson. *Discourse Analysis: Investigating Processes of Social Construction*. Thousand Oaks, Calif.: Sage, 2002.

Physicians for Human Rights. *Broken Laws, Broken Lives: Medical Evidence of Torture by U.S. Personnel and Its Impact: A Report.* Cambridge, Mass.: Physicians for Human Rights, 2008.

——. *Leave No Marks: Enhanced Interrogation Techniques and the Risk of Criminality.* Cambridge, Mass.: Physicians for Human Rights, 2007. https://s3.amazonaws.com/PHR_Reports/leave-no-marks.pdf.

Pilkington, Ed. "Obama Under Fire Over Detention of Terror Suspect on US Navy Ship." *Guardian*, July 6, 2011. http://www.theguardian.com/law/2011/jul/06/obama-detention-terror-suspect-us-navy-ship.

Pincus, Walter. "Waterboarding Historically Controversial." *Washington Post*, October 5, 2006, http://www.washingtonpost.com/wp-dyn/content/article/2006/10/04/AR2006100402005.html.

PollingReport.com. "Bush: Job Ratings." Accessed April 26, 2014. http://www.pollingreport.com/BushJob.htm.

——. "Bush: Job Ratings (1)." Accessed April 26, 2014. http://www.pollingreport.com/BushJob1.htm.

Pollner, Melvin. *Mundane Reason: Reality in Everyday and Sociological Discourse.* New York: Cambridge University Press, 1987.

Porpora, Douglas V., Alexander Nikolaev, Julia Hagemann May, and Alexander Jenkins. *Post-Ethical Society: The Iraq War, Abu Ghraib, and the Moral Failure of the Secular.* Chicago: University of Chicago Press, 2013.

Potter, Jonathan. *Representing Reality: Discourse, Rhetoric, and Social Construction.* Thousand Oaks, Calif.: Sage, 1996.

Potter, Jonathan, and Alexa Hepburn. "Discursive Constructionism." *Handbook of Constructionist Research* (2008): 275–93.

Priest, Dana. "CIA Puts Harsh Tactics on Hold; Memo on Methods of Interrogation had Wide Review." *Washington Post*, June 27, 2004. http://www.washingtonpost.com/wp-dyn/articles/A8534-2004Jun26.html.

Purdy, Matthew. "A Nation Challenged: The Law; Bush's New Rules to Fight Terror Transform the Legal Landscape." *New York Times*, November 25, 2001. http://www.nytimes.com/2001/11/25/us/nation-challenged-law-bush-s-new-rules-fight-terror-transform-legal-landscape.html.

Quinn, Carolyn. "Transcript of Wilkerson Interview." *BBC News*, November 29, 2005. http://news.bbc.co.uk/2/hi/middle_east/4481092.stm.

Redacted. "E-Mail from [Redacted] to [Redacted]." *ACLU.org*, Accessed April 26, 2014. http://www.aclu.org/torturefoia/released/FBI_5053_5054.pdf.

Rejali, Darius. "Review Essays: 'American Torture Debates.'" *Human Rights Review* 9, no. 3 (2008): 393–400. doi:10.1007/s12142-007-0056-9.

——. "Speak Frankly About Torture." Accessed July 4, 2010. http://academic.reed
  .edu/poli_sci/faculty/rejali/rejali/articles/Speak_Frankly.htm.

——. *Torture and Democracy*. Princeton, N.J.: Princeton University Press, 2007.

——. *Torture and Modernity: Self, Society, and State in Modern Iran*. Boulder,
  Colo.: Westview Press, 1994.

Riessman, Catherine. *Narrative Analysis*. Newbury Park, Calif.: Sage, 1993.

Risen, James, David Johnston, and Neil A. Lewis. "The Struggle for Iraq: Detainees; Harsh C.I.A. Methods Cited In Top Qaeda Interrogations." *New York
  Times*, May 13, 2004. http://www.nytimes.com/2004/05/13/world/struggle
  -for-iraq-detainees-harsh-cia-methods-cited-top-qaeda-interrogations
  .html?pagewanted=all&src=pm.

Risse, Thomas. "International Norms and Domestic Change: Arguing and Communicative Behavior in the Human Rights Area." *Politics and Society* 27, no. 4
  (December 1999): 529–59. doi:10.1177/0032329299027004004.

Risse, Thomas, and Kathryn Sikkink. "The Socialization of International Human Rights
  Norms into Domestic Practice: Introduction." In *The Power of Human Rights: Inter-
  national Norms and Domestic Change*, edited by T. Risse-Kappen, T. Risse, S. C
  Ropp, and K. Sikkink, 1–38. New York: Cambridge University Press, 1999.

Roberts, Carl W., ed. *Text Analysis for the Social Sciences*. New York: Routledge, 1997.

Rosen, Jeffrey. "Conscience of a Conservative." *New York Times*, September 9,
  2007. http://www.nytimes.com/2007/09/09/magazine/09rosen.html.

Rosenthal, Alan. "Legislative Behavior and Legislative Oversight." *Legislative
  Studies Quarterly* 6, no. 1 (February 1, 1981): 115–31. doi:10.2307/439716.

Sachs, Richard C. *Hearings in the US Senate: A Guide for Preparation and Procedure*. Washington, D.C.: Congressional Research Service, 2003.

Saletan, William. "Koh Is My God Pilot." *Slate*. Accessed April 26, 2014. http://
  www.slate.com/articles/health_and_science/human_nature/2011/06/koh_is
  _my_god_pilot.html.

Sands, Phillip. *Torture Team: Rumsfeld's Memo and the Betrayal of American
  Values*. New York: Palgrave, 2008.

Sartre, Jean-Paul. *Colonialism and Neocolonialism*. New York: Routledge, 2001.

Savage, Charlie. "Closing Guantánamo Fades as a Priority." *New York Times*,
  June 25, 2010. http://www.nytimes.com/2010/06/26/us/politics/26gitmo.html.

——. "Election Will Decide Future of Interrogation Methods for Terrorism
  Suspects." *New York Times*, September 27, 2012. http://www.nytimes.com
  /2012/09/28/us/politics/election-will-decide-future-of-interrogation
  -methods-for-terrorism-suspects.html.

——. "Kuwaiti Prisoner Held for Thirteen Years Is Released from Guantánamo." *New York Times*, November 5, 2014. http://www.nytimes.com/2014/11/06/us/guantanamo-kuwait-fawzi-al-odah-released.html.

Scarry, Elaine. *The Body in Pain: The Making and Unmaking of the World*. New York: Oxford University Press, 1985.

Schmidt, Randall, and John T. Furlow. *Investigation into FBI Allegations of Detainee Abuse at Guantanamo Bay, Cuba Detention Facility, US Department of Defense*. Accessed April 26, 2014. http://www.defense.gov/news/Jul2005/d20050714report.pdf.

Schmitt, Eric. "Abuse Panel Says Rules on Inmates Need Overhaul." *New York Times*, August 25, 2004. http://www.nytimes.com/2004/08/25/politics/25abuse.html.

Schneider, Joseph W. "Social Problems Theory: The Constructionist View." *Annual Review of Sociology* 11 (1985): 209–29. doi:10.1146/annurev.soc.11.1.209.

Scott, James C. *Seeing Like a State*. New Haven, Conn.: Yale University Press, 1999.

Scott, Marvin B., and Stanford M. Lyman. "Accounts." *American Sociological Review* 33, no. 1 (1968): 46–62. doi:10.2307/2092239.

Seelye, Katharine Q. "A Nation Challenged: The Prisoners; Troops Arrive at Base in Cuba to Build Jails." *New York Times*, January 7, 2002. http://www.nytimes.com/2002/01/07/us/a-nation-challenged-the-prisoners-troops-arrive-at-base-in-cuba-to-build-jails.html.

Shane, Scott. "Holder Rules Out Prosecutions in C.I.A. Interrogations." *New York Times*, August 30, 2012. http://www.nytimes.com/2012/08/31/us/holder-rules-out-prosecutions-in-cia-interrogations.html.

——. "Waterboarding Used 266 Times on 2 Suspects." *New York Times*, April 19, 2009. http://www.nytimes.com/2009/04/20/world/20detain.html.

Shor, Eran. "Conflict, Terrorism, and the Socialization of Human Rights Norms: The Spiral Model Revisited." *Social Problems* 55, no. 1 (2008): 117–38. doi:10.1525/sp.2008.55.1.117.

Silverleib, Alan. "Poll: Terrorism Fears Are Fading." CNN.com, July 2, 2008. http://www.cnn.com/2008/POLITICS/07/02/terrorism.poll/.

Smith, Dorothy E. *The Conceptual Practices of Power*. Boston: Northeastern University Press, 1990.

——. "Texts and the Ontology of Organizations and Institutions." *Culture and Organization* 7, no. 2 (2001): 159–98. doi:10.1080/10245280108523557.

——. *Texts, Facts, and Femininity: Exploring the Relations of Ruling*. New York: Routledge, 1990.

Smith, Philip. "Codes and Conflict: Towards a Theory of War as Ritual." *Theory and Society* 20, no. 1 (1991): 103–38. doi:10.1007/BF00160735.

——. *Punishment and Culture*. Chicago: University of Chicago Press, 2008.

Smith, R. Jeffrey. "Memo Gave Intelligence Bigger Role." *Washington Post*, May 21, 2004. http://www.washingtonpost.com/wp-dyn/articles/A43708 -2004May20.html.

Smith, R. Jeffrey and Josh White. "General Granted Latitude at Prison." *Washington Post*. June 12, 2004. http://www.washingtonpost.com/wp-dyn/articles /A35612-2004Jun11.html.

Sontag, Deborah. "'Who Is This Kafka That People Keep Mentioning?'" *New York Times*, October 21, 2001. http://www.nytimes.com/2001/10/21/magazine /who-is-this-kafka-that-people-keep-mentioning.html.

Sontag, Susan. *On Photography*. New York: Farrar, Straus and Giroux, 1977.

——. *Regarding the Pain of Others*. New York: Picador, 2003.

——. "Regarding the Torture of Others." *New York Times Magazine* 23 (2004): 23–29.

Soufan, Ali. "My Tortured Decision." *New York Times*. April 22, 2009. http:// www.nytimes.com/2009/04/23/opinion/23soufan.html.

Spector, Malcolm, and John I. Kitsuse. *Constructing Social Problems*. New York: de Gruyter, 1987.

Stewart, Phil, and Jeff Mason, "U.S. Captures Suspected Ringleader of 2012 Attack in Benghazi," *Reuters*, June 18, 2004, http://uk.reuters.com /article/2014/06/17/uk-usa-politics-benghazi-idUKKBN0ES24I20140617.

Sugiyama, Tara M., and Marisa Perry. "The NSA Domestic Surveillance Program: An Analysis of Congressional Oversight During an Era of One-Party Rule." *University of Michigan Journal of Law Reform* 40, no. 1 (2006): 149–89. http://heinonline.org/HOL/LandingPage?handle=hein.journals /umijlr40&div=10&id=&page=.

Sweig, Julia E. "Give Guantanamo Back to Cuba." *Washington Post*, May 3, 2009. http://www.washingtonpost.com/wp-dyn/content/article/2009/04/29 /AR2009042903940.html.

Sykes, Gresham M., and David Matza. "Techniques of Neutralization: A Theory of Delinquency." *American Sociological Review* 22, no. 6 (1957): 664–70. doi:10.2307/2089195.

Talbert, Jeffery C., Bryan D. Jones, and Frank R. Baumgartner. "Nonlegislative Hearings and Policy Change in Congress." *American Journal of Political Science* 39, no. 2 (May 1, 1995): 383–405. doi:10.2307/2111618.

Taylor, John. *Body Horror: Photojournalism, Catastrophe, and War.* New York: New York University Press, 1998.

——. "Iraqi Torture Photographs and Documentary Realism in the Press." *Journalism Studies* 6, no. 1 (2005): 39–49. doi:10.1080/1461670052000328195.

Tétreault, Mary Ann. "The Sexual Politics of Abu Ghraib: Hegemony, Spectacle, and the Global War on Terror." *National Women's Studies Association Journal* 18, no. 3 (Fall 2006): 33–50. doi:10.1353/nwsa.2006.0064.

Thiessen, Marc. "Could a Captured Taliban Leader Have Warned Us of the Times Square Plot?" *National Review*, May 11, 2010. Accessed May 5, 2014. http://www.nationalreview.com/corner/199225/could-captured-taliban-leader-have-warned-us-times-square-plot/marc-thiessen.

——. "Yglesias Admits His Ignorance." *National Review*, February 9, 2010. Accessed May 5, 2014. http://www.nationalreview.com/corner/194573/yglesias-admits-his-ignorance/marc-thiessen.

——. "Yglesias and the Slow Learners at Think Progress." National Review Online, February 8, 2010. Accessed May 5, 2014. http://www.nationalreview.com/corner/194550/yglesias-and-slow-learners-think-progress/marc-thiessen.

Todorov, Tzvetan. *Torture and the War on Terror.* New York: Seagull Books, 2009.

U.N. General Assembly. *The Universal Declaration of Human Rights.* 1948. Accessed October 17, 2014. http://www.un.org/en/documents/udhr/.

——. *Convention Against Torture and Other Cruel, Inhuman, or Degrading Treatment or Punishment.* 1984. Accessed October 17, 2014. http://www.ohchr.org/EN/ProfessionalInterest/Pages/CAT.aspx.

U.S. Department of Defense. "Defense Department Operational Update Briefing." May 4, 2004. http://www.defenselink.mil/transcripts/transcript.aspx?transcriptid=2973.

U.S. Department of the Army, *Field Manual 2-22.3 (FM 34-52) Human Intelligence Collector Operations.* Washington, D.C.: Department of the Army, 2006. Accessed October 23, 2014. http://www.loc.gov/rr/frd/Military_Law/pdf/human-intell-collector-operations.pdf.

——. *Field Manual 34-52 Intelligence Interrogation.* Washington, D.C.: Department of the Army, 1992. Accessed October 23, 2014. http://www.loc.gov/rr/frd/Military_Law/pdf/intel_interrrogation_sept-1992.pdf.

VandeHei, Jim, and Josh White. "Guantanamo Bay to Stay Open, Cheney Says." *Washington Post*, June 14, 2005. http://www.washingtonpost.com/wp-dyn/content/article/2005/06/13/AR2005061301513.html.

Van Reenen, Piet, and Dan Jones. "Torture: What Can Be Done." In *A Glimpse of Hell: Reports on Torture Worldwide*, edited by Duncan Forrest, 197–210. New York: New York University Press, 1996.

Van Wagenen, Aimee. "An Epistemology of Haunting: A Review Essay." *Critical Sociology* 30, no. 2 (March 1, 2004): 287–298. doi:10.1163/156916304323072116.

Veyne, Paul. *Writing History: Essay on Epistemology*. Middletown Conn.: Wesleyan University Press, 1984.

Voltaire. "Torture." In *A Philosophical Dictionary* (1764), vol. 7 of *The Works of Voltaire: A Contemporary Version*. Translated by William F. Fleming. New York: E. R. DuMont, 1901.

Wallach, Evan. "Drop by Drop: Forgetting the History of Water Torture in U.S. Courts." *Columbia Journal of Transnational Law* 45, no. 2 (2007): 468–506. http://heinonline.org/HOL/LandingPage?handle=hein.journals/cjtl45&div=17&id=&page=.

Walker, Lauren. "Remember the Abu Ghraib Torture Pictures? There Are More That Obama Doesn't Want You to See." *Newsweek*, October 22, 2014. http://www.newsweek.com/remember-abu-ghraib-torture-pictures-there-are-more-obama-doesnt-want-you-see-279254

Walsh, Edward. "Treatment of Detainees Defended; FBI Official Says Risks Justified Policy." *Washington Post*, June 26, 2003.

Walton, Kendall L. "Transparent Pictures: On the Nature of Photographic Realism." *Critical Inquiry* 11, no. 2 (December 1984): 246–77. doi:10.1086/448287.

Washington Post. "A Failed Investigation." September 10, 2004. http://www.washingtonpost.com/wp-dyn/articles/A10281-2004Sep9.html.

——. "An Inadequate Response." May 8, 2004.

——. "Text of President Obama's May 23 Speech on National Security." May 23, 2013. http://www.washingtonpost.com/politics/president-obamas-may-23-speech-on-national-security-as-prepared-for-delivery/2013/05/23/02c35e30-c3b8-11e2-9fe2-6ee52d0eb7c1_story.html.

Watkins, Ali, Jonathan S. Landay, and Marisa Taylor. "CIA's Use of Harsh Interrogation Went Beyond Legal Authority, Senate Report Says." *McClatchy*, April 11, 2014. http://www.mcclatchydc.com/2014/04/11/224085_cias-use-of-harsh-interrogation.html.

Weiser, Benjamin. "Since 2011 Guilty Plea, Somali Terrorist Has Cooperated with Authorities." *New York Times*, March 25, 2013. http://www.nytimes.com/2013/03/26/nyregion/since-2011-guilty-plea-somali-terrorist-has-cooperated-with-authorities.html.

White, Josh. "Abu Ghraib Tactics Were First Used at Guantanamo." *Washington Post*, July 14, 2005. http://www.washingtonpost.com/wp-dyn/content/article /2005/07/13/AR2005071302380.html.

Williams, Scott. "ABC, NBC Let Children Ask Questions About the Gulf War." *AP News Archive*, 1991. Accessed May 5, 2014. http://www.apnewsarchive .com/1991/ABC-NBC-Let-Children-Ask-Questions-About-the-Gulf-War /id-ae7bc214175119859db0a76c57322571.

Wood, Diane P. "The Rule of Law in Times of Stress." *The University of Chicago Law Review* 70, no. 1 (winter 2003): 455–70. http://www.jstor.org/stable/1600569.

Woolgar, Steve, and Dorothy Pawluch. "Ontological Gerrymandering: The Anatomy of Social Problems Explanations." *Social Problems* 32, no. 3 (1985): 214–27. doi:10.1525/sp.1985.32.3.03a00020.

Yglesias, Matthew. "If Marc Thiessen Doesn't Want to Be Compared to the Spanish Inquisition, He Should Stop Advocating Torture Techniques Used in the Spanish Inquisition." *ThinkProgress*, February 8, 2010. Accessed May 5, 2014. http://thinkprogress.org/yglesias/2010/02/08/196096/if-marc-thiessen -doesnt-want-to-be-compared-to-the-spanish-inquisition-he-should-stop -advocating-torture-techniques-used-in-the-spanish-inquisition/.

——. "No One Expects the Spanish Inquisition." *ThinkProgress*, February 8, 2010. Accessed May 5, 2014. http://thinkprogress.org/yglesias/2010/02/08/196102 /no-one-expects-the-spanish-inquisition/.

Zagorin, Adam. "'Twentieth Hijacker' Says Torture Made Him Lie." *Time*, March 3, 2006. http://content.time.com/time/nation/article/0,8599,1169322,00 .html.

Zagorin, Adam, and Timothy J. Duffy. "Inside the Interrogation of Detainee 063." *Time*, June 20, 2005. http://www.time.com/time/magazine/article /0,9171,1071284,00.html.

Zeleny, Jeff, and Thom Shanker. "Obama Moves to Bar Release of Detainee Abuse Photos." *New York Times*, May 13, 2009. http://www.nytimes.com /2009/05/14/us/politics/14photos.html.

Zveržhanovski, Ivan. "Watching War Crimes: The Srebrenica Video and the Serbian Attitudes to the 1995 Srebrenica Massacre." *Southeast European and Black Sea Studies* 7, no. 3 (2007): 417–30. doi:10.1080/14683850701566377.